NO SL
CANVEY ISLAND
The Great Pub Rock Revolution

NO SLEEP TILL CANVEY ISLAND

The Great Pub Rock Revolution

Will Birch

For Lesley and Rupert

This book is dedicated to the memory of
Lee Brilleaux.

'If you read the word culture in this tome,
return as a faulty product.'

This edition first published in 2003 by
Virgin Books Ltd
Thames Wharf Studios
Rainville Road
London
W6 9HA

First Virgin paperback edition published in Great Britain in 2000 by
Virgin Publishing Ltd

A catalogue record for this book is available from the British Library.

ISBN 0 7535 0740 4

Typeset by TW Typesetting, Plymouth, Devon
Printed and bound in Great Britain by Clays Ltd, St Ives PLC

CONTENTS

ACKNOWLEDGEMENTS

Welcome to this updated edition of *No Sleep Till Canvey Island*. The publication of the first edition, in April 2000, resulted in many messages with welcome comments and suggestions and also brought to my attention to a number of small errors, which I hope I have now corrected. I was surprised to receive so many requests for more stuff about my own group of the time, the Kursaal Flyers and I have gone some way towards redressing this.

Sadly, Ian Dury died just as the first edition was going to press. Ian's death received a huge amount of media coverage and his funeral was one of most widely reported non-royal send-offs in recent times. An excellent biography of Ian, by Richard Balls (Omnibus Books), appeared in 2000, just as I was starting to put together my own story of Ian Dury's life. This is now taking shape, and I hope my biography of Ian will appear one day.

Also no longer with us is Barry Richardson, leader of Bees Make Honey, who died from cancer in Belgium in 2001.

Researching *No Sleep Till Canvey Island* was a joy. It involved frequent trips to the new British Library, where I had to suppress a pathetic 'Yuss!' each time I uncovered a crucial nugget of information. I spent endless minutes on the Internet, often in vain, seeking something – anything – that would lead me to the person who held the key to a vital clue. I met, or reacquainted myself with, dozens of chaps and chapesses who were, mostly, only too pleased to spill the beans. And I enjoyed some splendid lunches over which the anecdotes flowed as fast as the wine.

From the outset, I tried to locate and interview all of the leading players. I needed first-hand recollections throughout, as I did not want to lift quotes from the pop publications of the day, which, in any event, barely reported anything that happened below the surface. I am pleased to say, therefore, that I have not 'cut' or 'pasted' any interview quotes. Dubious information was checked and double checked, although in two or three instances, I admit, I have had to rely on instinct. As a result, the complete story of the chain of events that led to the launch of Brinsley Schwarz and its significant aftermath is recounted here, in painful detail, for the first time.

My poor interviewees were often asked to recall events that occurred up to thirty years ago. The major problem was, of course, that for many of them, the entire period was a blur, brought about by the steady consumption of alcohol and other exotic stimulants. Staying 'high' during the era in question seems to have been the norm – a priority no less – almost across the board. Thankfully, however, many interviewees demonstrated an impressive recall of times, places and events.

Unfortunately, I have not been able to speak to everyone. Some of the players have died, in several cases during the period of my research. Those I was unable to reach before their deaths include: Chas Chandler, Mike Raven, Jon Goodchild, Monty Fresco, Martin Bayer and John Seymour. Although I often conversed with Lee Brilleaux during his lifetime, I regret that I was unable to grill him fully for this book.

Others have simply gone to ground. One of my biggest disappointments, perhaps, is that I was not able to locate Edward Molton and Stephen Warwick for their versions of events in the early years. Molton and Warwick set up Famepushers, the company that orchestrated the Brinsley Schwarz hype, yet it has been suggested to me, on more than one occasion, that they never actually existed! This scenario would have provided the perfect twist – the non-existence of two shadowy figures whose chance meeting sparked a rock 'n' roll revolution! But they did exist, although it seems 'Molton' was one of a number of aliases; the cunning old devil remains a mystery figure.

I have tried to show Edward Molton and Stephen Warwick in the appropriate light. I have been careful not to attribute to either of them any act based merely on hearsay or opinion. It has emerged, however, that Molton's business methods in the period 1969/70 were slightly unconventional and almost certainly led to financial problems for third parties with whom he was involved. But hey! It was the late 60s! (And even Edward Molton was on a learning curve.)

My starting point for the reconstruction of this early period was a selection of material loaned to me by Alan Wright, one of the *Melody Maker* competition winners in the great Brinsley Schwarz hype. I was originally put in touch with Alan by Mat Snow, the editor of *Mojo*, a publication to which I occasionally contribute. In early 1995, Mat commissioned my article on Pub Rock and mentioned to me that an Alan Wright had contacted *Mojo* about his Fillmore experience. I soon met with Alan, who supplied me with a great deal of original material relating to the Fillmore trip, including press releases, airline menus, hotel room keys, press cuttings and a copy of the 'Cadillac Allocation List', which helpfully identified every passenger who was theoretically on the junket.

Additional material relating to the Fillmore trip was supplied by Andrew Lauder, former A&R head of United Artists Records, who signed Brinsley Schwarz to a ('long-term, world-wide') recording contract in 1970. I interviewed Andrew together with Dai Davies, Pub Rock entrepreneur and ex-manager of Ducks Deluxe and Brinsley Schwarz. Andrew and Dai put the whole Pub Rock era into perspective for me and supplied a great deal of background information.

Next stop was John Eichler, who gave me invaluable assistance and an overview of the events of 1969/70. Once a partner of Dave Robinson in the post-Fillmore 'Down Home' venture and later landlord of the Hope & Anchor, Eichler was literally the man in the middle. He was almost as much a catalyst as the artist Barney Bubbles in the events that unfolded. In the mid-80s, John had attempted to co-write a book about Pub Rock with Man guitarist Deke Leonard. Although their project never saw the light of day, John let me view the transcripts of interviews that he and Deke had conducted for their ill-fated book.

For years, Dave Robinson was reluctant to discuss his involvement with Pub Rock – the scene he helped to create. He would ward off prospective interviewers with one terse statement: 'I went into the pub – it rocked.' After the traumas of the collapse of Stiff Records, the label he took on a rollercoaster ride between 1976 and 1987, Robinson became even more circumspect. I am therefore extremely grateful for the contribution Dave has chosen to make to this story.

Leading archivist and Rock Family Tree creator Pete Frame responded to my request for information by sending me a package labelled: 'This shit may be of immeasurable assistance to you.' Its contents were, indeed, very useful. Since then, Pete has always been ready to help with information and cut through the bullshit that surrounds the legendary Fillmore trip, for he was there. Pete also read various chapters as they neared completion and responded with positive suggestions and wise words.

I am also extremely grateful to Charlie Gillett, former manager of Kilburn And The High Roads and author of the seminal rock 'n' roll book, *The Sound Of The City*. As well as granting me a most illuminating interview, Charlie was happy to look at very early drafts and provide support and encouragement. In fact, it was Charlie who suggested the idea for this tome in the first place; when I told him I was writing the Pub Rock story for *Mojo*, he replied, 'It has to be a book!' Thanks Charlie. The same sentiment was quickly echoed by Jonathan Morrish at Sony. Thanks Jonathan.

I would also like to thank the following people for kindly furnishing printed information and visual material: Malcolm Addison (his diaries, photographs), Dot Burn-Forti (various items), Greg Cox (press cuttings), Paul Bradshaw (his scrapbook), John Eichler (various items), Chris Fenwick (various items), Ian Gomm (his diaries, photographs), Eric Goulden (various items relating to Stiff's Greatest Stiffs Live), Andrew Lauder (numerous items), Mr and Mrs Drain Lowe (correspondence), Deke O'Brien (his scrapbook), Jake Riviera (original artwork by Barney Bubbles and numerous items), Jodi Routh (various items), Richard Treece (scrapbook cuttings, photographs), Ricky Blears (press cuttings) and Alan Wright (numerous items relating to the Fillmore trip).

All of the following people provided help and/or crucial contacts: Ann Adley, Julian Alexander, Dave Anderson, Neda Armian – assistant to Jonathan Demme, Cora Barnes, Peter Barnes, Ann Barr, Stuart Batsford, George Blevings, Valerie

Boyd, Naomi Brookes, Geoff Brown, Dan Burn-Forti, Lucy Burn-Forti, John Butterfield, Ian Campbell, Tim Chacksfield, Andy Childs, Gavin Clive-Smith, Susan Coelho, John Collis, Glen Colson, Mary Costello, Gareth Davies, Roger Dopson, Paul du Noyer, Ray Etzler, Chris Fenwick, Rodney Fitch, Pete Frame, Phil Franks, Charlie Gillett, Mike Gott, Neil Greenway, David Hepworth, Liz Hills, Julia Honeywell, Barney Hoskyns, Bobby Irwin, Val Jennings, John Jobson, Tony Judge, John Kalinowski, Cynthia Lole, Tracey MacCleod, Jonathan Morrish, Phil Nolan, Maureen O'Donnell, Terry Pond, Judith Riley, Paul Riley, Alan Robinson, Amanda Robinson at Conran Group, Christian Routh, Andy Saunders at Creation, Henry Scott-Irvine, Dave Shannon, Tom Sheehan, Ned Sherrin, Jan Simmons, Barry Sinclair, Doug Smith, Ken Smith, Mat Snow, Christopher Somerville, David Sturge at *The Oldie*, Gill Taylor, Judy Thomas, Eddie Thornley, John Tobler, Alan Trist, Justin Tunstall, Kosmo Vinyl, Brendan Walsh, Val Walsh, Trisha Wrench and Peter York.

I would like to add a special word of thanks to Jill and Brian Jewiss, sister and brother-in-law of the late, impossibly great, Barney Bubbles.

Thanks also to my dear friend, Keith Smith, for drawing my attention to important matters that I would not otherwise have been aware of.

I would like to thank the following research sources: Mark Popham at *Racenews*; Mr Wood at The London Meteorological Office; Vi Bellamy at Companies House, London; Sylvia Jones and Steve Alexander at Companies House, Cardiff; the staff of The British Newspaper Library, Colindale; the staff of The British Library, St Pancras; past and present members of staff at Southend Library; Aileen Healey at BECTU; and Jill Tulip and Naomi Lees at the *Time Out* library.

All of the interview quotes in *No Sleep Till Canvey Island* are taken from first-hand interviews conducted by the author between April 1995 and July 2002. (There are three exceptions, noted below.)

Many thanks, therefore, to: Malcolm Addison, Bob Andrews, Roger Armstrong, Paul 'Diceman' Bailey, Martin Belmont, Ricky Blears, Lee Brilleaux, Shirley Brilleaux, Dot

Burn-Forti, Paul Carrack, Ted Carroll, Dave Charles, Andy Childs, Giana Cioffi, Stafford Cliff, Virginia Clive-Smith, John Coleman, John Collis, Glen Colson, Paul Conroy, Elvis Costello, George Darby, Dai Davies, Justin de Blank, Austin de Lone, Jeremy Deedes, Ian Dury, John Eichler, Sue Eichler, B.P. Fallon, Chris Fenwick, Pete Frame, Phil Franks, Charlie Gillett, Ian Gomm, Eric Goulden (Wreckless Eric), Fred Grainger, Jonathon Green, Dave Higgs, Gerry Hogan, Tony Howard, Peter Jenner, Brian Jewiss, Jill Jewiss, Wilko Johnson, Derek Kavanagh, Pauline Kennedy, Andrew Kerr, Miles Kington, Shelagh Laslett-O'Brien, Andrew Lauder, Dick Lawson, Nick Lowe, Gered Mankowitz, Alan Marcuson, John Martin (The Big Figure), Alan McGee, Graham McPherson (Suggs), Mick Molloy, Kate Moon, Mouse, Stanley Mouse, John Muggeridge, Frances Newman, Deke O'Brien, Jack O'Hara, Humphrey Ocean, Graham Parker, Alan Parsons, Frances Pemberton, Warwick 'Rocky' Prior, Phil Rambow, Billy Rankin, Barry Richardson, Paul 'Bassman' Riley, Jake Riviera, Tommy Roberts, Dave Robinson, Jodi Routh, Rat Scabies, Brinsley Schwarz, Blue Sheppard, Ken Smith, Doug Smith, John B. Sparks, Christie Sutton, Pete Thomas, Geoff Travis, Richard Treece, Kosmo Vinyl, Trevor Wiffen, Terry Williams, Bob Wilson, Colin Wiltshire and Alan Wright.

I am deeply indebted to John Eichler and Deke Leonard for allowing me to quote from their May 1986 interviews with Sean Tyla and Jake Riviera at relevant points in the story. Although Jake has been extremely helpful to me in my research for this book, he is no longer comfortable with the idea of being interviewed in front of a tape recorder and my requests to record our conversations were politely declined. So, instead, I had to rely on my memory and the hastily scribbled notes I made whenever we met or talked on the telephone. Covertly recording Jake was out of the question, as I nervously recalled the time when a *Record Mirror* journalist once attempted to 'interview' Elvis Costello with a hidden tape recorder.

I am also indebted to Nigel Cross for letting me use quotes from his interview with Larry Wallis.

Thanks to Jonathon Green for allowing me to view 'out-takes' from his essential oral history, *Days In The Life* –

Voices From The English Underground 1961–1971, especially interviews with Pearce Marchbank, Doug Smith, Andrew Bailey and Keith Morris.

I must also thank my editor, Ian Gittins of Virgin Publishing. Ian and his colleagues had the balls to take on this book, which, I admit, is about a relatively uncommercial corner of pop history. Massive sales, I do not think, were the objective. Virgin also provided the book's snappy title (when I was tinkering with loftier, rather pretentious, alternatives).

Thank you to my copy editor, Martin Noble.

A big 'Ahoy there!' to my colleagues in the Kursaal Flyers: Paul Shuttleworth, Graeme Douglas, Vic Collins, Richie Bull, Dave Hatfield, Barry Martin and John Wicks; our manager Paul Conroy, and Pete Thomas, Jake Riviera, Jonathan King, Peter Barnes and David Gentle for their crucial help at a time when you could get pissed for two quid and still have change for a fish-and-chip supper.

Most of all, I would like to thank my family for their support.

Sorry to anyone I forgot. Yes, you. Let me know!

Hardware by Sony and Toshiba. Software by Bells.

Some sections of *No Sleep Till Canvey Island* have previously appeared in *Mojo*. The author wishes to thank Mat Snow, editor of *Mojo*, and its publishers, EMAP Metro, for allowing these sections to be reproduced. Special thanks also to Paul du Noyer, founding editor of *Mojo*, for getting me into this writing lark in the first place.

The author would like to hear from anyone who enjoys this book, or does not, or who has something to contribute that may enlighten future revisions of the text.

Elusive characters, or those I may have overlooked, are welcome to step forward. Come on; don't be shy; send your e-mail to: pubrocker@bigfoot.com

INTRODUCTION

Timing, we are told, is everything.

If you happened to be a male of the pop persuasion, born in Britain in the late 1940s, you could not wish to have arrived at a more opportune time. The Second World War was over and the Yanks had gone home, leaving crafty American inventions like denim jeans and chewing gum to find their own way across the Atlantic to England. After several years of early childhood, during which you absorbed the novelty songs of the day on the family gramophone, you reached record-buying age at precisely the point when the craftiest American invention of them all materialised.

If, perhaps, your parents were hoping to steer you away from the perils of popular music, Elvis 'The Pelvis' represented their first serious hurdle. If you slipped now, and succumbed to Presley's beguiling ways, you would be scarred for life. Your path would be irreversibly mapped out. Although a large proportion of ten-year-olds cleared The Presley Obstruction with ease, taking only a superficial interest in rock 'n' roll (and being given bicycles as tokens of gratitude), other dangers lay ahead.

The next obstacle was home-grown and, therefore, a threat more real. Lonnie Donegan, spearheading the skiffle craze, was a prototype Johnny Rotten, for he led you to believe that it was within your grasp to become a pop star. With Lonnie as your role model, showbiz was a viable proposition. Surely you could master the three basic chords, as the Eleven Plus loomed, to become a 'Worried Man' (and sing a worried song).

A couple of years later, when The Shadows ruled the roost, your paper-round money would have gone towards the down payment on some drums or a cheap electric guitar. Buddy Holly had perished a year or so earlier, but his horn-rims had been inherited by the UK's first guitar hero, Hank 'B' Marvin, whose bespectacled, acne-ridden face launched a million red guitars. Marvin oozed cool, at around the same time you were doing a bit of oozing of your own, without any help from Hank. I'm referring, of course, to teenage spots.

The very early 60s, it has been said, were rock 'n' roll's fallow years, but for those psyching up to the idea of that nerve-racking 'first date', the songs then emanating from New York's Brill Building provided the perfect soundtrack – 'Take Good Care Of My Baby'; 'Will You Love Me Tomorrow'; 'It Might As Well Rain Until September'. Bolstered by slightly tougher material from the likes of Dion, Sam Cooke and Tommy Roe, this sumptuous pop era culminated in the awesome racket of Phil Spector's early productions. So far, so fantastic.

Then, in 1963, things changed dramatically. If you'd spent the last four years 'training' your hair to emulate the Quiff of Fury, it had all been a waste of time. The Beatles had introduced a new coiffeur, soon to be publicly endorsed by The Rolling Stones and, on the first edition of *Ready Steady Go*, the defiant Billy Fury looked sadly dated. What went up, had definitely come down and after half an hour with a sachet of Vosene and your mum's pinking shears, you too could achieve a convincing 'mop top'.

At the time you left school, there were plenty of jobs to choose from, but it was hard to focus on work each morning with the roar of James Brown, Tamla Motown and Stax still ringing in your ears. As you approached your teenage introspective phase – an ideal time to appreciate and analyse Bob Dylan's mysterious songs – drugs reared their head. Along came the West Coast sound of Jefferson Airplane, Love and The Doors. It was obviously a conspiracy.

At around 20, with a couple of items of faded denim in your wardrobe, you were man enough to tackle the Blues Boom, and even if you couldn't quite manage the droopy moustache, you would soon be ready to move on to the laid-back country rock of The Byrds and The Band. Furthermore, after reading *Rolling Stone* from cover to cover for some time you were probably sussed enough to give the elbow to Emerson, Lake & Palmer and their progressive ilk.

Now in your early twenties, you were perhaps 'in a band' yourself (if you'd learnt a musical instrument), or a fully qualified pop pundit if you hadn't. David Bowie, Roxy Music and The New York Dolls flashed by in a smear of mascara. There was much loose talk of 'Pop Music' – a guaranteed wind-up for the great-coated millions, still immersed in all things 'progressive'. You, on the other hand, had cast off your loon pants and long hair and moved on, to embrace the new pop ethos, guided, in part, by the hip rock critics who were plugging Iggy Pop And The Stooges, The MC5 and The Flamin' Groovies.

It was now the mid-70s. The seeds of revolution were in the air and, as luck would have it, even after two decades of hanging around in record shops, you were still young enough for punk! Amazing timing. You had absorbed nearly every development in rock 'n' roll and enjoyed a comprehensive pop education. From this vantage point you naturally felt you knew what was what in the wheat/chaff stakes. For example, in your heart you knew that the early recordings of Elvis Presley were unlikely to be equalled for sheer exhilaration. In your head, you knew that 1966 represented the pinnacle of pop, at least as far as creativity was concerned, with *Pet Sounds*, *Blonde On Blonde*, *Revolver* and 'Reach Out I'll Be There'. And in 1976, in your heart, your head and your feet, you recognised, in The Ramones, the sound of a brave new tomorrow.

The Ramones, along with another American group called Television, had been mentioned in dispatches from New York, arousing great curiosity. The *New Musical Express* (*NME*), in particular, had been reporting on this scene for some time, but now, with the release of The Ramones' debut LP, it was actually possible to hear what all the fuss was about. It was a mighty noise. Two-minute pop songs with attention-grabbing hooks and minimal lyrics, performed at breakneck speed.

There was just one nagging thought though: that mono-chrome sleeve shot, that stripped-down sound – wasn't it all a bit familiar? For the last couple of years, you'd been digging Blighty's own Dr Feelgood. Surely they were the future of rock 'n' roll, you were thinking. Now along come these Noo Yawk upstarts called The Ramones, doing a very similar thing. All right, the Feelgoods were R&B and The Ramones were fast pop, but these two groups had attitude to burn. Soon they would be sharing the title for the world's most influential rock group of the post-Led Zeppelin era.

Actually, you might have wondered how The Ramones could have got to this point, at this time, without having been exposed to the influence of Dr Feelgood. They had certainly come into contact with each other – in May 1976 The Ramones had opened for the Feelgoods at New York's Bottom Line – but both groups had established their style(s) long before this historic event. Yet, while the Feelgoods had probably never even heard of The Ramones, or Television for that matter, the New Yorkers themselves were a little more switched on.

Confirmation of the Feelgoods' undoubted influence on the New York scene eventually surfaced in 1999, when Gary Valentine, an early member of Blondie, wrote in *Mojo*:

> Clem [Burke] went to London for a six week adventure . . . When Clem returned from England he brought back the first Dr Feelgood album. We threw a party at the loft and invited everyone. They all came. We had more people there than at any of our gigs. Johnny Thunders, Jerry Nolan, Richard Hell, The Ramones, The Miamis, The Marbles, Lance Loud And The Mumps, The Dictators, Talking Heads, Suicide. Conspicuous by their absence were [Tom] Verlaine and Patti Smith . . . Clem played the Dr Feelgood album over and over. Strange the give and take between New York and London. The stripped down straightforward R&B of Dr Feelgood inspired everyone there that night to go on . . .

Valentine then went on to acknowledge the cultural exchange between London's pioneers and New York's trail-blazers: 'not too long after, the torn shirts of early Television would turn up in the whole Sex Pistols aesthetic, shipped back to us via Malcolm McLaren.'

Punk Rock's side of the story has been done to death. What we're dealing with here are the events that occurred in

London immediately before punk. This is commonly referred to, and often dismissed as, Pub Rock, but it was a scene that gave Dr Feelgood a platform upon which to wield their undisputed influence and, a couple of years later, helped to make *the quick acceptance* of Punk Rock, possible. In fact, Pub Rock was a scene that, had it not existed, would have left the Feelgoods languishing in obscurity and the evolution of rock taking an altogether different and probably less entertaining turn.

Just for the record, Pub Rock, in the context of this book, does not refer to lacklustre boogie bands swathed in denim, knocking out interminable Chuck Berry numbers or, even worse, jazz-rock musos immersed in widdly-widdly 'fusion'. Pub Rock refers to a small number of extremely exciting combos that burned with flair and imagination in London in the early to mid-70s, exemplified by 'the Brinsleys', 'the Ducks', 'the Kilburns' and 'the Feelgoods'. As Suggs, singer with Madness, says:

> We used to hang around the Hope & Anchor. You had so many great bands playing there. We saw The Pretenders and, not that they were an influence, Dire Straits too. The Kilburns and Ian Dury were a huge influence on Madness. The sound that they made was almost exotic and their lyrics were very London. We also saw The Kursaal Flyers, Dr Feelgood, Lew Lewis – great bands. Some of them were slightly theatrical, which punk didn't have any room for when it came along, but fortunately Madness had been creeping along in a lay-by and punk shot past us at 100 miles an hour. We crept back out into the fast lane after punk had passed, breathing in its exhaust fumes.
>
> But seeing the Pub Rock groups gave us the inspiration and the confidence to do it ourselves. It was a revelation. Punk is credited with that ethos, but it certainly came from before that. The idea that you could play in a local pub seemed somehow to circumvent the whole notion of the music business. You didn't have to go and get any fancy backing or management. We got a

residency at the Dublin Castle and built up an audience. We told them we were a jazz band. The only association we had with jazz is that we played wrong notes most of the time, and we had a saxophone. But we later played at the Hope & Anchor and John Eichler was very supportive.

Madness soon signed to Stiff Records. Suggs recalls:

Stiff seemed to be the best place to be at that time. Ian Dury we'd seen from the beginning and his real success was just beginning. Elvis Costello, who we all liked, had been on the label. Mainly it was the do-it-yourself ethos. Dave Robinson took us to a pub and enticed us with a few pints of light and bitter. Dave had a very direct idea about what could be done, whereas EMI didn't have a clue about what we were all about.

Stiff Records was a label that evolved from the Pub Rock scene and was the forerunner to, and an influence on, the dozens of independent labels that sprang up in the UK in its wake. The marketing scams and promotional gimmicks employed by underdog labels like Stiff were later seized upon by the major record labels and are seen now as 'fair play'.

Today's aspiring pop musician is well versed in the machinations of the record industry, and accepts the marketing stunt as a necessary evil in the rags-to-riches process. More importantly, today's aspiring rocker is quick to extol the virtues of the three-minute pop song and the songwriter's craft, but it wasn't always this way. Let us not forget that 'songs' were an endangered species in the Yes/ELP/Genesis-dominated early 70s.

But by the mid-70s, the tide was on the turn, with Americans like Bruce Springsteen, Nils Lofgren, Bob Seger and Steve Miller pointing the way. On a more humble level, it was The Flamin' Groovies who led the revolt. By 1976, pop was cool once again and Stiff was there to ram the message home. Within a few years, everybody would be 'getting it', but the origins of this sensibility and the almost universal acknowledgement of marketing flair and the snappy song as the central currencies of pop, following the 'heavy years' of the progressive era, can be traced directly back to 1976 and the launch of Stiff, spearheaded in the UK by the release of Nick Lowe's 'So It Goes'/'Heart Of The City'.

This was modern pop, fast and witty, rocking and tuneful, but with more depth than much of the 60s output. It also sported narrow slacks and a happening haircut and was packaged in a slick new way and, even if Stiff's early releases did not achieve immediate commercial success, they were a considerable influence on countless musicians and taste-makers. The Stiff effect can still be felt a quarter of a century later and its spirit permeates the best of today's pop. Alan McGee, for instance, founder of the internationally successful Creation Records, pays his respects:

I'm one removed from Stiff really, but in the context of the music business in 1976/77, Stiff was fantastic. They put out the first punk single, didn't they? The Damned's 'New Rose'. It was one of the greatest records ever made. I also bought Elvis Costello's first LP, and the Yachts'. Stiff went on to become one of the most successful independent labels there's ever been with Madness, who had over 20 hits. Creation took it a stage further. We ended up spawning Oasis – the biggest group in the world in 1996, which is pretty unbeatable in taking a blueprint and going the full way, but, when I was a kid, Stiff definitely gave me encouragement. They made me realise that maybe you could be an independent and actually have hits! You could never wake up and imagine yourself like EMI or MCA, but maybe you could be like Stiff. All it takes is somebody that knows about music and has a lot of bollocks. Dave Robinson was there in the beginning and he did it. He was obviously a maverick and he did it on his own terms.

Along with Punk Rock, Stiff's pop vision, referred to in some quarters as New Wave, came out of Pub Rock and changed the way we listen to rock 'n' roll. But whereas punk has always enjoyed lavish reportage, much less is known about the other side of the coin.

No Sleep Till Canvey Island attempts to tell the story of how this turning point in rock history came about. I have made no attempt to write in depth about the music itself – it is best listened to. There is no analysis here of Elvis Costello's lyrics, or track-by-track details of the Brinsley Schwarz LPs. This book is about the crucial events that occurred in London in the early 70s and the people who made it all happen – the artists and entrepreneurs whose paths crossed and whose own roots lie in the Mod era of the mid-60s and, a little later, London's underground music scene.

Barney Bubbles, the legendary graphic artist, was the unwitting catalyst. In his desire to entertain and communicate ideas, Bubbles unconsciously brought together all of the leading players. Although Bubbles was 'an awful hippie', according to the writer Jonathon Green, he craved organisation and structure. Sadly, this did not extend to Bubbles's own business arrangements and a crippling tax liability, a hangover from the early 70s, would dog him throughout his career.

Dave Robinson, co-founder of Stiff Records, was the architect of Pub Rock – a phenomenon that is often derided but which was, in fact, a musical revolution. For unknown groups with a bit of flair, the pubs provided a fast track to recognition. Some years before inventing Pub Rock, Robinson had pulled off the biggest pop publicity stunt of all time with the infamous launch of Brinsley Schwarz. Throughout these events, the word 'can't' was not in Robinson's vocabulary. 'Dave should have been in the Marines,' says musician Barry Richardson. 'He knows no fear.'

Jake Riviera, human dynamo and the true inspiration behind Stiff Records, had the wit and style to repackage what was essentially 'Limey Americana'. The selling of Elvis Costello was Riviera's greatest commercial achievement. The general perception of Costello as a 'New Wave' artist was a triumph of packaging over content. There was nothing 'new' about Costello's debut LP *My Aim Is True*, although he was, of course, a uniquely gifted artist who quickly developed his own style. But without Riviera's guiding touch, Costello would never have gained the notoriety that kick-started his long and successful career.

Nick Lowe, former front man of the doomed Brinsley Schwarz, survived his own psychedelic nightmare to become the sharpest musician and record producer of the New Wave era. It could be said that Lowe is simply a rock 'n' roll chameleon with a brain full of pop templates that he plunders shamelessly when the need arises. But, at his best, Lowe is easily the most talented, self-contained British songwriter of the post-Beatles era.

These four men – Riviera, Robinson, Lowe, and Bubbles – were the essence of Stiff Records – the 'Rockethead of a Revolution', to quote writer B.P. Fallon. With Elvis Costello and Ian Dury added into the equation, they eventually brought their vision into the British living room and inspired the next generation.

Pub Rock gave these creative individuals the breaks, yet, even at its height, Pub Rock attracted a relatively small audience. Compared with the mainstream rock scene, it was something of a close-knit community. One would often see familiar faces at key gigs, creating the impression that the core audience was the same twenty or thirty people, moving very quickly from pub to pub.

The fact that the venues were so tiny also contributed towards the atmosphere. The audience was close to the music. There was nowhere to hide. When, for example, a hundred souls were gathered in the cellar of the Hope & Anchor, it felt like something important was happening, although applause, even for the most entertaining performance, was often muted. It was not easy to clap with a beer glass in one hand.

Also, the scene was populated with some priceless characters. You could meet up at the bar with charismatic performers like Ian Dury or Lee Brilleaux. Whereas the big name artists of the day were untouchable, Pub Rock removed the barriers between the fan and the artist and the artist and the music business. If you had the determination, everything was accessible and anything was possible. This was the one vital lesson inherited by the incoming punk groups.

The Pub Rock era was a marvellous time – don't believe its detractors. As the story that follows will show, it changed the course of popular music. Yet, unbeknown to many, it had its origins in a most unlikely set of circumstances. And like many good things, it began with The Beatles.

PART I
MALPRACTICE

1. THE FAIRY GODFATHER

In 1968, the Beatles' Apple organisation was in its first flush of success, exerting a powerful influence over the movers and groovers of London's underground community. While supposedly radical publications such as *International Times* (*IT*) and *Oz* were, on the one hand, busy promoting anarchy and sexual liberation, they were also helping to cultivate an atmosphere in which, it was thought, an 'alternative economy' might flourish. As *IT*'s Barry Miles wrote:

> Paul McCartney asked me to point out that Apple is not in competition with any of the underground organisations, rather it exists to help, collaborate with, and extend all existing organisations as well as start new ones. The concept, as outlined by Paul, is to establish an underground company above ground as big as Shell, BP or ICI but as there is no profit motive The Beatles' profits go first to the combined staff and then are given away to the needy.

It was the dawn of a new entrepreneurial era and the world's most famous pop group had caught the bug. Since the emergence of the teenager in the 50s, the youth pound had firmed up and was now in growth. Young people had begun to create their own products and services. The Beatles would branch out into films, electronics, music publishing, recording studios, artiste management and retail shops. In a blaze of publicity, Apple offered to help fund creative projects, placing advertisements in the press urging those with talent to submit their tapes and photographs.

'This man has talent . . .' ran Paul McCartney's copyline in the Apple ad, accompanying a photograph of a busker, loaded down with musical instruments. 'He wrote [to Apple] . . . sent the tape . . . This man now owns a Bentley.' The Beatles' message was simple and it sent out a powerful signal to their audience. It was okay to live in a commune, share out the organic food and attend 'Legalise Pot' rallies, but it was equally okay to aspire to the luxury of an expensive motor car, although, even at Apple, there were never quite enough Bentleys to go round.

'We all believed The Beatles were like us and we were like them,' says John Eichler, who was, at the time, trying to enter the film industry. 'Apple was a wonderful idea . . . unlimited money and artistic development. It was that cusp when the hippie thing was still reasonably underground and you couldn't buy hippie clothes in the high street. You had to go somewhere and hunt down beads.'

All this fervent activity had a most profound effect on one Stephen Warwick, a 26-year-old 'head' who floated around the fringes of the film industry. With John Eichler, who was a close friend and neighbour in Barnes, south-west London, Warwick had started making a number of pilot films for children's TV. 'We were in our twenties,' recalls Eichler, 'and old enough to be confident in our stupidities.' Their films included a proposed series entitled *Rollercoaster*, all about the exploits of five young people sharing a house, which was inspired by the atmosphere at the nearby home of their friend Chris Higson.

When The Beatles started to distribute their money, Warwick was at the head of the queue, applying for a grant to fund his fledgling company, Breydon Films Ltd. Unfortunately, Warwick and Eichler's ideas failed to catch the imagination of the decision-makers at Apple and their application was among hundreds that were unsuccessful in the early months of 1969. Undeterred, Stephen Warwick set about building his own Apple-style empire.

Stephen Paul Warwick was born in 1943, son of the eminent film cameraman Norman Warwick. On leaving school, Warwick, whose family was Catholic, became a novice monk. 'He thought he was going to take orders,' says Eichler, 'but discovered Pat-a-Cake and sex.' Pat-a-Cake was the family nickname given to Warwick's wife Patricia Anne, whom he had married the previous year.

Warwick had set up Breydon Films in 1967 to handle his income as an assistant film sound editor. He had worked on a number of the James Bond movies produced by Albert 'Cubby' Brocolli, including *Goldfinger*, *Thunderball* and *You Only Live Twice*. Although Warwick enjoyed his work to the point of obsession, he desperately wished to head a film production company. 'He was always interested in finding his own Cubby Brocolli – an entrepreneur who could conjure up the millions he needed to put his ideas into action,' says Eichler.

Seeking new outlets for his creative talents, Warwick conceived the idea of building 'The Pleasuredome' – a futuristic leisure resort where fellow heads could relax, take soft drugs and philosophise long into the night. 'At that time we thought the world would be different,' remembers Eichler. 'It wasn't going to be Maggie Thatcher; there was going to be room for pleasuredomes!' Warwick's hippie holiday resort was to be built on a disused wartime fort located at Red Sands in the Thames Estuary, approximately nine miles to the north of Whitstable in Kent.

In his book *The Battle of the East Coast 1939–1945*, historian J.P. Foynes describes the steel anti-aircraft platform at Red Sands as 'a spectacular innovation'. It was one of seven such forts placed in the Thames Estuary and was built in situ between mid and late 1943. This enormous 'Maunsell Fort', named after its designer, Guy Maunsell, was Army property and consisted of seven towers mounted on four legs apiece and linked by catwalks. Of the seven towers, four mounted 3.7-inch guns, one a Bofors gun, one a searchlight and one the gunnery control gear.

The towers at Red Sands stood desolate from the end of the Second World War until June 1964, when the platform was boarded by one Harry Featherbee, owner of Invicta, the pirate radio station. Radio Invicta commenced full broadcasts on 17 July, with Featherbee himself spinning the discs under the pseudonym Tom Pepper. After five months of successful broadcasting, tragedy struck. On 16 December, Featherbee, fellow deejay Barry Hoy aka Simon Ashley, and engineer Martin Shaw were all drowned when the launch *David* sank on a return trip from Red Sands to Faversham. Two months later, Radio Invicta closed.

This was only one of a number of unfortunate incidents that befell the pirate radio stations, the most notorious of which was the shooting of pop impresario and Radio City owner Reg Calvert. Calvert was shot dead in June 1966 when he went to the Essex home of Major Oliver Smedley, a business associate with whom he had fallen out. Smedley was initially charged with murder, later reduced to manslaughter. Pleading self-defence, Smedley was found not guilty and walked free.

Following the closure of Radio Invicta, Red Sands was next occupied by Radio K.I.N.G., which commenced broadcasting in March 1965, but the venture was short-lived. In its last days, K.I.N.G.'s announcers started to plug another new station, Radio 390, which took over Red Sands on 21 September. 390's most influential deejay was Mike Raven, a cousin of the aforementioned Oliver Smedley. Raven was instrumental in introducing to British ears a great deal of American blues and soul music in his programme *Raven Around* and the station soon built a loyal following.

Under pressure from the Home Office, 390 was forced to come off the air temporarily in November 1966, but soon returned, claiming immunity from prosecution because, 390 said, Red Sands was beyond the then 'three-mile limit', outside British territorial waters and therefore beyond the jurisdiction of United Kingdom law. The High Court countered with the claim that a nearby sandbank, Middle Sands, was exposed at low tide, making it inside the limit. In response, station boss Ted Allbeury hired a hydrographer to disprove this. The hydrographer stated that Middle Sands was always covered in at least five inches of water, but the Royal Navy later gave evidence that Middle Sands was uncovered at low tide and produced a photograph of Lieutenant Commander John Mackay standing on the sands, bearing a Union Jack.

By the summer of 1967, Radio 390's days were numbered. In any event, the Marine etc. Broadcasting (Offences) Bill, designed to outlaw the pirate stations, was getting its second reading in Parliament and would become law on 15 August. On 28 July, Radio 390 closed down. A week later, five men raided Red Sands and removed £500 worth of radio equipment, and were subsequently caught and charged with theft.

Eighteen months later, Red Sands was under the control of Stephen Warwick. He had become loosely involved in pirate radio through his friendship with a deejay named Max Stamp, to whom he offered the use of his attic as a base for 'London Free Radio' and it was through this contact that Warwick acquired the fort.

Warwick then drew up plans for The Pleasuredome. In addition to the resort's accommodation and leisure areas, the fort would also house a new off-shore radio station, whose advertising revenue would help fund other branches of the Warwick empire. The execution of these plans, however, was far beyond Warwick's practical capabilities and his own financial status and so he began searching for a business partner who could help to transform his dreams into reality. He found one in Eddie Molton.

Stephen Edward Molton was a 28-year-old entrepreneur who was unattuned to the ways of the alternative society. Slightly overweight and immaculately groomed, with a neatly trimmed beard, the enigmatic Molton was a most fastidious man. He would frequently indulge in manicures at Simpsons in Piccadilly and Turkish baths at Queensway's Porchester Hall and always dressed conservatively to blend in with the bankers and the venture capitalists on whose input he relied. Operating under a number of aliases, 'Eddie' Molton was always on the lookout for an exciting scheme.

On Saturday, 29 March 1969, Molton hit pay dirt. His girlfriend, Liz Robertson, a young West Indian nurse, had accepted a babysitting assignment at 119 Cowley Road, Mortlake, to look after Alexander and Lyndsey, the children of Stephen and Patricia Warwick. Molton, who had no other pressing engagements that evening, accompanied his girlfriend and so met Stephen Warwick for the first time.

Molton and Warwick hit it off immediately. When Warwick enquired about Molton's recent business activity, Molton explained that he had just returned from Canada and that he had been handling business affairs for the fashion designer, Zandra Rhodes. Sensing an important business opportunity,

Warwick told Molton about his plans for the Pleasuredome and his inside knowledge of the film and TV industries.

Molton was already attracted to the entertainment business and had been looking for a way to break into this potentially lucrative area for some time. He now saw Warwick as the key and offered his services as financial consultant. Warwick could not resist Molton's smooth and confident approach and the duo immediately struck up a partnership. At this point their combined bank balance totalled £15.

In the days that followed, Molton and Warwick worked fast, planning a number of ambitious and off-the-wall business ventures, based on new ideas that were beginning to occur to them at a rapid rate. The most exciting option, by far, was the pursuit of Stephen Warwick's central dream – the Pleasuredome. Molton had initially presented himself to Warwick as a money man, but his first suggestion was a practical one – the fort at Red Sands needed guarding. A small advertisement would be placed in the London *Evening Standard*, giving Warwick's home telephone number as the point of contact.

Molton then suggested that they might look for some office space. Some days later, while working in the cramped conditions of Cowley Road, Molton chanced upon a sheet of Breydon Films headed notepaper and asked Warwick about its origin. When Warwick replied that it was the work of a graphic designer who operated out of a studio in West London, Molton insisted on meeting the artist.

On 14 April, Molton found himself in Portobello Road, talking to a small thin man by the name of Colin Fulcher.

Colin Fulcher was born during an air raid in July 1942 in Tranmere Road, Whitton, Middlesex. He attended the local Nelson School, then Whitton Boys and Isleworth Grammar. At Isleworth, he showed signs of artistic talent, creating a particularly striking model of an Egyptian temple, and became fascinated by the various bold shapes found in Egyptian architecture.

On leaving school, Fulcher went to Twickenham College of Art, where he met fellow student Chris Higson, who had first introduced him to John Eichler and Stephen Warwick. Also at Twickenham during this period was future Small Faces star, Ian McLagan.

In his autobiography, *All The Rage*, McLagan recalls:

> I hung around with the coolest people I could find, hoping they wouldn't let on. Colin Fulcher was one of them. A very talented artist, he was interested in the blues as well . . . he could play pretty good gut-string guitar in that folk blues style. He had a ready grin and when he laughed, he laughed from his long nose to his toes, as if Gerald Scarfe had drawn him. He was like a cartoon character.

In June 1965, Fulcher joined The Conran Group as a designer. Another new recruit at Conran was Virginia Clive-Smith, who says, 'We were the bright new kids. Conran was at 5 Hanway Place, off Oxford Street, and we used to go for lunch at Fiori, an Italian greasy spoon. I remember Colin Fulcher holding a slice of Mother's Pride bread up to each ear and saying, "Anything suits me . . ." He was waving the bread around like giant earrings.'

'Colin was awed by almost anybody,' continues Clive-Smith, recalling Fulcher's admiration for, among others, Jon Goodchild and Martin Sharp at *Oz*; the photographer David Larcher and beat poet, John Esam:

> Larger-than-life characters came bounding onto the scene with wild colour and hair and ideas and Colin's eyes would swivel and he'd say, 'Wow, this is fantastic.' He was so receptive and wanting to know about the world, and sensitive and delicate. He was too gentle to flourish, like a wayside elfin character. Had he the ego, he could have pushed his way up through that lot, but he didn't do that. It wasn't in his nature.
>
> Colin didn't like to ask people to pay him. Given his vulnerability and his delicacy, he was such a gent, from another time. He didn't have a high opinion of his abilities. He was very humble. I used to cuddle him. He

looked like he needed it. The amount of drugs that were going around were the last thing he should ever have gone near. His imagination was too finely balanced to handle hallucinogenics. He didn't have too many defence strategies.

Colin loved rock music. He and I made an eight-millimetre movie to the music of 'My Generation'. It was one of his favourite records. We mixed up a bathful of flour-and-water paste and filmed an enormous custard-pie fight in the bathroom of his flat. I also remember him leaping onto the plan chest, holding his T-square like a guitar, pretending to be Jimi Hendrix or Pete Townshend. We talked about putting on a concert at the Albert Hall, where anyone could get up and perform, using whatever object they liked . . . tennis racket, T-square, anything.

'Colin Fulcher was into fantasy,' says Stafford Cliff, another former colleague at Conran. 'He made a film in Kensington Gardens, where everyone had to dress up as characters from *Alice In Wonderland*. He was drawn towards the pop scene and underground publications such as *Oz*, in which he desperately wanted to be involved.' In May 1968, Fulcher achieved this ambition by co-designing, with Stafford Cliff and others, some pull-out inserts for issue number 12 of *Oz*, described many years later by design writer Julia Thrift as, 'An exuberant collage of favourite hippie imagery'.

This was the era of the psychedelic poster, an art form that had originated in San Francisco with the work of Rick Griffin, Victor Moscoso, Wes Wilson, Stanley Mouse, Alton Kelly and others. In London, artists like Michael English and Nigel Waymouth, who went under the name of Hapshash And The Coloured Coat and the Australian, Martin Sharp, whose designs graced *Oz* Magazine, all made a tremendous impact on Colin Fulcher.

Such was Fulcher's desire to immerse himself in all things psychedelic that, in the summer of 1968, he set off for the USA. In San Francisco, he met up with the legendary poster artists Stanley Mouse and Alton Kelly and hung around the

West Coast scene, visiting the Fillmore Auditorium, where he was awed by the liquid light shows.

San Francisco was a turning point in Fulcher's life and, in the mind of his family, it was not for the better. 'When he came back from America he was a different person,' says his sister, Jill. 'He had a breakdown. He felt he was useless and he wasn't achieving anything. He'd lost his self-confidence. After America his work went from being what I call normal to containing lots of weird shapes. There was always a monster in the picture.'

'Colin hated America,' says Clive-Smith. 'I know that when he got back to London airport he burst into tears. He had been completely overwhelmed by America. He was such a sensitive creature.' Nevertheless, Fulcher returned from the States with a head full of inspiration and now had ideas about starting his own liquid light show in London, based on those he had seen at the Fillmore Auditorium in San Francisco.

Back in London and trading as 'OK Designs', Fulcher briefly returned to his job at Conran, but when creative director Justin de Blank left the company in late 1968 to start his own design and marketing consultancy, Fulcher was invited to join him. In January 1969, Fulcher quit his flat at 1a Leigh Court, in West Kensington's Avonmore Road and acquired the lease on a three-storey building at 307 Portobello Road. There he would live and have his own studio where he could concentrate on his work for Justin de Blank and others.

As a sideline, Fulcher operated a light show for the rock group Gun and took his lights to various underground events and 'happenings', often at the Roundhouse in Chalk Farm, the Electric Cinema or Middle Earth, where he was billed as 'Sexy Barney Bubbles Light Show'. Partly to elude a pressing income-tax bill, the move to Portobello Road also coincided with Colin Fulcher reinventing himself as 'Barney Bubbles'.

Portobello Road was, in Barney Bubbles's mind, the centre of the universe. Fellow psychedelic traveller, Blue Sheppard, recalls, 'Barney and I just worked away in the divine madness of that time and place, just two doors away from each other.' Sheppard was involved in the hippie boutique, Forbidden Fruit, that would soon loom large in the business affairs of

Edward Molton. 'The atmosphere in Portobello was electric,' continues Sheppard. 'Roger Cross had gotten the Electric Cinema going and at the Roundhouse all-night gigs wore through the fabric of reality to a chemical new world . . . we felt like the first Christians in a land that had not awakened from darkness.'

A number of Bubbles's friends had also seen the light and were soon living together at 307 Portobello Road. These included 'Record John', who had a stall in Kensington Market; Rod Baker, an American draft dodger Bubbles had met in San Francisco; and Giana Cioffi, who became Bubbles's girlfriend. Cioffi says, 'He'd met a lot of people in the States who then all proceeded to come to England and stay at the house.' The most celebrated visitor was Stanley Mouse, who recalls Barney as 'a bright light and a happy-go-lucky artist'.

'There was an art studio on the ground floor,' continues Giana Cioffi. 'On the first floor, where there were two bedrooms and a toilet, there was actually a black family living there. They had to be bribed to leave. Barney was good at carpentry and built a bathroom and kitchen on the top floor, where our friend Record John had a room. Barney made up a rota and we all had our domestic jobs. Barney would organise everyone. He didn't want anyone to lay about and not do anything. We had to be productive.'

Barney Bubbles himself was totally productive. 'I don't know how he got his work,' continues Cioffi, 'but he started his business with a hamburger design on brown paper and did cider labels.' Bubbles's most famous design from this period is the Strongbow Cider label for H. P. Bulmer, featuring a helmeted archer with crossbow.

Bubbles was also involved in a company called A1 Designs, also known as A1 Good Guyz, but resigned when the company became involved in the publication of a sex magazine. In a loose partnership with Justin de Blank, Bubbles designed wine labels, menus and a brochure for de Blank's floral service, as well as work for nearby businesses including the menu for a Cypriot restaurant and stationery for Tom Spear's garage. Despite such industry, however, Barney Bubbles was consistently broke, due mainly to late payment by clients.

When Molton and Warwick arrived at 307 Portobello Road to meet with the impecunious Barney Bubbles, his bank balance was three shillings and a penny. When Molton heard all about Bubbles's plight, he immediately offered to collect his debts in return for a 10 per cent commission. Bubbles agreed, whereupon Molton proposed setting up a graphic design business, to be called, at the artist's suggestion, Teenburger Designs.

As Molton glanced around the interior of Bubbles's combined home and business premises that afternoon, he considered that the building was not being utilised to its full potential and asked Bubbles if he and Warwick could rent some space. They would soon be launching The Pleasuredome and there was the prospect of much design work in the pipeline. Bubbles was enticed by this proposition and so agreed to let Molton and Warwick use 307 as their business address.

On 22 April, Breydon Films lodged documents with Companies House notifying a new registered office – 307 Portobello Road, W10.

On Thursday, 1 May, all of the usual down-and-outs were lurking around the cafeteria at London's Charing Cross Station. It was the practice of some of these homeless individuals to observe the cafeteria's clientéle carefully and focus on anyone who was constantly checking his wristwatch. Such a person might be about to make a last-minute dash for a train and therefore be forced to abandon a half-finished snack. At this point the quickest-witted scavenger would pounce.

Fast off the mark that afternoon was Malcolm Hardy Addison, a 30-year-old former Royal Navy submariner down on his luck. After quietly observing the wristwatch brigade, Addison slid deftly into the cafeteria and claimed a half cup of lukewarm tea and a mint copy of the *Evening Standard*.

'I'd been on the streets for about a year,' says Addison, recalling his incredible story. 'The millionairess I'd been living with had killed herself. She was an acute alcoholic and had been stuck to one side in Chalk Farm by her family because of her drinking and it had affected me as well. We met whilst

I was a private detective.' In fact, having left the Royal Navy in 1965, Addison had worked for three years as a private investigator. 'I kept saying I would leave her,' continues Addison, 'which I finally did, returning to my own flat in Kilburn which I'd maintained. The next day she committed suicide. I got a phone call asking me to go down and identify the body.'

Picking up the *Evening Standard*, Addison turned to the General Vacancies section.

I don't know why, because I was unemployable for God's sake, but I saw this advert. It read: 'Interesting Caretaking Job At Sea. No Money. Food and Fags. One Month. Telephone 01 876 9887'. I phoned up and got an interview the next day. It was at an office in Portobello Road. In order to make myself presentable for the meeting, I went via my old flat, which my flatmate, Pat O'Donnell, had kept on. Pat had to steam my shoes and socks off my feet, it was that bad.

I remember thinking that Molton and Warwick were absolutely ace. Stephen Warwick was svelte, almost unctuous. He had a very smooth line and never stopped moving, walking round the office, papers in hand, never still. Molton was more sedentary. They were going to open a resort at Red Sands Towers and whilst it was under construction it would be my job to repel boarders.

They said there was another guy, the notorious Roy Bates, a Southend businessman who operated a radio station at Knock John Tower, who was also trying to get on the towers. I was to be armed with petrol bombs to stop him taking over. I pointed out that I'd had experience at sea and that I'd also worked as a private detective and security guard. My most recent job had been Security Officer at the New Zealand Embassy. I'd also done a bit of undercover work for the Inland Revenue investigation branch. Mainly divorce work.

Addison appeared to have all the right qualifications and was considered by Molton and Warwick to be the most suitable applicant. Addison was immediately dispatched to Queenborough on the Isle of Sheppey. After a choppy ride in a fishing boat called the *June Francis*, owned by local garage owner Bill Black, Addison soon found himself marooned 80 feet above the waves in the rusting fort, waiting for the workmen to arrive. 'A chap called Hugh was on the tower with me,' recalls Addison. 'Ex-public schoolboy, long-haired hippie, six foot two. I was an ex-copper as far as he was concerned, from a completely different background.'

With the hired muscle ensconced at the fort, Molton then suggested to Warwick that they set up a limited company to handle the affairs of The Pleasuredome. On 8 May, Sea Tribe Ltd, an off-the-shelf company with a share capital of £100, was registered at Companies House, 'To carry on business of promoting dances, concerts, theatrical agents, to transmit films, TV, Radio, and Records'. Its registered office was also given as 307 Portobello Road and shares of one pound each were issued to Edward Molton, Stephen Warwick and Patricia Warwick. Molton and Stephen Warwick were named as directors and Barney Bubbles, signing as 'C Fulcher', witnessed their signatures. Molton and Warwick soon announced plans to open a 'hippie fun palace' at Red Sands Towers.

To close observers, it seemed that Molton was in the habit of proposing business partnerships with everyone he encountered. 'He'd have a go at anything that moved,' confirms neighbour Bob Wilson, who with his partner Elio Mitzi, occupied 305 Portobello Road. In fact, Wilson was another member of the local business community who would soon receive an offer from Molton that was difficult to refuse.

Wilson and Mitzi were in the antiques business. Says Wilson:

> We sold junk actually, and curios, plus a few
> second-hand records. I'd come up to London from
> Gloucestershire, hoping to be a reporter, but Fleet Street
> wasn't quite ready for me. Our first shop in Holland Park
> was demolished to make way for the Shepherds Bush
> roundabout, so we moved to Portobello Road. We were

beginning to get drawn into the underground community because we sold publications such as *International Times* and *Oz*. First we took some stalls in the street market; then we noticed a TO LET sign on 305, down the cheap end of Portobello, towards Golbourne Road, near Forbidden Fruit and I Was Lord Kitchener's Valet. I think it might have been one of Rackman's old properties.

Elio and I then planned our oddball shop which was to be called Much Ado. We would sell pine, which was quite fashionable then, metalworks, demolition stuff, puppets. We weren't into antiques by any means, just trappings and ephemera. Barney did the graphics for us but nothing happened very quickly in those days.

In fact, it had taken Wilson and Mitzi several months during the winter of 1968/69 to renovate the building. 'We occupied all of 305, converting it and restoring the flats above. The shop was to occupy the ground floor and the basement.'

One afternoon in June 1969, Molton decided he should acquaint himself with Bob Wilson and through Barney Bubbles and Stephen Warwick, a meeting was set up. Wilson recalls:

Warwick introduced Ted Molton as his business manager. Molton was looking for somewhere to live and the middle flat at 305 was empty. He moved in. We were all hopeless with money. We'd dropped out, whatever that means, and we didn't worry about anything. There were lots of opportunities in music, film, publishing and fashion. We were having a good time. We had great ideas, but we just wanted someone to sort out the money.

Ted came along and he was like the fairy godfather, waving his magic wand saying, 'You can have anything you want, children'. In fact I can see Molton now, flamboyantly waddling around with his glasses up on his head and the silk cravat, talking deals.

Once ensconced in the flat, Molton began to keep a watchful eye on developments downstairs. Bob Wilson, who would be his next target, recalls:

> I had a big pantechnicon truck in which we all used to go round the festivals with twenty people piled in. It was also being used to store the shop's opening stock. I'd been round the country to auctions and demolition sites to collect items for Much Ado. When I got back to London one afternoon, I parked the truck on the corner of Oxford Gardens and Portobello Road and popped next door to see Barney. We had a cup of tea and when I came out the truck was gone, along with all of our stock. At this point my partner Elio wanted out and sold his share in Much Ado to Molton for a few hundred pounds. Suddenly I had a new partner.

Molton was gradually acquiring more pies than fingers, but he enjoyed the company of his new associates, finding the 'alternative society' a stark contrast to his earlier working environment and something of a novelty. Quickly picking up on the hip vernacular of his new colleagues and inspired by Barney Bubbles's quiet sense of humour, Molton christened 305/307 Portobello Road 'Motherburger' and in the summer of 1969 began to imagine himself as the benevolent overlord to a myriad of underground enterprises. Not unlike a far-out version of Apple, thought an excited Stephen Warwick.

2. FAMEPUSHERS

Throughout the summer of 1969, Addison continued to guard the fort at Red Sands, but there was still no money to build the Pleasuredome. Consequently, Stephen Warwick returned to freelance film work, editing sound for *The Virgin Soldiers*, where he met and befriended the film's assistant producer, Ned Sherrin. Some cash started to flow into Warwick's company, Breydon Films and on 4 July, Warwick appointed Molton director and company secretary after Molton had undertaken to make the money work. Various characters started to become involved in the growing empire, including Rudolph Russell, son of the 13th Duke of Bedford, who had been made a director of Breydon Films on 26 June.

One of Molton's first priorities was to find a bank to service the various enterprises. The Olympia branch of one of the 'Big Five' high street banks, where Barney Bubbles held his modest current account, was perfect for Molton's purposes. After an initial meeting with the branch manager, a Mr Holborn, Molton opened a number of accounts, such as those for Sea Tribe, Breydon Films and Teenburger Designs. Each time the smooth-talking Molton entered the building, Mr Holborn was only too pleased to listen to the endless name-dropping and the forecasts of success that awaited Molton's business projects.

As Stephen Warwick became inextricably entangled in the complex financial web being spun by the audacious Molton, his erstwhile partner, John Eichler, had taken a 'straight' job as a production manager and colour matcher at Strand Cosmetics in Barnes. The job also involved hiring personnel and Eichler, who was keen to enter the entertainment industry, decided that a novel way to meet musicians would be to recruit them as staff. 'I actually put an advert in the newspaper that read "Wanted: Process Workers With Musical Ability",' says Eichler. Two of the musicians hired by Eichler to make cosmetics were Malcolm Morley and Richard Treece, who would later form the basis of the group Help Yourself.

John Eichler lived with his wife Sue and daughter Sara at Burford Villa, in First Avenue, Barnes, the home of Dorothy Burn-Forti. Dorothy, or Dot to her friends, was the estranged wife of the actor Jonathan Burn-Forti, who had appeared in the musical *Hair* and various television productions. 'I first met John Eichler when he used to work in the off-licence on the corner,' recalls Dot Burn-Forti. 'He wore beads. Then he lost his job and the flat that went with it and he and Sue were each forced to live apart with their respective parents. I asked the Eichlers if they'd like to move into Burford Villa on a trial basis.'

Following the break-up of her marriage, Dot had learned to type and, in November 1968, got a job as a secretary to music publisher and agent Bryan Morrison. The Bryan Morrison Agency represented an Irish group called Eire Apparent, whose main claim to fame was that their debut album had been produced by Jimi Hendrix. Eire Apparent's tour manager was a former Hendrix roadie by the name of Dave Robinson.

Dave Robinson was born in Dublin in 1942. On leaving school, Robinson worked as a printer and then became a photographer for a magazine chain. After starting a club called Sound City at Burgh Quay in Dublin, Robinson briefly became Van Morrison's manager, during a period when Morrison had returned to Ireland, disillusioned with the music business after his hits with Them. Robinson's next managerial role was with the Irish group The People, who, in 1969, went to London and changed their name to Eire Apparent.

On his visits to the Bruton Place office of the Bryan Morrison Agency, Robinson would often encounter Dot Burn-Forti and, in the summer of 1969, they started to date. Soon, Robinson moved into Burford Villa, after a number of comical episodes in which he was repeatedly discovered climbing through a window of the three-bedroomed house in the middle of the night. Most evenings at Burford Villa were spent around the coffee table as Robinson, Eichler and Burn-Forti discussed what might be their collective next move in the music industry. 'Burford Villa was the epicentre of creativity,' remembers Eichler, 'but none of us had any money.'

A number of ideas were mooted. Robinson could possibly manage the solo career of Eire Apparent's vocalist Ernie Graham and Eichler might oversee the Malcolm Morley/ Richard Treece partnership. Dot, who was about to lose her job following a merger between the Bryan Morrison Agency and NEMS Enterprises, would assist. Eichler, still working at Strand Cosmetics, was now the sole breadwinner in the house, but with two potential acts and a network of contacts, it was resolved that Robinson, Eichler and Burn-Forti would form a management company as soon as suitable backers could be found. They would call their new enterprise 'Famepushers'.

Lack of funds notwithstanding, it soon became apparent that Malcolm Morley and Richard Treece were far from ready to be propelled towards fame. There was simply not enough work for three partners, so Eichler opted out, considering a return to films. In September 1969, Eichler got back in touch with his old friend and neighbour Stephen Warwick. 'We met in a Chinese restaurant,' recalls Eichler, 'and Stephen told me he'd met this guy, Eddie Molton.' Eichler then heard how the Pleasuredome at Red Sands had been put on the back burner while numerous business enterprises had consumed the duo's energies. However, none of these ventures had yet met with any success and Molton and Warwick were desperate for a new scheme that would raise cash quickly.

'A foray into pop was suggested,' recalls Eichler, 'and Stephen asked whether I wanted to form a management company. I told him that as I was the only person in our house who was working, supporting Dave and my own family; I couldn't do anything. So I mentioned to Stephen that Dot would like to do something.' At Warwick's suggestion, a meeting was arranged for the following day, so that Molton could meet Dot Burn-Forti.

'The experience I had gained working for Bryan Morrison was supposed to have equipped me for this,' says Dot Burn-Forti. 'It was a great opportunity for me, but daunting. I was aware that it was a man's world out there in the music business and at that time I couldn't even drive. I needed the advice and support of someone with greater experience, so I took Dave Robinson along. His vast experience and energy were the vital factors for success.'

At the White Hart, a public house in Mortlake, Dave Robinson dominated the meeting. Molton and Warwick sat transfixed as the charismatic Irishman revealed his plans for conquering the music industry. They had finally encountered someone whose dreams and ideas were as big and fearless as their own. Molton and Warwick immediately wanted to be involved and agreed to fund Famepushers in return for a share of the profits. At the same time, John Eichler was invited to join Warwick on various film projects. For the time being, everyone's prayers had been answered.

The following week, at Molton's invitation, Dave Robinson and Dot Burn-Forti moved Famepushers into the basement of 305 Portobello Road. Robinson and Burn-Forti were soon joined by 29-year-old Ricky Blears, who was drafted in to handle press and marketing. Ricky Blears had previously been employed by the film division of United Artists and was one of Molton's early targets in the quest for design commissions for Barney Bubbles.

Ricky Blears recalls, 'Pat-a-Cake Warwick came to see me on a sales call representing Barney Bubbles's Teenburger Designs. Notwithstanding my being married with two kids at that stage and Pat-a-Cake being wed to Stephen, we fell instantly and madly in love. Pat-a-Cake was Anglo-Asian and absolutely stunningly attractive. We had a wildly dangerous affair.'

Soon after joining the Famepushers organisation, Blears brought in Rosalind Pearce, who had been his secretary at Tandy Halford Mills, a design consultancy. Blears says, 'I recruited Ros to bring some professional skill and sanity to an office full of half-baked, half-stoned airheads. She was from Aylesbury and seemed to thrive on the more anarchic atmosphere of sex, drugs and rock 'n' roll.'

Famepushers now had an office and some staff, but very little work to do. Although Ernie Graham and the Treece/

Morley partnership showed promise, the roster needed a focus, so Famepushers set about finding an unknown group that they could propel to international stardom.

'Eddie Molton asked me how long it would take to find such a group,' recalls Dave Robinson. 'I told him it would take about three months. He then asked me how much money would be required to fund the operation. I told him five-thousand pounds, a figure I plucked out of the air.' Unfortunately, Molton didn't have the necessary five-thousand pounds and suggested to Robinson that the cash might be drip-fed on a weekly basis. Robinson found this proposal unacceptable and immediately threatened to pull out, leaving Molton desperately in need of a quick injection of capital.

Just along the street from Motherburger, at 293 Portobello Road, was the thriving hippie boutique Forbidden Fruit. Molton visited the shop's proprietors, Duncan and Bob Laurie, to see if they would not be averse to the idea of a bank overdraft facility, something Molton said he could arrange if Forbidden Fruit would appoint him its business adviser. Molton said he had a good relationship with a bank in West Kensington and suggested that Forbidden Fruit might easily qualify for an overdraft of, say, £5,000. The Laurie brothers agreed to let Molton apply for the overdraft on their behalf and signed the necessary papers, but the application was rejected. Although disappointed, Forbidden Fruit's proprietors nevertheless admired Molton's suave confidence and retained him to seek out other business opportunities.

Molton soon returned to Forbidden Fruit with another proposal, inviting the Laurie brothers to invest in a new film production. This they did, parting with £2,500 in return for a share of the film's profits. The film was never made, but Molton was now in a position to present Dave Robinson with a cheque for £2,500, while suggesting that Famepushers should be set up as a limited concern.

On 16 October, Molton purchased an off-the-shelf company called Wornet Ltd., which would, in due course, register a change of name to Famepushers Ltd. Dave Robinson would be at the helm as managing director, although Warwick would have a controlling interest with 52 per cent of the shares. The remaining 48 per cent would be divided equally between Robinson and Burn-Forti, both of whom would handle the day-to-day running of the company.

With cash in the bank, Dave Robinson took the time-honoured step of placing a classified advertisement in the Situations Vacant section of the *Melody Maker*, Britain's leading pop paper. The ad would appear in two consecutive editions, for the weeks ending 18 and 25 October 1969.

YOUNG PROGRESSIVE MANAGEMENT COMPANY

require

YOUNG SONGWRITING GROUP
with own equipment

Tel 969 5633

Dave Robinson says, 'As Molton didn't appear to have a huge amount of money I thought it would be wise to find a group that had its own van and equipment, having been through periods with groups without these basics.' Robinson also considered it would be to everyone's advantage if said group could write its own material. Within a week of placing his advertisement, Robinson had received around 85 replies and went through two weeks of 'self-inflicted torture' listening to all the tapes and going to see the best of the aspiring young groups perform in obscure towns across Britain.

By far the best submission, in Robinson's opinion, came from Tunbridge Wells. The group was called Brinsley Schwarz and comprised: William Hector Rankin III, aged 18 (drums); Robert Charles Andrews, aged 20 (organ and vocals); Brinsley Ernst Pieter Schwarz, aged 22 (lead guitar and vocals); and Nicholas Drain Lowe, aged 20 (bass and lead vocals).

Nick Lowe and Brinsley Schwarz had first met in 1962 when they were pupils at Woodbridge, a boarding school in Suffolk. Lowe's father, Drain, was a group captain in the Royal Air Force and, at that point, was stationed in Germany. The young Lowe had mastered the banjo and learnt a number of Lonnie Donegan songs by his eleventh birthday, which were dutifully performed at family gatherings. Schwarz, whose parents lived in Sevenoaks, Kent, had been playing guitar for two years, having originally been inspired by The Shadows' 'Apache'.

In 1963, Lowe and Schwarz formed a school beat group which they named Sounds 4+1. Other members were organist Barry Landeman and guitarist Phil Hall. In the summer of 1964, through Lowe's father's contacts, the group undertook a short tour of British air bases in Germany, travelling in Schwarz's parents' Commer Caravanette. The group's repertoire consisted of 90 songs, all cover versions, including songs by Chuck Berry and Little Richard.

In 1965, Schwarz left Woodbridge School and went to live in Tunbridge Wells, where he formed a trio called Three's A Crowd, with drummer Pete Whale and bassist Dave Cottam. With the addition of former Sounds 4+1 organist Barry Landeman in 1966, the group changed its name to Kippington Lodge, named after Schwarz's parents' house in Sevenoaks, Kent. They soon acquired a manager, Irving Press, an optician by trade, who also had connections with Herman's Hermits. In 1967, Press arranged a recording test with EMI and the group were immediately awarded a contract with EMI's Parlophone label.

The first single by Kippington Lodge, 'Shy Boy' c/w 'Lady On A Bicycle', was produced by Mark Wirtz, who had enjoyed success as the mastermind behind Keith West's 1967 hit 'Excerpt From A Teenage Opera'. 'Shy Boy' was released in October 1967, but bombed miserably. The follow-up, 'Rumours', again produced by Mark Wirtz, was, unfortunately, another flop.

Meanwhile, on leaving school in the summer of 1965, Nick Lowe had aspirations to become a journalist. After a year at Cassio College, Watford, with one O-level in English Language to his credit, Lowe secured a job as an editorial assistant with King & Hutchins, publishers of the *Middlesex Advertiser* and other local newspapers. 'I wanted to be a journalist, a war correspondent,' says Lowe, 'but I ended up reporting on flower shows. I soon realised I didn't have what it took.' Nevertheless, Lowe held the job down for nearly 18 months, until the day he received a phone call from Schwarz.

Cottam had quit Kippington Lodge after a disagreement over musical policy. He had wanted the group to perform more Motown numbers, but Schwarz preferred to adhere to harmony pop. In February 1968, Nick Lowe accepted Schwarz's invitation to replace Cottam and joined Kippington Lodge just in time to appear on the group's third single, 'Tell Me A Story', followed at the end of the year by 'Tomorrow Today', composed by hit writers Roger Greenaway and Roger Cooke.

The Kippington Lodge recordings and publicity photographs of this period suggest a post-psychedelic pop group, reminiscent of The Herd. But despite their heavily orchestrated recordings and Nick Lowe's Andy Bown hairstyle, Kippington Lodge lacked The Herd's commercial edge and teen appeal and their records failed to chart.

In addition to ballroom tours backing artists such as Billie Davis and J.J. Jackson, the group's most prestigious live work was their regular support slot at the Marquee, where they would open for headliners such as The Nice and Yes. The latter of these two groups was a particularly strong influence on Kippington Lodge towards the end of 1968. 'Yes were seriously good and made a big impression on us,' says Schwarz. 'They were so incredibly tight and dynamic that I stood with my mouth open, although I must add that I did not find Yes so appealing a couple of years later.'

Kippington Lodge were on the verge of becoming a progressive rock outfit and sensing that the group were moving away from their pop roots, organist Landeman quit at the end of 1968 to join Vanity Fare. In January 1969, the group advertised in the *Melody Maker* for a new keyboard player and recruited Bob Andrews, from Leeds. With his background in R&B and soul, the group's sound hardened and Andrews soon moved south to share a flat with Lowe in Tunbridge Wells.

The fifth and final single by Kippington Lodge, a cover of Lennon and McCartney's 'In My Life', features Bob Andrews's

Hammond organ to the fore and was clearly inspired by the Yes arrangement of The Beatles' 'Every Little Thing'. The B-side, 'I Can See Her Face', marked Nick Lowe's singing and songwriting debut on record and is closer to the sound of Traffic. Released in May 1969, the record bombed.

On 5 July, a few hours after the Rolling Stones free concert in Hyde Park, Kippington Lodge made one of their regular Marquee appearances and came dangerously close to losing their bass player. Approaching the microphone to make an introduction, Nick Lowe received a severe electric shock that sent him flying to the ground. Bob Andrews immediately responded by pulling Lowe away from the faulty equipment, effectively saving his life. 'It was like when you read about people drowning,' recalls Lowe. 'I really did see my whole past life flash before me and I thought, "Hang on a minute, I'm only 20, I thought I might have done a little more with my life than this." '

The following month Kippington Lodge undertook a four-week residency at the seaside resort of Margate in Kent and it was during this period that a chasm opened up between drummer Pete Whale and the rest of the group. 'Pete had a day job whereas Bob, Nick and I were full-time musicians,' says Schwarz. 'Also Pete's musical tastes and personality were different.' The group talked about sacking Whale and thought they had the perfect opportunity on the final night of the Margate engagement. Whale's father had, that day, suffered a heart attack. Shortly after hearing the ominous news, Whale threw a major tantrum, putting his foot through the skin of his bass drum.

On the journey home from Margate, the atmosphere in the van was strained. As the group were trying to pluck up the courage to tell Whale he was out, the drummer had overcome his anger and became quite talkative. 'It's great to be in a band,' chirped Whale. 'I'm really looking forward to the future . . .' His three colleagues quietly listened to this sudden declaration of commitment and were filled with guilt at the thought of sacking him. Unable to bear the suspense any longer, Nick Lowe suddenly spoke out. 'Sorry Pete, but you're not in the group any more.' Whale went quiet for ten minutes and then piped up again, 'Well, never mind, I still feel really good about the future!'

The group had already had talks with their prospective new drummer, Billy Rankin, whom they first saw playing with The Martin James Expression at a talent competition at the Dowgate Hall in Tonbridge. In the interim, Rankin had joined a ten-piece soul band called The Luther Morgan Relationship. Rankin ran into Kippington Lodge in Munich. 'I got fed up with Luther Morgan,' says Rankin. 'Eleven guys in one van and no money. I thought Kippington Lodge were fantastic, even if they'd gone a bit progressive. They used to play "Nights In White Satin".'

In September 1969, Rankin joined Kippington Lodge, but the group were beginning to question their future as a minor EMI recording act with five failed singles to their debit. 'We really couldn't get arrested as Kippington Lodge and things were changing quite drastically,' says Nick Lowe. 'We'd been known as a Parlophone pop group, which at that time – 1969 – wasn't a very cool thing to be.'

To make matters worse, the group was getting less and less live work, despite the fact that their 'sole agent', Peter Johnson, regularly took advertisements in the music press to publicise the acts in his stable which, in addition to Kippington Lodge, included Jason Crest and Leviathan. Nick Lowe says, 'He was the son of a local vicar. A switched-off kind of guy. His non-swinging address was Kilndown, Cranbrook, Kent. Who was going to think this was a happening organisation?'

Influenced by the recently released CBS budget price sampler *The Rock Machine Turns You On* and Captain Beefheart's *Safe As Milk*, the group was also beginning to suspect that a musical revolution was in the air, spearheaded by American acts such as Blood Sweat And Tears and Electric Flag. 'We were also very into Crosby, Stills & Nash,' says Nick Lowe. 'I loved their first album and we developed this look, a sitting-on-stools look, and I remember we used to go round to Brinsley's house to hear his stereo. It was a treat – two speakers!' Another album that also influenced the group heavily at this time was *Music From Big Pink* by The Band.

'We figured times were changing,' says Lowe. With a shift in musical direction and the substitution of a new drummer, the group decided it needed a change of name and a fresh start. 'We agreed that we'd all try to think of a name and then we'd meet and choose one,' says Schwarz. 'When we met, I was informed by the others that they had already decided. We were going to be called Brinsley Schwarz. I opposed it, but I was gradually talked round.'

On 16 October, Billy Rankin obtained the latest issue of *Melody Maker* and scoured the classified advertisements. Famepushers' classified ad leapt from the page and Rankin urged Schwarz to make the telephone call that was to shape his group's destiny. 'Billy and I went and met Dave Robinson at 305 Portobello Road,' recalls Schwarz. 'It was certainly a long meeting and I remember Dave talking about his experiences with Hendrix and Eire Apparent quite a lot. We thought at last we'd met someone who'd been involved with groups and knew what musicians were all about.'

Soon Nick Lowe and Bob Andrews met with Robinson and Dot Burn-Forti, who visited Tunbridge Wells to see the group play at Frant Village Hall. 'This guy was extremely wild,' says Lowe. 'He'd done some serious shit, like Hendrix, whereas we were playing the *Radio One Club*.'

Robinson stated that his basic concept was to find a group who wrote their own songs, and had their own van and equipment. Through honest hard work, Famepushers' contacts and the group's musical abilities, the group would get gigs and work up from the bottom. Robinson gave two reasons for this approach. First, Famepushers simply didn't have the money to buy the group on to a big tour or launch a high-profile publicity campaign and secondly, it would be a mistake to promote the group aggressively as they were somewhat inexperienced and might find it extremely difficult to live up to the hype.

The group liked Robinson's reasoning. 'Dave was a very conscientious, thinking manager,' says John Eichler, 'I don't think he wanted to rush it originally.'

To Nick Lowe, Robinson sounded like just the sort of manager the group needed and it was now necessary to win him over. 'Both Dave and his girlfriend seemed like real exotic creatures to us,' says Lowe. 'Very hip, cool threads, they were *nice* people.' Robinson and Dot Burn-Forti were cordially invited to Tunbridge Wells. In honour of their guests the group laid on a sumptuous feast, specially prepared by their friend, Jean-Claude, who ran a local banqueting business.

When Robinson visited Lowe's flat, he was shocked by what he found. 'Jean-Claude's food was terrific,' says Robinson, 'but Nick's flat had condensation that ran down the walls like a river and he looked terribly ill.' Not only did the group 'live like pigs', in Robinson's opinion, but the van they claimed they owned was actually rented. Worst of all, they already had a manager, the aforementioned Irving Press, who owned all the equipment. To Robinson, it was starting to look like a less attractive proposition, but for the songwriting talents of Nick Lowe.

Robinson returned to London to think things over. Still trying to convince himself that he had discovered a truly talented group, he thought about how he might persuade Edward Molton to back the venture and played heavily on the songwriting angle. But it wasn't only Robinson that was lacking in confidence at this stage. Back in Tunbridge Wells, Lowe was starting to realise that his group was skating on very thin ice, so he quickly composed some new songs and sent them to Robinson, who was favourably swayed.

'I thought Nick had a little something,' says Robinson, 'so I talked to him about the songs and suddenly he'd written two more, which I thought was very quick for those days. This guy was a songwriter. I had in the back of my mind that if you're gonna sign a group, and it's one of the things I said to Molton, you should try and sign somebody who writes because the idea of finding songs and going through that kind of poppish bit was painful. Having spent several years in the States with Eire Apparent, who didn't really write, or if they did it was average, made me realise the value of having a writer.'

After quickly securing a management agreement with the group, Famepushers now had a number of key objectives. They had to get the group into a recording studio and find an agent and get some live work. They also needed to move the group nearer to London, so that they might soak up some of the atmosphere and be on hand for any eventuality.

Within six months of meeting, Edward Molton and Stephen Warwick had become involved in no less than five separate business ventures, all operating out of 'Motherburger' at 305/307 Portobello Road.

Their bulging portfolio consisted of: Breydon Films Ltd, Sea Tribe Ltd, Teenburger Designs, Much Ado, Famepushers Ltd and *Top Pops And Music Now*, edited by Tony Norman. None of these companies was yet showing a profit, but this did not prevent Molton from further diversification. With film, leisure, graphic design, antiques, pop music and publishing sewn up, it was now time for Molton and Warwick to add another string to their ever-straining bow. Their next target would be the underground press.

3. GOING UNDERGROUND

In 1969, the world's premier rock read was *Rolling Stone*, the fortnightly tabloid that had been founded by Jann Wenner in San Francisco two years earlier. Small numbers of early issues found their way into the UK and were sold from London's 'head shops' and specialist record stores, such as One Stop and Musicland, alongside the underground publications *International Times* and *Oz*. *Rolling Stone*'s masthead boasted two 'London staff' – writer Jonathan Cott and photographer Ethan Russell.

The UK was an important market for Wenner, himself a fan of the British rock scene and the Rolling Stones in particular. In March 1969, Wenner had travelled to London for a meeting with Mick Jagger, who had become interested in magazine publishing. A deal was discussed whereby the magazine's namesakes – the Rolling Stones – would help to expand the UK operation, although it was rumoured that the Stones had originally expressed dissatisfaction over the inclusion of their name in the magazine's title. The threat of litigation may have given Jagger the upper hand in negotiations with Wenner, but after Jagger and Wenner reached agreement, the matter was quietly dropped.

In May 1969, Mick Jagger ploughed £5,000 into the venture, setting up the Trans-Oceanic Comic Company Ltd. Operating out of the Stones' office at 46a Maddox Street, London W1, Trans-Oceanic produced a British version of *Rolling Stone*, edited by Jane Nicholson. Initially, this was simply the American magazine wrapped in an adapted, UK-produced outer cover, laid out each fortnight by Gene Mahon, a graphic artist who had recently helped to design The Beatles' Apple logo. *Rolling Stone* (UK) also included some local advertising, hustled by one Alan Marcuson.

Alan Hugh Marcuson was the son of a wealthy South African businessman. He had come to England as a student in 1965 but, after being thrown out of Leeds University for failing to attend lectures, arrived in London at the intersection of flower power and student unrest. Marcuson recalls:

I got into the whole underground scene. LSD . . . LSE . . . I was named as an outside agitator during the London School of Economics sit-in. I was banned from entering the building. All we were doing was a bit of mild vandalism. 'Smash the place up' was where it was at!

Rolling Stone was the cult magazine in London. It was imported and treasured. People used to read every bloody word! I got very interested and although I knew nothing about journalism, I'd developed an obsession about magazines. When I heard that *Rolling Stone* was hiring staff, I went along and applied for the job as advertising manager. I was interviewed by Jo Bergman, the Stones' assistant. I remember Brian Jones was there, looking pathetic in an office all by himself, having just left the group. He was shaking, with sweat pouring down him. Nobody wanted to talk to him.

I got the job, £25 a week. I couldn't believe it, working for Mick Jagger, who would sweep in, in his cape, to give us a little pep talk. I didn't know what selling advertising entailed. I went to all the record companies and it was a struggle. I didn't know what to say, I'd had no sales training. But because it was such a strange period, I'd end up selling advertising to the guy at Track Records and dropping a tab of acid with him at the same time. It was crazy times. I was incredibly naïve about business. I was keen to sell ads, but I never saw any figures or any such thing as a spreadsheet!

In June 1969, Jagger moved Trans-Oceanic into a palatial Georgian building at 19 Hanover Square, in Mayfair. *Rolling Stone* (UK) was now expanding, adding UK news pages and more local advertising. Former pirate radio DJ Mike Raven wrote a fortnightly column and writer Mark Williams joined the editorial staff. Designer Jon Goodchild joined Gene Mahon in the art department. Dick Lawson, who also contributed, says:

There was a cultural upheaval happening right across London and I have to say also that it was London, rather than anywhere else in the country at that point. It was a few people. You had a base of a dozen people, working in Hanover Square with Mick Jagger's money, who were being paid to tell people what they knew. There were two great new albums every week that you could draw people's attention to. The same thing happened with cinema and theatre and art as well and it was quite easy to pull all those things together from a dozen people who knew exactly what was happening in the city. I think we all felt that if you had an interest in music it wasn't just music, it was everything around it. We were all in Grosvenor Square. I remember Alan Marcuson being heavily criticised during the Grosvenor Square march for wearing brown leather trousers when he was trying to be an anarchist.

During the course of the next two months, more and more British copy was added to *Rolling Stone* (UK), sometimes at the expense of the American content.

Wenner was not amused [says Marcuson]. We'd started messing around with the magazine big time. Jagger told us, 'Go your own way! Fuck Jann Wenner! It's going to be a British magazine. I'm paying for it; I say what goes in the magazine!' Jagger told us to develop UK *Rolling Stone* and to make it more political if we wanted.
Rolling Stone came from the States on film, and we'd started doing our own covers and using those of Wenner's pages we wanted. It was getting up his nose. When Jane Nicholson did an article on Bob Dylan and we spelt it 'Dillon', it was embarrassing. Wenner got pretty uptight. Then Jane Nicholson had a nervous breakdown or something and Jo Bergman offered me a promotion.

By October, Alan Marcuson had become the editor of *Rolling Stone* (UK) and, with recently appointed news editor Jonathon Green, began making radical changes. Issue number 44 contained no US copy whatsoever and made no reference to the American office. 'One of the reasons for the all-British issue was that Wenner eventually refused to send the plates,' says Marcuson. 'I asked the Stones' office what I should do. I told them I could produce a magazine called *Rolling Stone* and they said, "Go right ahead." I wasn't obeying orders, but I was getting the endorsement of the Stones' office to do this stuff. So we brought it out, with the blessing of Mick Jagger. Wenner was freaking. I can't remember what tipped him over the edge.'

What had tipped Jann Wenner over the edge was Marcuson's bold editorial in issue number 44. 'This is the first issue of *Rolling Stone* in which all the editorial pages are British . . . Sure the music is important – very important – but a million and one other things have their own potential . . .' Taking his cue from Jagger, Marcuson was indeed pushing the magazine in a more political direction, much to Wenner's annoyance. A number of warnings from the proprietor arrived by telegram, via the Stones' office.

By October 1969, *Rolling Stone* (UK) had achieved a degree of celebrity in certain circles and, like Apple, its offices had become a Mecca for hippies and the new breed of underground entrepreneurs with big dreams. Guys like the American Bobby Steinbrecher, who had arrived in London convinced he could replace Allan Klein as the Beatles' manager and guys like Edward Molton and Stephen Warwick, who had targeted *Rolling Stone* (UK) to help launch their own publishing empire and lend a veneer of underground credibility to their organisation.

'Steve and Eddie just walked into the office one day,' recalls Alan Marcuson. 'They started making noises about getting involved.' Molton and Warwick were unaware that they had arrived at a crucial point. In San Francisco, Wenner was making plans to shut down the London office after Marcuson had ignored an ultimatum to submit all his copy to the American office for approval and concentrate on selling advertising space. Marcuson responded by turning up the heat. With the assistance of John Esam, the charismatic poet and counter-culture guru who was responsible for launching LSD on London in 1965, Marcuson composed his next daring editorial.

High on acid and loosely quoting the *I Ching*, Esam and Marcuson wrote:

A Message – The Younger Son Leaves Home; No Blame. Reluctantly, and in response to realities not necessarily of our own choosing, this magazine is in the process of disassociating itself from *Rolling Stone* USA . . . San Francisco is not Europe yet . . . It leaves two cells alive . . . we would like to state that we feel no animosity towards American *Rolling Stone*, but for various good reasons, it is better that we change the name. The next issue will therefore be known as *Friends of Rolling Stone*. In time we will most likely become simply *Friends*. The Staff.

Published in issue 45, Marcuson's prankish yet astonishingly naïve stance was greeted by a swift retort from Wenner. When Marcuson and his colleagues arrived at Hanover Square the following day, they found a large padlock on the door. He recalls:

A man from the Stones' office had been sent to lock the building. We were then allowed to come and get our personal effects and leave. I can now see why Wenner closed us down. We were bringing out a completely different magazine with his logo on it! But I had sold a lot of advertising, about £1,200 worth, booked for the next issue. I'd gone round to all the advertisers, told them we were bringing out a British magazine, hinting that it would be called *Friends of Rolling Stone*, with lots of music and no politics. The advertisers hated the politics and so did Wenner because it chased the advertising away. That was the position the underground press was in. Wenner very cleverly said, 'Stick to the music, that's where the revenue is,' and that's how he became a multimillionaire.

Issue 45 of *Rolling Stone* (UK) had also contained a full-page advertisement wishing *Friends of Rolling Stone* every success. It was signed by a number of well-wishers, including Famepushers; Molton and Warwick in the guise of 'Motherburger'; and Ned Sherrin, the well-known film and television executive who had befriended Stephen Warwick during the making of *The Virgin Soldiers*.

But Jann Wenner was not about to allow Marcuson to use the words 'Rolling Stone' in the title of his breakaway publication and immediately threatened an injunction. Marcuson instinctively turned to Mick Jagger for help, but by now the Rolling Stones were departing for the American tour that would culminate at Altamont. 'There was no way that Jagger was going to give another moment's attention to the magazine, or any of us,' reflects Marcuson, who was now itching to launch his new publication.

'I just wanted to get a newspaper out every two weeks and I didn't give a toss ... whatever it took,' says Marcuson. 'Money was a necessary evil; something you had to have. We used to say, "Money's like petrol; you've got to put it in the tank to drive the car." That's all it represented to us at that time. I had the odd fantasy that we'd get distributed by W. H. Smith and make lots of money, but Smith's wouldn't even touch *Private Eye* in those days.'

Jonathon Green, also working on the new publication, recalls:

When Jon Goodchild left to go to *Oz*, I was expected to do the layout. Goodchild was part of that full-bloodied, acid-soaked hippie thing whereby it was awfully good fun to make the pages illegible and say, 'Hey man, let's put an umlaut over that.' We needed a designer, so I phoned up my friend Pearce Marchbank who was at *Architectural Design* and asked him if he'd like to art-edit *Rolling Stone*. Of course he said, 'Yes I would.' By the time Pearce arrived, the magazine had turned into *Friends of Rolling Stone*; then we went for a drink and it was *Friends*.

Pearce Marchbank respected Barney Bubbles, who was an awful hippie, but a great designer. Every third word from Pearce was 'Clean ... clean design! Straight lines! Right angles! Lots of white space!' The hippies didn't like that.

Marchbank started work on the design of *Friends* at the Earls Court flat of *Time Out* advertising manager John Leaver and his partner Pat Bell, who had worked on *Rolling Stone* (UK). Soon, the operation moved to another makeshift HQ in Knightsbridge provided by would-be Beatles manager Bobby Steinbrecher. 'Bobby's flat was wonderfully over the top,' recalls Jonathon Green. 'Pearce and I laboured over the boards at a kitchen table, albeit in a smart kitchen, but *Friends* needed somewhere permanent. At this stage Alan presented us with these two hustlers, Steve and Eddie.'

Meanwhile, Malcolm Addison was still guarding the fort at Red Sands, awaiting news from Molton and Warwick. 'It all seemed very professional at first,' recalls Addison. 'But I spent a lot of time filling milk bottles. Then we had to build a bloody helicopter pad.' Forty railway sleepers were towed out from Queenborough behind the *June Francis* and Addison had to haul them 90 feet up on to the towers, lash them down and construct the landing pad. But the helicopters failed to arrive, as did any communication from the mainland. Hugh had long departed and there was no sign of any workmen to build the Pleasuredome.

Naturally, with little more to do than make Molotov cocktails, Addison became disillusioned. The final straw was yet to come. 'I was left for eleven days, stranded without any food or water,' says Addison. 'I was completely out of supplies. It was a bastard period. It was dreadfully cold and windy. I was very pissed off and this marked the end of my time on the fort.' Eventually the *June Francis* arrived. A frozen and dejected Addison peered down from the central tower to be greeted by Molton, making a token appearance at Red Sands. 'There was a brief attempt at an apology,' says Addison, 'but there wasn't a great deal of time before the tide changed and the boat had to go back to Queenborough.

'Hugh and I were just caretakers, mere tools,' says Addison. 'They may have considered employing us as labourers once the thing got going but I don't think we had anything to offer other than that. When the plan fell through, it was abandoned. In hindsight I think it was the safety considerations that made it impossible to build the Pleasuredome. I stayed down on the Isle of Sheppey, ran the *June Francis* and took out the odd fishing party and worked as a butcher in Queenborough. But anybody with long hair was regarded with suspicion. The fishermen didn't like all the weird hippies being down there.'

As Edward Molton continued to diversify his interests, Stephen Warwick's creative impulses were left unfulfilled and he too was becoming disillusioned. The prospects for the Pleasuredome had deteriorated to the point where only an injection of serious money could rescue the project. Moreover, Warwick still hankered after an opportunity to produce a movie or, at least, a television feature. He pestered Molton day and night, but his partner was simply devoid of contacts in the entertainment world. As Warwick's frustration was nearing its limit, Molton got lucky again.

4. BRIDGE-O-RAMA

Enjoying a quiet drink in a Mayfair pub, Edward Molton overheard a conversation. Standing nearby and holding court was the journalist Jeremy Flint, soon to become the BBC bridge correspondent. Flint was boasting about how much money there was in tournament bridge and rubber bridge and was expressing the opinion that there might be some crossover between bridge and television. Molton seized the moment and introduced himself to Flint.

In the discussion that followed, it was suggested that a television series based on the game of bridge would be of great interest to the American TV networks, the rationale being that US advertisers were always looking for new ways to reach the more affluent consumers. These people did not watch very much television, but they did play a great deal of bridge. After an exchange of telephone numbers, Molton dashed over to Warwick's Mortlake home, exclaiming that he'd met a man in a pub who wanted to make a film about bridge.

'The words that were on our lips the whole time were "production values",' says John Eichler. 'Stephen, knowing that the world-famous screen star Omar Sharif played bridge to an international standard, felt the two things – Sharif's celebrity and TV bridge – naturally slotted together.' Pursuing this idea, Molton and Warwick set up a meeting with Omar Sharif's manager and fellow bridge player Leon Yallouze, then resident at the Westbury Hotel in London's Bond Street. 'Yallouze had always wanted to have a part of the film action,' continues Eichler, 'and he was prepared to put up a considerable amount of Sharif's money, around £100,000.'

For Molton and Warwick, this was by far their most exciting and daring venture to date. If they could sell the series in the USA, enough cash would flow into the organisation to fund everything, including the Pleasuredome and Brinsley Schwarz. On 5 December 1969, Molton registered Grand Slam Productions Ltd at Companies House and the following day shares and directorships were allotted to Leon Yallouze, Stephen Warwick and Martin Bayer, a South African solicitor who had been introduced to Molton by Alan Marcuson. Bayer, also known as Mr X, was the secret head of The Defence & Aid Fund for Southern Africa, a network set up to support political prisoners and their families. Bayer had smuggled millions of pounds into South Africa without detection.

Stephen Warwick's concept was to make a 12-part television series following the progress of the most expensive card game in history – a bridge tournament between Jeremy Flint and Jonathan Cansino, versus 'The Omar Sharif Bridge Circus', consisting of the Italian players Giogio Belladonna, Benito Garrozzo and Claude Delmouly, plus Leon Yallouze and Sharif himself. John Eichler says, 'This was to be Rubber Bridge, a pound a point, which meant there was anything up to £10,000 on the table. Jonathan Cansino was the young wild boy of bridge and Omar Sharif's Blue Team were the world champions.'

In early December, with Leon Yallouze's £100,000 in the bank, Molton and Warwick were able to start making arrangements for the event and engage all of the necessary talent. Christopher Morahan was appointed director and Derek Kavanagh was hired as production manager. Ned Sherrin accepted an unpaid role as producer, 'to keep a fatherly eye on things'. With underground movie director John Palmer, whose films included *Ciao Manhattan!*, starring Edie Sedgwick, Molton and Warwick set up yet another company – JPM&W – to handle the titles.

'Stephen went for all the people he knew in the business from around the James Bond scene,' says John Eichler. 'He gave it a huge look and spent a lot of money. There was lots of beige and cream baize on the walls. The game room was a soundproof box within the ballroom. There would be security men, who would look after the cards and hand the packs to the players as they went into the sealed box.'

Another part of the set contained The Bridgorama – a giant scoreboard in the shape of a cross. 'It was to be operated by worthies,' recalls Eichler, 'bridge people, who were giving up their holidays to come and operate it. It would display the hands the players were holding and you could see who had what. Bridge people in the audience could read the progress of the game and imagine what they would play.'

We also built an international press box [recalls Derek Kavanagh]. It was, of course, totally phoney. There were 13 booths with actors of various nationalities and flags representing their supposed countries. Each had a microphone and it was as if he was reporting the event in his own language to his own country. We had three cameras trained on the audience and, as a gimmick, the TV wrestling commentator Kent Walton announcing each game's progress, as if it was being broadcast live. In the game room there were three cameras – one overhead, looking straight down on the table so you could see the hands as they were played and two cameras looking over shoulders at opposite faces so that you would always have an east–west partnership or a north–south partnership in camera revealing the facial expressions of Omar Sharif and the other players.

As Christmas 1969 approached, Molton and Warwick distributed invitations to the media and the bridge community.

Grand Slam Productions Limited cordially invite you to a Challenge Match between The Omar Sharif Bridge Circus and Jeremy Flint & Jonathan Cansino at The Piccadilly Hotel London . . . a remarkable event – a challenge match of 100 rubbers . . . £1 per point with a further £1,000 every four rubbers.

At the beginning of January 1970, an executive jet brought Omar Sharif and his team from Italy to Heathrow Airport where they were met by a fleet of five Rolls Royces and three Humbers, laid on by Grand Slam. Strategically positioned cameras filmed the convoy as it made its way along the M4 motorway and into London. The tournament commenced on

6 January and play continued for a further four days. Each day consisted of two sessions, the first commencing at 2 p.m. After a break for dinner, play continued until midnight.

It all got out of hand and turned into a huge production [says Eichler]. When the event started, Stephen and I stood in the doorway. Omar walked in, there were TV cameras everywhere, those big ones that looked like fridges on stands, and we were going, 'Wow!' This was insane. It happens to nearly everybody that does anything like that. You don't do it with confidence. We thought we'd get found out at any minute. Upstairs we had three suites that we used as production rooms. A day into the event, Stephen had decided that his documentary would be a fly-on-the-wall film, exposing the bridge scene. Stephen had also fallen in love with Omar's daughter, thinking she was his secretary.

There had been a few threats on Omar's life. We hired a guy called Bobby Ramsey to be Omar's bodyguard. He was short, square and flat-faced and his business card said: 'Have _____ Will Travel'. He also carried a briefcase with him and I always had the vision that it contained a gun. He was good at getting in between people. On the first day that Omar arrived we started getting pestering phone calls. Two Middle Eastern guys arrived at the office, asking to speak to Omar. On the third day they'd found their way into the production suite and were ranting, 'Where is Omar? You hide him from us.'

We called Bobby Ramsey up and told him. Bobby said to them, 'I've seen you lads before. I like you but I'd like you to go away now. I don't want any problems.' They didn't know he was frisking them while he was talking to them. We were slack-jawed watching this. They continued ranting and Bobby said, 'You don't want to step over the line with me . . .' They carried on ranting. Then it just happened. Suddenly Bobby went 'Whack!' into the guy's face. He went down. Then he punched the other guy up the hall. Every time the guy got up, Bobby

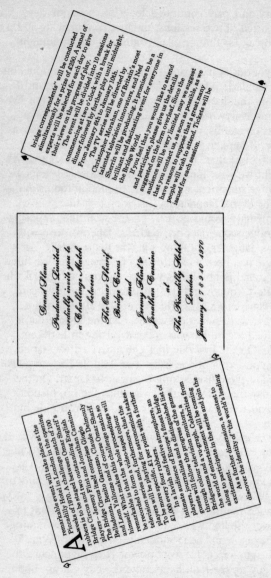

Take it to the Bridge-O-Rama; Molton and Warwick's first daring adventure (courtesy Malcolm Addison)

hit him in another direction and punched him all the way to the lift. He threw them both in, pressed the button and the doors closed. He came back and said, 'Right, I'd better go and look after Omar now. I don't think we'll have any more trouble with them . . .'

On 10 January 1970, Grand Slam hosted a gala night at the Piccadilly Hotel:

We had the media, minor royalty and bridge-playing celebrities [says Eichler]. Molton had a suit made for the event, a green tuxedo. Sandie Shaw was there, Godfrey Wynn and Ned Sherrin. A lot of people wanted to come because Omar was there and the champagne was flowing. I'd become quite friendly with Bobby Ramsey, having had breakfast together. I suddenly said, 'Look Bobby, it's driving me up the fucking wall. What is in that briefcase?' He replied, 'Well, I like to carry it with me, just in case.' He opened the briefcase and it contained his press cuttings – a huge bunch. 'This is me with Reg and Ronnie Kray; this is me with Barbra Streisand; this is me with Frank Sinatra, Peter Sellers . . .' They were all there. That was his life, in that briefcase.

On 12 January, the Challenge Match moved to the Monte Carlo Suite at the Mayfair Hotel. Play continued for a further two days after which it was time for Stephen Warwick to consider the intended TV series and documentary. Eichler recalls:

We had huge amount of footage in the can, all on videotape, which was very expensive to edit, but we had no money left over for post-production. Also, one of the main problems was that the overhead camera didn't work. Quite a lot of the action wasn't captured, which was a nightmare. Key shots were missing. We'd also built up a network of various businesses. As the Omar thing grew, we'd taken on all these little things. JPM&W, Much Ado, *Friends* and numerous little offshoots that were helped by the money that was coming in to the

Bridge Circus. Our focus the whole time was to raise money for the Pleasuredome.

Friends magazine was considered by Molton and Warwick to be one possible source of revenue. With this in mind, Molton offered the magazine accommodation at 305 Portobello Road, in the two upstairs rooms that had been his home for the last six months. 'When we moved into Portobello, we paid rent,' says Alan Marcuson, emphasising that Molton's gesture was not purely altruistic:

I think Steve and Eddie made some sort of proposal. They had a lot of verbal, but there was no actual money. They were making business suggestions, but they weren't putting anything into it. They may have paid the wages for a couple of weeks, but the wages were about ten quid each. I'd registered two companies, T.F. Much and F.F. Out. The bank wanted to know who T.F. Much was. I said he was a graphic designer I admired . . . my hero. They believed me. People would write out cheques to the 'Too Fucking Much Co Ltd'. The bank manager used to freak out. It was early days. But I never let Steve and Eddie near the company. I retained control.

'*Friends* gave Molton credibility,' says John Eichler. 'The other heads thought that if Molton was dealing with *Friends*, which was part of the whole underground scene, then he must be alright.'

The first issue of *Friends* appeared in December 1969. The tabloid format required folding, an operation that could not be carried out easily at Portobello Road. Molton offered *Friends* the use of some offices he'd acquired at 140 Park Lane as a base for *Bridge-O-Rama*. 'We moved into Park Lane,' recalls Jonathan Green, 'and folded all the copies of *Friends* No.1 by hand. The offices were quite grand, on the corner of Park Lane and Oxford Street, overlooking Marble Arch. Coming from two rooms with no heating above a junk shop in Portobello Road, it was quite something.'

* * *

In a little under nine months, Molton and Warwick's sprawling empire had grown out of all control. In addition to several smaller businesses, they had deeply involved themselves in four extremely ambitious ventures: the Pleasuredome, Famepushers, *Bridge-O-Rama* and *Friends*. The lives of dozens of people were tied up in their elaborate plans, yet none of these companies was showing any sign of profit. Cash flow was virtually nonexistent and Molton was desperately juggling the finances.

To the outsider, it may have looked as if Edward Molton was a financial Svengali with unlimited resources, but, in reality, Molton had little or no money, only growing debts. The numerous businesses under his control may have appeared to interact harmoniously with one another, but it appears that they were sharing the same tranche of limited cash.

According to Ricky Blears, Molton's financial equilibrium was achieved by the dubious cash-juggling technique known as 'kite flying'.* As Ricky Blears says:

Eddie Molton had about 14 cheque books and he was cross-firing. Let's not beat about the bush. He was keeping all these companies going by moving the same money in and out of all of them. One minute there would be £20,000 in the bank, then it would be gone. He'd built up a lot of confidence with a lot of bank managers. There was money around from the Omar Sharif deal, a huge amount of money, but Molton was a flamboyant character who was used to taking about 200 people out to dinner at expensive restaurants like The Minotaur, The Genevieve or Mr Chow's.

---

*The basis of kite flying, or cross-firing, is that the perpetrator uses the time between banking a cheque and having it clear, assuming that it does, to falsely inflate his account balance. In this window of opportunity there may be an attempt to draw cash or raise credit. In another version of the same scam, the perpetrator issues multiple cheques against a nominal deposit to secure goods and services. However, a problem arises when a number of cheques, the total of which exceeds the account balance, arrive simultaneously at the issuing bank.

For the moment, Molton was managing to keep things moving forward, but the 60s were coming to an end and, although the halcyon days of the get-rich-quick merchant were not exactly over, a new hard realism was beginning to bite. Trying desperately to keep his balls in the air, Molton needed one more life-saving wheeze.

PART II
STUPIDITY

5. REVERTING TO HYPE

On the evening of 14 December 1969, 22-year-old Andrew Lauder, boy wonder of United Artists Records' A&R department, left his Kensington flat for the Country Club on Haverstock Hill. His mission was to assess the talents of Formerly Fat Harry, a four-piece rock band assembled by Bruce Barthol, former bassist with Country Joe And The Fish. Just three months earlier, Barthol's old hippie ensemble had appeared at the Woodstock Festival of Arts and Music in upstate New York, urging the mud-encrusted audience to give them: 'An F! . . . a U! . . . a C! . . .', but much had happened in the intervening quarter.

Creedence Clearwater Revival were in power, assaulting the US Hot Hundred with a rapid succession of three-minute broadsides; The Band had just released their critically acclaimed second long-player and Van Morrison was in New York's A&R Studios cutting *Moondance*, his soul-inspired follow-up to the ethereal *Astral Weeks*. These developments were perceived by many to represent rock's long-awaited return to basics.

This new direction had been inspired, perhaps, by The Band's 1968 debut, *Music From Big Pink* and the recent appearance of rock's first 'bootleg' – the illicit release of *Great White Wonder*, featuring the recent and unissued recordings of Bob Dylan. These two records had certainly been influencing the Beatles, who were about to endorse the proceedings with the rootsy 'Get Back', but were otherwise quietly disbanding. The Rolling Stones were also in retro-mode with their new release *Let It Bleed* – an unintentionally ironic title; during their recent performance at the Altamont Raceway in California, the Stones had witnessed the bloody murder of 18-year-old Meredith Hunter just a few feet from the stage.

Anticipating a packed Country Club and concerned that his name might not be on the guest list, Andrew Lauder quickened his pace. He needn't have worried; headliners Formerly Fat Harry were not yet in the 'standing room only' league and the club was almost bare. Unsure of the evening's precise programme, Lauder was heading for the bar when he heard the club's promoter, Stuart Lyons, announce the next act: 'Ladies and gentlemen, please welcome ... Brinsley Schwarz!'

'My immediate thought was that I'd arrived too early,' recalls Lauder, 'and that I would have to wait ages for the proper group to come on!' He watched, half-interested, as the members of Brinsley Schwarz filed on stage, resplendent in contemporary fashion – scooped neck T-shirts emblazoned with stars; tight-fitting suede jackets with appliqué cartoon motifs; velvet bell-bottom trousers and snakeskin boots – the finest that Ruskin of Kensington Market could offer.

Lauder was dubious, but four numbers in, as the organist held down a series of swirling sustained chords, the young A&R man felt excitement. He thought he recognised this one and his sudden expectations were confirmed as Brinsley Schwarz launched into The Band's 'Chest Fever'. 'I liked them,' continues Lauder. 'They sounded like The Band. In fact they were quite unlike any English group that had come before.' Lauder made a mental note to keep an eye on the group's progress and then, awaiting the on-stage arrival of Formerly Fat Harry, he casually mentioned to promoter Lyons that he had enjoyed the support act.

A few days later, Lauder received a telephone call from Dave Robinson, managing director of Famepushers and co-manager of Brinsley Schwarz. 'Dave wanted to talk,' recalls Lauder. 'I wasn't ready to sign the group, but I certainly wanted to hear their demos.' It was nearing Christmas and, as the UK record industry was preparing to shut down for its traditional ten-day break, Lauder was busy making plans for his first visit to the USA early in the new year.

The tail end of 1969 was a bizarre period for Brinsley Schwarz. On the one hand they were struggling to get work in their reinvented state – their appearance at the Country Club had been an isolated engagement – and on the other hand they were still fulfilling their contractual obligations as Kippington Lodge, including their headlining Saturday night residency at the Marquee. The group were suffering from an identity crisis, pondering whether they should hang on to their established circuit and survive, or persevere with the new approach and starve.

Dave Robinson had no doubts and was busy making recording and accommodation arrangements for his protégés. 'We had to get the record started,' says Robinson. 'So I got a few quid together and we cut a couple of tracks at Olympic.' Then he rented some rooms for the group above the Red Lion public house, conveniently located opposite the studio.

Hiring Olympic Studios, in Barnes, south-west London, where rock luminaries such as the Rolling Stones and Jimi Hendrix had recorded, was an extravagant way in which to commence the group's recording career. To pull it off, Robinson says he had to rely on a few favours and forego the services of an established producer:

> I was scamming the studio a bit, and there was no way
> there were any well-known producers who would do it.
> The band was together and I thought an engineer would
> be all right – he'd hold it together. That's how I became
> the producer. I did try approaching a couple of record
> companies and producers. I spoke to Tony
> Stratton-Smith at Charisma and Mickie Most. I always
> felt that you should go and talk to people. Words are
> sometimes the only way round it. I wanted Mickie Most
> to produce it.

At this point Mickie Most, was very busy getting his own label, RAK, off the ground but, after talking with Robinson, Most agreed to a session with Brinsley Schwarz, to take place at Morgan Studios in Willesden, north London. 'Mickie was very polite,' recalls Robinson. 'I think he did it much against his will.'

'We were doing very few gigs at this time,' says Nick Lowe. 'We weren't doing much self-composed material but we did have one terrible thing called "Life Is Dead", which was one of mine.' Bob Andrews elaborates, 'It was a rotten song that we would never have put on an album. "Life Is Dead" was a 20-minute progressive dirge. To us, Mickie Most was a pop person, so we gave him a hard time.' Lowe continues: 'We understood this to be a test recording, but Mickie said, "This is much too long, it should be three minutes." We thought it was shocking that he was gonna machete his way into our intricate arrangement and axe the fifteen-minute guitar solo.'

Mickie Most declined any further involvement with the group, so they went back into Olympic with Robinson at the controls. With the studio bills mounting up and Famepushers' own bank balance dwindling, Robinson's ideal-istic notion of carefully and slowly building the group's career was starting to fade and he began to focus clearly on the need for a serious recording contract.

Robinson concentrated his efforts once again on Andrew Lauder. 'Molton didn't really have enough money to support the band for six months,' says Dave Robinson, 'which was the basis on which we'd signed them. I'd even drawn up a cashflow document, but there was also a bit of a Catch 22 situation, because you couldn't get live work without having an official agent and the agent wouldn't take you on unless you had a record deal.'

To make matters more pressing, a bombshell was about to be dropped from another corner of the Molton and Warwick empire. *Bridge-O-Rama* had run into extreme financial diffi-culties. With over 50 hours of footage in the can, a number of outstanding bills had not been paid and there were absolutely no funds left for the crucial editing process. Molton and Warwick were forced to raise serious money fast, otherwise the proposed TV series would never see the light of day and Omar Sharif's manager, Leon Yallouze, would be calling for the return of his substantial investment.

Just as *Bridge-O-Rama* had been the focus to raise money for the Pleasuredome, a new focus was now required to raise money for *Bridge-O-Rama*. Edward Molton anxiously scrolled through the list of business ventures under his wing until his finger landed at Famepushers. Pop music, he reasoned, was where the fast money was. What, Molton wondered, was happening with Brinsley Schwarz? He phoned Robinson, who reported that the sessions were going well and there were many interested record labels – RAK, United Artists, some others, but Robinson reiterated that he still wanted to take things at a cautious pace. This was not what Molton wanted to hear.

Molton called an immediate meeting, to take place at Burford Villa. 'Rock 'n' roll was the obvious area in which to raise money,' says Eichler. 'Present at the meeting were Dave Robinson, Edward Molton, Stephen Warwick, Ricky Blears, Dot Burn-Forti and myself.' The essence of the conversation was as follows:

Molton:	How can we get the band a deal, quickly?
Blears:	We need a showcase.
Warwick:	Where would be the best venue?
Robinson:	We'll put them on at the Speakeasy.
Blears:	Not big enough. Where else is there?
Eichler:	Why not the Albert Hall?
Blears:	No – too ordinary. Where is the biggest and the best venue in the world, the rock 'n' roll mecca? Where the group could play a gig and attract a lot of press?
Robinson:	The Fillmore East, New York.
Blears:	Great – couldn't we put a gig on there?
Robinson:	There would be a few hurdles to overcome. Bill Graham amongst them.
Molton:	That shouldn't be a problem for you Dave.
Blears:	If we had a gig somewhere really exciting, maybe we could get some sponsorship from somebody . . .

'In a couple of hours, we'd talked it up from the Speakeasy to the Fillmore,' continues Eichler. 'Then it became, "Let's see if we can charter a little plane. Let's see if we can get a bigger plane. Let's see if we can fill it up with journalists." Dave said he had a mate at Aer Lingus whom he could contact and everybody went, "Yeah!" Ricky Blears was very good at dealing with the press, and proposed a competition with the *Melody Maker*. We had to get some serious dosh, some American dosh. There was a lot of stadium rock going on at the time and hype wasn't such a dirty word. We didn't think of it as such. It was a laugh. We laughed ourselves stupid.'

Everyone in the organisation was excited by the sheer audacity of the idea, but it would be Dave Robinson's task to pull it all together. He needed two big favours: the first, from an international airline and the second from the promoter at the world's then most famous rock 'n' roll shrine. The fact that Brinsley Schwarz were totally unknown was not an issue. For Robinson, securing a deal with Aer Lingus was relatively straightforward. He started to negotiate a charter flight at a discount price of £7,000, because of the publicity that the airline would receive from having one of its aircraft 'full of journalists'.

On this basis, Ricky Blears started to draw up the press invitation list, which included a number of reporters from some highly improbable publications. John Eichler explains the reasoning. 'Why take journalists we knew wouldn't be into it, like the guy from the *Jewish Chronicle*? Because we were totally barmy. Fashion editors, the *Sporting Life* . . . it was a big plane, we had to fill it! We could of course have filled it up with our friends and relatives, but the deal with Aer Lingus was that the aircraft would be literally full of journalists!'

Obtaining a booking at the Fillmore East was rather more difficult. In 1970, the Fillmores East and West were two of the world's most important and prestigious rock venues and the auditoria's promoter, Bill Graham, was a powerful and respected player. His well-publicised motto – 'Though I walk through the valley of the shadow of death, I fear no evil, for I am the meanest son of a bitch in the valley' – struck fear into the hearts of lesser managers and agents. Robinson, however, was undeterred, phoning Graham's West Coast office incessantly until he eventually got through to the legendary impresario.

When Robinson finally got to speak with Graham, he immediately sensed that the self-confessed son of a bitch wasn't staying on the phone for too long. There were only a few moments in which to make an impression. 'Brinsley Schwarz are going to be massive!' Robinson exclaimed nervously. 'Don't pass up the opportunity of having them play the Fillmore!' Bill Graham wasn't buying, and told Robinson, 'I've got a thousand record companies on my back. It's No!'

Then, thinking it would see off the mad Irishman, Graham quickly terminated the conversation, 'Look Dave, any time you're in San Francisco, drop by.'

It was 6 p.m. London time. Robinson grabbed his passport and took a cab to the airport. Early the following morning he was in San Francisco, not even sure if Graham was in town, but he'd been in the air long enough to refine and rehearse his pitch. Without a hotel reservation or luggage to contend with, Robinson made for the offices of Bill Graham's Winterland Productions on Market Street, opposite the Fillmore West Auditorium. There, the receptionist asked him to wait in the corridor.

At midday, Bill Graham showed up. Graham was so astonished to find Robinson waiting for him, less than 24 hours after their transatlantic telephone conversation, that he agreed to a five-minute meeting. Robinson, nervous as hell, attempted to break the ice by asking Graham for a cigarette. Then he launched into his spiel. 'Bill, I have to have this gig . . . the press want to see Brinsley Schwarz in the right setting . . .' As Robinson continued, Graham started to warm to him and promised to give the matter consideration.

Back in England, everyone was on tenterhooks. Brinsley Schwarz were kept busy at De Lane Lea Studios in Soho, producing some incidental music for Stephen Warwick's proposed *Bridge-O-Rama* documentary. 'We used some of the bits from our progressive phase,' recalls Schwarz. 'Music to accompany set-building. We were handed a bit of paper saying they needed 30 per cent drums or 90 per cent brass. It was really tedious.'

When Robinson returned from San Francisco with a less-than-rosy report, he was reluctant to give the group or his management colleagues false hopes and a week passed without a response from Graham. 'Then the call came,' remembers Robinson. ' "Yes," said Graham, "there is a weekend in April at the Fillmore East. I've got Van Morrison and Quicksilver Messenger Service. Brinsley Schwarz can open." It was extraordinary.'

Dave Robinson now had a tangible plan with which to ensnare a record company.

* * *

Andrew Lauder returned from his first US trip in February 1970, to discover that a massive campaign had evolved. 'The group is making its world debut in New York . . .' announced Robinson excitedly, '. . . at the Fillmore East . . . with Van Morrison and Quicksilver Messenger Service. I've been over to see Bill Graham and it's all set up!'

Lauder listened to Robinson's salvo knowing instinctively what would be coming next. 'He still needed a record deal,' he remembers. 'Deadlines were suddenly imposed because of the US trip and Dave was saying to me, "If you want to do this, you've got to do it quickly." '

Andrew Lauder had very much enjoyed his first visit to the States and, with the prospect of a swift return trip in the back of his mind, agreed to pop down to Olympic Studios to listen to the group's recordings. It was sounding good. By now, Robinson was bombarding Lauder with more exciting plans. 'We're inviting the world's press,' he said, matter-of-factly. 'And we're chartering a jet to take everybody to New York.'

'I thought it smelt of disaster,' says Lauder, 'and I felt the hype beginning to build, but I thought that Robinson might just be able to pull it off.'

As Lauder sat in the Olympic control room, tapping his A&R foot to the group's gentle country-rock rhythms, Robinson produced the finished artwork for 'the album'. It had been designed by Barney Bubbles and featured a full-colour illustration of a Red Indian astride his horse, glancing over his shoulder at the planet Earth. The sleeve copy listed all the song titles, group members and so forth and Dave Robinson was credited as producer. On the spine of the sleeve was a small white square, ready to accept the catalogue number and identity of the record company that would be willing to take the plunge. Robinson passed the artwork to Lauder, who immediately focused on the small white square.

Lauder reported back to Martin Davies, head of business affairs at United Artists and soon Robinson was summoned in to discuss a deal. Accompanied by his lawyer, Jeff Abrahams of Gerald Black & Company, Robinson again carried with him a copy of the sleeve artwork, this time containing one minor alteration. As the meeting commenced, Robinson unpacked the artwork and casually passed it to Lauder, who quickly spotted the difference between this and the earlier version. The small white square, previously blank, now contained the legend 'RAK Records'!

RAK, now successfully launched by Mickie Most, was the new home of former Apple pop band Hot Chocolate – 'Not the sort of label,' thought Lauder, 'to sign a quasi-progressive group like Brinsley Schwarz.' It also occurred to Lauder that if Robinson was talking to RAK, he may well have shown Mickie Most a copy of the sleeve artwork bearing a United Artists logo!

During this period, Andrew Lauder had already signed, or was about to sign to United Artists, a number of groups with one common attribute. These were former 60s beat groups who had changed their image and name to greet the new 'heavy' era. These included: Family (formerly the Farinas), Man (formerly the Bystanders), Gypsy (Le Gay), and Cochise (Plastic Penny). Brinsley Schwarz (formerly Kippington Lodge) fell neatly into this pattern, although Lauder recognised that 'the Brinsleys' were one of only a handful of bands in the UK at that time performing American-influenced country rock. This, however, might have been just the thing to distinguish Brinsley Schwarz from the herd.

With the prospect of a major promotional campaign in place, to be funded, thankfully, by the group's management company, and a reasonable debut album already recorded and packaged, Lauder and Davies offered the group a £22,000 advance against an 8 per cent royalty to sign with United Artists.

News of the recording contract was music to the ears of Edward Molton and Stephen Warwick. With £22,000 coming into Famepushers' coffers, it would now be possible to borrow some of this money and commence the editing of *Bridge-O-Rama*, before talking to prospective buyers among the various American TV networks. A deal for *Bridge-O-Rama* would net large sums in advances, surely enough to repay Brinsley Schwarz and also finance the Pleasuredome.

Molton and Warwick had not forgotten, of course, that the Fillmore launch was fast approaching and reminded Robinson that firm deals now had to be struck with Aer Lingus, Head Limousines and the Grand Metropolitan hotel chain, including, wherever possible, comprehensive credit facilities.

But even if all of this could be achieved, unimaginable problems lay ahead for Brinsley Schwarz and their intrepid managers.

6. VISA TROUBLE

Now, just six months after recruiting Brinsley Schwarz, Robinson had secured a recording contract with United Artists Records and acquired an agent – Tony Howard at NEMS. 'I had 20 or 30 acts at the time,' says Howard. Brinsley Schwarz were pretty low on the totem pole for me at that point. But they were a good band and had made a reasonable record and I got swept along in the Dave Robinson hype.'

As February 1970 was drawing to a close, Famepushers began making plans for the group's appearance in New York, which those involved were now routinely referring to as 'The Hype'. Nick Lowe recalls:

> It was presented to us as a *fait accompli*. We thought it was the greatest. We were gonna go to the Fillmore and we'd be famous. End of story. We could short-circuit all those unpleasant miles in a Transit and the horrible club dates – we wouldn't have to do them. Of course, we were very inept. We'd been playing Goudhurst Village Hall two days before we left for the States. All I knew was that I wanted to climb on a big plane to North America and get down to the groupie club.

The Fillmore dates were set for Friday, 3 April and Saturday, 4 April 1970, two houses per night. With only six weeks to go, the office at 305 Portobello Road was far too small to accommodate the small army of workers who would have to put in long and arduous hours organising the trip. More importantly, Famepushers needed more than one telephone line. Stephen Warwick had recently found some office space for the *Bridge-O-Rama* production team at 44 Park Road, close to Regents Park and there was a spare room available for Famepushers. In addition to Dave Robinson, Dot Burn-Forti and Rosalind Pearce, the team was joined by Sue Crafts and John Cowell. Ricky Blears, now trading as Messagemakers, also moved to Park Road, with his new assistant Christie Sutton.

Ricky Blears had already begun devising a competition in conjunction with the *Melody Maker*. The five winners would each receive a pair of tickets to see the world debut of Brinsley Schwarz in New York. The *Melody Maker* competition was run in the issues dated 14 and 21 March under the banner 'Win a free weekend in New York with Brinsley Schwarz'. Entrants were asked to place, in order of importance, seven qualities needed by the successful group of the 70s. These were, in the eventual winning order: Originality, Musicianship, Composing Talent, Visual Appeal, Showmanship, Having A Message, Clothes. (By 1977, the reverse order would prove to be nearer the mark.)

Meanwhile, Robinson was working on the logistics of the trip, including the scheduling of the press flights; booking rehearsal time and equipment rental in New York; arranging seats and photo passes for the journalists at the Fillmore; hiring a fleet of limousines to ferry the entire party around New York and firming up record release dates and promotion.

It was decided that the press entourage would fly out on the Saturday to catch that evening's first show. The normal flight time from London to New York was seven hours, with New York five hours behind London. Theoretically, this meant that the journalists could fly out in the morning and arrive in plenty of time to be at the Fillmore for showtime at 8 p.m. On the Sunday, after some free time for sightseeing, the journalists would attend a press reception at The Royal Manhattan Hotel, before returning home on an overnight flight.

Famepushers' rationale for such an extravagant promotion was contained in Ricky Blears's colourfully worded information sheet that accompanied the invitation mailed initially to 74 prominent UK journalists, broadcasters and taste-makers. The invitation read:

It's because you're such a hard lot to woo. If we'd invited you to hear Brinsley Schwarz at the Sale Locarno and offered to pay your bus fare, I doubt if we'd have such a distinguished group of guests . . . it's part of the Twentieth Century myth that if you go somewhere far and fast, whatever's at the other end is necessarily superior.

Not all of the journalists invited would be taken in quite so easily. Writing in *Zigzag*, Pete Frame was publicly wrestling with his conscience.

Would I like to go to New York and see Brinsley Schwarz play at the Fillmore. Free, gratis, and for nothing? Jesus Christ, of course I would. Bloody right . . . But then I had a sit down and thought about the whole business . . . and I got to thinking that any writer with an ounce of integrity is going to denounce the whole thing as a giant, blatant con . . . but I knew all the same that I was far too selfish to turn down a free trip to New York.

If I dig the group and gush with superlatives will anybody believe that I haven't been sucked into the vat of bought publicity . . . if I think they're the worst load of crap since The Archies, will I have the courage to say so, and then will I be condemned for miserable ingratitude . . . would anybody care about what I thought anyway?

When Frame then heard that Andrew Lauder, a man whose taste he respected, had signed the group to United Artists, he became even more baffled, concluding, 'I couldn't be in a more confused pre-trip state if I tried.'

As the trip drew nearer, Pete Frame was not alone. Although the press response to the invitations was encouraging, Ricky Blears was suffering a crisis of confidence. John Eichler recalls, 'At one point Ricky said he wanted to talk to me and offered me a ride home in his Mini. He said, "This isn't going to work. They're going to turn on us, I know it." Ricky was panicking. It was understandable. We all realised there was a risk element, but it was too late. We were going to New York.'

Nobody considered that the Brinsleys themselves might be slightly nervous about their monumental launch. Nick Lowe recalls:

We had a rehearsal just before the trip and our backers came down. They were horrified because we weren't doing any of the new tunes from the album that featured our Crosby, Stills & Nash harmonies. We could do these when we were sitting round in a circle, or in a studio, but when it came to getting up on stage and opening our mouths and singing through amps, well, we didn't know how to do it. We could only do all our Kippington Lodge stuff like 'Life Is Dead'. Steve and Eddie were appalled that we couldn't do the harmonies live.

It was also Famepushers' intention to film 'The Hype', even though *Bridge-O-Rama* and Stephen Warwick's documentary about it remained unfinished. This new project would fall in the lap of 19-year-old Jodi Routh, son of television personality and writer Jonathan Routh. He recalls:

I had been working for a company called O Films. We made pop promos and I'd also worked as a junior cameraman on *Stones in the Park*. Then I inherited some money from a long-lost aunt and set up Jodi Routh Entertainments Ltd in January 1970. I assembled a team of people to help me make experimental pop films and one of these people was John Eichler, whom I knew from the fringes of the music scene.

Then I met Edward Molton and Stephen Warwick. They realised that I had a lot of contacts and that my father, who was famous at the time, was in a liaison with Olga Deterding, who was an oil heiress. I think it was this contact that Molton and Warwick were interested in, as a source of money for production. I arranged meetings between them and Olga and at one of these meetings they wanted me out of the way so that they could talk about money with Olga. It was my blue-eyed innocence at the time. I said, 'OK, fine, no problem', so I let them talk about money.

Olga Deterding was the 42-year-old daughter of the late Captain Henri Deterding, founder of the Royal Dutch Petroleum Company and one of the wealthiest men in the world. Olga had led a varied and interesting life, including a stint with Dr Albert Schweitzer at his West African leper colony, and was now an extremely astute business woman. Olga was usually cautious about share dealings and investments, but when Edward Molton mentioned to her that money was badly needed as a down payment on the Aer Lingus charter flight, she had no hesitation in investing £5,000. Simultaneously, Jodi Routh was named as producer of the film to be made of the event. Jodi says, 'Molton and Warwick realised Olga might have been a good source of finance for these various ventures and by stroking me, as it were, I would be the key to Olga.'

Jodi Routh's first job, as producer, was to locate a director. He immediately thought of Tony Palmer, with whom he had worked on the Jack Bruce documentary, *Ropeladder to the Moon*. Palmer had also made two well-received rock documentaries for the BBC – *All My Loving* and *Farewell Cream*. Two weeks prior to the Fillmore trip, Palmer commenced filming and, with his crew, travelled around London and Tunbridge Wells, shooting footage with the four members of Brinsley Schwarz, including a lunchtime concert at the Conway Hall in Holborn on 24 March. 'He took the group to Regents Park Zoo and had them jumping up and down like monkeys,' recalls John Eichler. 'We saw the rushes and said, "No, this isn't what we want." We wanted Pennebaker ... cameras up the nose. So Stephen and I sacked Tony Palmer.'

Meanwhile, as Dave Robinson was honing the fine details, Dot Burn-Forti contracted hepatitis, but decided she would still go to the Fillmore. It was Famepushers' intention for Brinsley Schwarz to go to New York a week ahead of the shows to acclimatise 'like footballers' and rehearse at the Fillmore, using specially hired state-of-the-art equipment. With ten days to go before the trip, Robinson applied to the London branch of the Musicians Union for work permits for the group and then to the US Embassy for visas. It was this final detail that proved the most irksome.

At the time, the Musicians Union and the American Federation of Musicians operated an exchange system, theoretically to protect the livelihood of their respective members. In order that four British musicians could work in the USA, engagements had to be found in the UK for a similar number of American musicians. In the case of Brinsley Schwarz, the group's work permits had been arranged by the Musicians Union on an exchange basis with the US West Coast group Love. But Love had cancelled their UK tour at the eleventh hour, effectively making exchange impossible.

Tony Howard recalls, 'I had a reciprocal deal with people in America, but there were always problems. As agents, we all did deals. Harold Davidson might have been bringing Count Basie in. That's 16 musicians doing a lot of dates and that's a lot of man-days. Davidson, who brought in many American bands, was the key to the Musicians Union. There was a lot of back-scratching going on, but the Brinsleys were only doing the one gig. That might have been the problem.'

'In the euphoria and excitement, little oversights were made,' says Brinsley Schwarz. 'Dave's ability to transcend normal thought may have left his administrative capabilities lacking. One of us had a drugs conviction but that didn't really hinder it. Dave's idea of getting visas was that if you were leaving on Friday, you just go down a few days beforehand and get your passport stamped.'

Nick Lowe says, 'I'd been busted for possession of dope the previous year. It was a microscopic amount – a five bob deal – but in Tunbridge Wells in 1969, that was extremely serious. The cops mounted a huge raid. I got fined seventy quid, but it might as well have been £700,000. Robbo paid the fine for me.' When, on Monday, 30 March, the members of Brinsley Schwarz went to the US Embassy in Grosvenor Square for their visas, minus work permits to substantiate their applications, Robinson encountered his first major stumbling block. The Fillmore engagement was four days away.

Brinsleys' drummer Billy Rankin possessed a US passport, so he was able to travel. On Tuesday, 31 March, Rankin and roadie John Seymour flew first class to New York on a Boeing 747, accompanied by the first film unit, consisting of cameraman Les Young; sound recordist Tony Hyde; production manager Derek Kavanagh; assistant director Terry Marcell; and Stephen Warwick, who had now appointed himself director.

Also in the advance party was Help Yourself drummer Dave Charles, whose job it would be to record Brinsley Schwarz's performances at the Fillmore. Dave Charles recalls, 'For the documentary we needed to make an eight-track recording of the group in the Fillmore, for the film soundtrack, but Bill Graham said, "We can't upset everyone else with recording gear and a mobile truck just for an unknown band from England." Because of this, we would be stuck for a soundtrack. Somebody suggested that I could do it with a Nagra, which was a state-of-the-art portable tape recorder used in the film industry. I am an engineer, so I said yes.'

For the next two days the first film unit waited for the rest of the group to arrive and filled in time by filming some location shots around the city. 'They filmed New York street scenes and anything they thought would be good to put into the film,' says Jodi Routh. 'Like a helicopter flying over Manhattan.' John Eichler adds, 'They'd also filmed Billy Rankin chasing the air hostesses in first class. It was a terrible waste of film.'

Back in London, unable to secure visas, Robinson considered the options. Cancelling or postponing the launch was out of the question, especially as United Artists had yet to part with a large portion of the group's advance. It occurred to Robinson that the group might take an unscheduled holiday in Canada – Toronto to be precise, conveniently just across the border from New York State. Robinson considered Canada's Customs and Immigration officials to be a little more relaxed than their US colleagues, especially when confronted with four young holidaymakers. Once admitted into Canada, the group would simply fly down to New York, hook up with Rankin, and commence rehearsals. Toronto was the obvious solution.

On arriving at Toronto airport on Tuesday, 31 March, Robinson, Lowe, Andrews and Schwarz sidled up to the immigration desk and presented their passports, posing as tourists. But their long-haired appearance was already causing the officials some concern and the four passports were studied in some detail. With entry into Canada starting to look unlikely, Bob Andrews piped up, 'We're only gonna be here for an hour – we're just popping over to the US Embassy to pick up some visas, then we're off to New York!' Amazingly, it worked. Canadian Immigration granted the party entry for just 24 hours so that they could visit the US Embassy in Toronto.

Arriving at the Embassy, the four visitors were given forms to complete, stating their reasons for entering America. Brinsley Schwarz recalls Robinson's instructions for completing the forms. 'Dave said, "Where it says HAVE YOU EVER APPLIED FOR A US VISA BEFORE?, put NO." So we all wrote NO.' Each applicant was then assigned a number and told to wait. Nick Lowe recalls, 'We had to sit in a long queue behind all manner of humanity including veiled women with screaming children whose own allocated numbers were in the 200s.'

The English musicians and their usually optimistic manager were starting to panic. Were they being deliberately put to the back of the line?

Eventually, Robinson and the three musicians were called to the desk. 'Who the hell do you think you are?' screamed the official. 'You're not gonna fool us!' Robinson stepped forward to calm the enraged immigration man, who continued his rant. 'We've got a million dollars worth of computer back there boy,' he said, jerking his thumb over his right shoulder, 'just to check up on your *type*! Do you think we're crazy? *You* applied for visas in London yesterday! You wanna go to the US of A? No fucking chance!'

Lowe, Schwarz and Andrews looked at Robinson who in turn looked back at his three slack-jawed clients as the prospect of walking on stage in New York that Friday was melting away. After much pleading and another long wait, there were now rather less than 24 hours in which to obtain visas. Realising that they were obliged to exit Canada by the following morning, the three musicians immediately went into hiding at a nearby Travel Lodge motel. 'We watched *Star Trek* continuously and ate hamburgers on room service,' recalls Schwarz.

Meanwhile, Robinson began making frantic telephone calls. He had friends in the city; people he had met during his tenure as tour manager for Jimi Hendrix. Over the next two days, phone calls were made, lawyers were engaged and a little bit of Famepushers' money changed hands. Just as the group were getting used to hotel life, albeit anxiously as it was now the eve of the first Fillmore show, the requisite visas and work permits suddenly materialised.

But just as a light began to appear at the end of their tunnel, the ill-fated musicians suffered yet another setback. A sudden Air Traffic Controllers' strike in the United States had brought all commercial flights to a standstill. 'I remember watching the news on the hotel TV,' recalls Lowe. 'We saw pictures of grounded aircraft all across the States.' Having come this far, Robinson was not about to give up easily. He managed to locate a six-seater plane to make the 350-mile trip to New York. Perhaps ominously, it would be operated by a Japanese pilot. After taking off from Toronto, it would be necessary for the plane to land briefly at Buffalo, just inside the US border, to clear immigration.

Ironically, the four freshly endorsed passports were not required. 'Nobody even looked in the fucking passports,' says Robinson. 'So maybe we could have done this in the first place!' En route to New York, the light aircraft encountered severe turbulence. 'It hopped around a lot in the sky,' continues Robinson, 'and Brinsley suffered very bad pressure problems and was in considerable pain.' But after the near-kamikaze experience, New York became a reality.

The aircraft touched down on a small landing strip in the New York borough of Queens, where the group was met by two huge cars, courtesy of Head Limousines. 'The driver was a head with a hat,' recalls Lowe, 'and he handed us all joints. We got extremely stoned on this very strong grass, another sensible move on the day of the first show.'

The group were driven to the Royal Manhattan Hotel for a brief stop and then on to the Fillmore, where they were reunited with Billy Rankin. 'When we walked into the Fillmore, we saw our plight for the very first time,' recalls Lowe. 'We'd ordered up lots of state-of-the-art equipment to use at the Fillmore. Another bad move. Fender Dual Showmen that deliver a very loud ding around the auditorium. We had no idea how to operate them.'

Countering Nick Lowe's self-deprecation, Billy Rankin says, 'The Fillmore was the best venue I'd ever seen. It had a great

Altec Lansing p.a. Everything on stage was mic'd up. The mixing desk was up in the gods. They had movable platforms on stage so that each group's equipment could remain permanently set up. Between sets they'd simply unplug the mics and move the platforms into place. Five minute changeovers. Beautiful sound.'

'We arrived at 7.15 p.m.,' says Schwarz. 'We met the crew, tuned up, did a short soundcheck, went upstairs to change and the next minute, we were on. I couldn't hear a thing.' Schwarz was forced to play the whole of the first show constantly watching Nick Lowe's hands to confirm the chord changes. 'The music had a lot of guitar solos,' recalls Robinson, 'so it was a bit iffy, but I thought they played all right, given the circumstances.' Nobody in the audience knew or cared that Brinsley Schwarz had made it to the Fillmore with only 45 minutes to spare. It had been a dramatic touch-and-go situation for the previous five days. Unbelievably, however, the group's difficulties in getting to New York were about to be dwarfed by the experience that awaited the press entourage the following day.

7. THE FILLMORE TRIP

In 1970, pop music, or bubblegum, as its most vociferous detractors referred to it, had no place in the thinking person's record collection. Even the recently disbanded Beatles were insufficiently 'heavy' for many young music fans. The fundamental language of pop had also been rewritten. Groups now called themselves 'bands', LPs had become 'albums' and live performances were either 'gigs' or, rather pretentiously, 'concerts'. The distinction between 'rock' and 'pop' was largely promoted by the *Melody Maker*, then at the height of its influence, with writers such as Chris Welch, Ray Coleman and Richard Williams.

'I was an avid *Melody Maker* reader,' says Alan Wright, who had won tickets to see Brinsley Schwarz in New York. 'I

Souvenir of a debacle: Fillmore East programme, 3–4 April 1970
(courtesy Malcolm Addison)

would digest it from cover to cover every week because it was the only serious read at the time. They gave full coverage of the artists with lots of detail. The competition to see Brinsley Schwarz was quite intellectual really, very *Melody Maker*. How they judged the answers, I don't know, but a weekend in New York seemed such an outrageous, unbelievable thing to do. I'd never entered a competition before, but I had a friend who'd won a Hillman Imp in a Heinz Baked Beans competition. That was in the back of my mind I suppose.'

Alan Wright had learnt of his good fortune just two weeks before the trip, when the following telegram arrived via the telegraph office in Bristol:

CONGRATULATIONS. YOU HAVE WON TWO TRIPS TO NEW YORK
WITH BRINSLEY SCHWARZ ON THE 4TH AND 5TH APRIL. PLEASE RING
COLLECT 01-723-3656 ON MONDAY MORNING AFTER 11.00. PLEASE BE
READY WITH DETAILS. YOUR AGE, YOUR GUEST'S NAME ADDRESS AND
AGE, TELEPHONE NO AT WHICH YOU CAN BE REACHED AND
PASSPORT DETAILS. I LOOK FORWARD TO MEETING YOU.
CONGRATULATIONS AGAIN. JOHN EICHLER.

Wright recalls how he decided to invite his girlfriend, Jacqui Powell, on the trip:

Jacqui was sixteen, coming up seventeen. We'd never been away together; in fact I don't think Jacqui even had a passport. I had to go and explain it all to her parents and they said OK. Jacqui's tastes were heavier than Brinsley Schwarz. She liked Black Sabbath and Fleetwood Mac. I was nearly nineteen and a first-year business student at Oxford Polytechnic. I was into progressive rock, for example Pink Floyd, Deep Purple, the Stones, Yes. I also really loved the blues and space/head music, so I considered the Brinsleys a bit soft. I had been aware of a single from Kippington Lodge, but that was pop, in other words, not to be taken too seriously.

As Brinsley Schwarz touched down in New York on Friday, 3 April 1970, Alan Wright and Jacqui Powell, together with the other four competition winners, each with a friend or partner in tow, were enjoying an eve-of-departure nightcap at London's Rembrandt Hotel. The Rembrandt was part of the Grand Metropolitan chain and had been booked by Famepushers in conjunction with New York's Royal Manhattan. John and Sue Eichler, representing Famepushers, had been appointed chaperones to the winners and kept a watchful eye on the proceedings, as Wright remembers:

> Jacqui's age was a concern of John Eichler's. It is unthinkable today, but my mother and father drove Jacqui and I all the way up to London from Cheltenham in the family's Vauxhall Victor, arriving at the hotel for the 7 p.m. rendezvous. Mum and Dad came inside, introduced themselves to everybody and handed us over for a rock 'n' roll weekend. I think my mother was a bit sceptical about all this being 'for real!' I remember wearing my best suit – I was so naïve and awed by the whole thing.

John Eichler took his role of chaperone very seriously. 'Boys' and 'Girls' were even allocated separate bedrooms at the hotel. 'I was supposed to share a room with a strange bloke,' recalls Wright, 'but after a few drinks, I quickly did a key swap so that Jacqui and I could be together. This was the first time I had ever slept the whole night with a girl!'

The following morning, at 8.30 a.m., an unusually colourful group of jet-setters gathered at Brompton Road terminus, where they would board a coach for Heathrow. The excitement of a visit to the USA and, for many of the party, their first, guaranteed a full turnout, much to the disappointment of Stan Barr, manager of the hippie group Quintessence. Barr, an American, turned up at the Aer Lingus check-in with his belongings in a rucksack, hoping to occupy the seat of a no-show. 'It'll be the first time I've been home for three years,' he told everyone hopefully, but the plane would be full.

Alan Wright and Jacqui Powell sat in the departure lounge at Heathrow, alternating their attention between the precise details contained in the Famepushers itinerary and a small group of bemused celebrities that they spotted about the building. These included Radio One DJs Jimmy Saville and Alan Freeman, who had been invited along to witness the departure of the junket. Ricky Blears recollects:

At Heathrow that morning I was satisfied that I'd got the entire voice of the pop business in Britain and part of Europe and they were going to meet the entire voice of the pop business in America. There would be all that interaction going on and there was going to be a great deal of excitement. The band were going to play their socks off and everyone was going to say they were the greatest thing they'd ever heard. United Artists had made the best investment they'd ever made and everyone was going to make millions. I'd dotted the 'I's and crossed the 'T's and nothing could possibly go wrong. I was an experienced advertising and publicity executive and I had it covered. We had a plane, a hotel, catering, cars and press packs. It was ambitious, but it was a standard PR exercise that happened to be stretched across two continents.

The Famepushers itinerary informed the party that the flight was due to leave at 10.40 a.m. and arrive at New York's John F. Kennedy airport at 2 p.m. local time. An hour had been set aside for clearing immigration and a further hour allowed for the party to travel to Manhattan in a fleet of stretch limousines for a press conference at the Royal Manhattan Hotel on 8th Avenue at 4 p.m. After this, there would be ample time for everyone to relax, freshen up and maybe watch a little American TV before leaving for the Fillmore, again by limousine, at 7.30 p.m.

It was an ambitious schedule and one that failed to allow for any flight delays, the first of which was about to occur. The Aer Lingus Boeing 707, in which the entourage was due to cross the Atlantic, had apparently been delayed on its way to London from Paris. 'We were told there was a technical fault,' recalls Alan Wright. 'Firstly it was a one-hour delay, which became two hours. There was a hubbub of anticipation. It was a rumour-monger's heaven.'

'There was no plane,' says Jodi Routh. 'Even though we'd ordered the plane I don't think Aer Lingus believed we would all turn up. When we did turn up it took them hours to find a plane.' Ricky Blears says, 'I think Aer Lingus had forgotten that they'd promised us a plane. I think that having got into this arrangement and having had the exchange of letters and meetings, Aer Lingus decided they'd like to see the colour of our money before they provided the hardware.'

After nearly a three-hour wait, during which time information was drip-fed and the journalists were placated with Aer Lingus coffee and sandwiches, a replacement aircraft eventually arrived. It was called the *St Lawrence O'Toole* and at 1.30 p.m. was ready for boarding. As the plane became airborne at 2 p.m., few of the passengers, outside of the Famepushers contingent, would have known that Famepusher-in-chief, Edward Molton, was not on board. Molton had told his colleagues that he'd decided 'to stay back at base, to hold the fort'. Molton's absence on the trip would later puzzle Dave Robinson. Why would someone who'd gone to such extraordinary lengths to launch a pop group not wish to be present for this epic promotion?

'Ted told us all he was terrified of flying,' says Christie Sutton, 'but actually he probably couldn't get a visa, although he was not going to tell us that.'

'I think that Molton didn't go to the Fillmore because he didn't have a passport, or at least a passport in the right name,' is John Eichler's opinion. 'If you're sitting next to your bank manager on the plane and your passport doesn't correspond . . . but he made it sound as if somebody had to stay back at base. He said to us, "You go and have a good time," but you could see he was really pissed off. It hurt.'

In accordance with Aer Lingus policy, the flight was scheduled to make a brief stop at Shannon, an airport with an unusually long runway. This turned out to be a most fortuitous route as the aircraft's brakes developed a mechanical problem over the Irish Sea. After some frantic fuel dumping, the 707 made an emergency landing. 'I remember speeding fire engines alongside the plane,' recalls Andrew Lauder. 'We could actually see the mud on the banks of the River Shannon,' adds Alan Wright, who thought he had come within a whisker of death.

At 3 p.m., the aircraft jarred to a halt just a few feet short of the river bank. 'They asked us if we would mind getting off,' recalls Eichler. 'Ricky Blears and I were supposedly the senior people on the plane, so they took us into the VIP lounge and said, "We're terribly sorry but you lost your brake fluid over the Irish Sea and you just landed without brakes." They'd had to rely solely on reverse thrust to stop. It was very dodgy.'

Eichler and Blears stressed to the Aer Lingus officials that the trip was running on a very tight schedule and they were already three hours late. Ricky Blears says, 'I made it fairly clear to Aer Lingus that we were on a time-critical trip and the world's press were not going to be impressed if a late plane screwed the whole thing up. Being the guy who was fronting the press side of things, I was running around like a scalded cat trying to fulfil the objective in the face of ever-mounting difficulties.'

'They told us they didn't have another plane,' continues Eichler. 'All they could do was top up the brake fluid, test the brakes and press on.' It fell upon Ricky Blears to inform the entourage that there would be another delay, without divulging the precise reason. 'I think even the hacks had noticed there was something slightly amiss,' says George Darby of the *Sunday Times*. 'Journalists can be flaky about things, but questions were being asked and it was the job of this poor harassed PR to wander around doing it by word of mouth.'

'The PR man from Aer Lingus at Shannon was an absolute gem,' says Ricky Blears. To keep the passengers entertained while technical adjustments were being made, Aer Lingus had no alternative but to throw open the bar. 'The airport lounge was awash with drink,' recalls Alan Wright, 'and I lost count of my vodka and oranges.' John Eichler says, 'The drinks were definitely flowing. I was introduced to Irish Mist – good stuff, especially in tumblers – and the people from the *Daily Sketch* and the *Daily Mirror* were really committed to it! We drank the free booze until it was coming out of our eyes.'

'It was definitely a case of "Put the cavalcade on hold!" ' says Pete Frame, whose name appeared on the passenger list alongside such past and future celebrities as Jonathan Demme, Hank Wangford, Jenny Fabian, Johnny Byrne and, worryingly, former *Candid Camera* japester Jonathan Routh, with his partner Olga Deterding. Other passengers included writer and broadcaster Charlie Gillett and *Oz* founder Richard Neville. 'Richard Neville took the opportunity to buy a new portable cassette recorder,' recalls Gillett, 'and sold me his old one for some small amount like three pounds. It became my cassette recorder for the next few years.'

It was also the day of the Grand National. As Richard Neville and his cohorts milled around the duty-free shop, Gay Trip, ridden by Irish jockey Pat Taaffe, romped home at 15–1, winning by some 20 lengths. 'The race was on every one of the wirelesses and TVs in the airport,' recalls Jeremy Deedes, then writing 'Londoner's Diary' in the *Evening Standard*. 'There was a certain sector of the party, with no real interest in racing, that was thrilled because Gay Trip had won it. They'd all backed it, and went round shouting, "Oh, I've won a hundred pounds dear!" ' Deedes's tone suggests that it was the first component of the horse's name that was the source of amusement, but what had really inspired the sudden outbreak of gambling mania, was the second, with all its druggy connotations.

At 4.30 p.m., the *St Lawrence O'Toole* was declared airworthy and the party re-embarked for the onward flight to New York. Once in the air, the drinks continued to flow and some of the passengers were now the worse for wear. Television personality Jonathan Routh wandered the aisles and, at one point, threw up. Remarkably, this incident was captured on camera by one of the more quick-witted press photographers.

'When that plane took off, it was the biggest drugs party that has ever taken place in mid-air,' says Alan Marcuson. 'It was pandemonium. At the front of the plane was the straight press who were drinking. At this time we hated the straight press. They were the enemy as far as we were concerned. There was a real clash of cultures. At the back we were taking

Mandrax, dope, acid and speed. The air hostesses completely freaked out.'

On eventually arriving at Kennedy Airport at 7 p.m., the journalists, many of whom were now seriously inebriated, faced the task of clearing immigration. Jeremy Deedes recalls;

I had a suit on. White shirt, tie, overcoat with velvet collar . . . my uniform in those days. I must have looked a bit strange with all the *Oz* crowd in their goatskin waistcoats. I certainly didn't have a clue what all this kit was they were smoking but when we approached immigration I thought, "Hang back a bit here Deedes old chap, because these boys are going to take hours to get through." But they all sailed through and I got worked over something rotten. I stood out so much they must have thought if anyone's carrying the stuff it must be that respectable-looking bloke. I was absolutely mortified.

Meanwhile, John Eichler and the film crew were attempting to get to the Fillmore ahead of the main party. Eichler recalls:

We hit the runway, they wheeled the steps up and we immediately tried filming, but the light had gone. And we were pissed. We were rushing round like loonies and I remember thinking I had to have some coffee and get sorted out. I poured it straight down my shirt. As the journalists were climbing into the limousines, the film crew and I jumped into a station wagon with an Italian driver who was going to get us to the Fillmore in double-quick time so we could start filming the journalists' arrival.

He remembers feeling slightly disappointed on seeing the Fillmore for the first time.

It had a run-down exterior and strange drugged-out people were hanging around the door. We walked up expecting to go straight in to set up, but the guy on the door said 'No'. We were getting a complete blank.

[Eichler became frustrated and resorted to drastic measures.] There was no way that I was not going to get in. I suddenly walked up to the doormen and shouted, 'Fuck off out of the way right now!' Amazingly they stood aside and we all walked in. It was just like I'd said 'Excuse me' in England.

Once inside the venue, Eichler met with more resistance.

We asked the usher where we could set up and he snapped back at us, 'Nobody sets up in here!' They'd got the word that we'd elbowed Tony Palmer who, unfortunately, was a very close friend of Bill Graham's. As soon as we'd fired him, he'd phoned Graham and told him he was not involved any more, so any arrangement he'd made to film the gig was now null and void! It was all over. A wrap.

As Eichler resigned himself to the fact that his film would have to do without the crucial footage of Brinsley Schwarz's performance, the journalists' motorcade was snaking its way towards Manhattan, dramatically accompanied by police motorcycle outriders (rumoured by some to be actors in hired costume). To further enhance the unreality of the situation, all cars had their ashtrays stocked with complimentary, illicit smoking material.

Due to the general chaos at Kennedy Airport, most of the journalists had jumped into the first limousine where they could find a seat, although Famepushers had drawn up a 'Cadillac Allocation List'. The list generally put all birds of a feather together, although a most illustrious mix of passengers was designed to impress bank manager, Mr Holborn, who found himself sitting alongside Shell heiress Olga Deterding and her famous partner, Jonathan Routh; Martin Bayer (a solicitor); Sam Hutt (a doctor); and George Darby from the *Sunday Times*.

With less than one hour to go before Brinsley Schwarz were due to take the stage, any ideas of freshening up at the hotel were shelved as the convoy of 22 stretch limousines converged with the mid-evening Bridge and Tunnel crowd, pouring into the city for their Saturday night entertainment. All approaches to the city were thick with traffic.

'The convoy was so long,' recalls Jeremy Deedes, 'that if the front cars got through a green light, the cars at the back were bound to go through red. Then the motorcycle escort started heading for the wrong venue and the whole cavalcade had to do a U-turn across the central reservation. It was during the course of that U-turn, where we all slewed across the traffic, that the accident happened. Several cars were damaged.'

After negotiating the jams and the gridlocks, the convoy screeched to a halt outside the Fillmore at 8.15 p.m. to unload the shaken passengers, now at the end of a 17-hour ordeal. A harassed Ricky Blears, who was holding all the press tickets and photo passes, was standing on the sidewalk desperately trying to identify the British journalists.

Blears recalls, 'The legendary Fillmore bouncers were under strict instructions not to let anyone who was stoned or drunk into the place. That included our entire party, which included me. I'd had one or two as you can imagine, to steady the nerves whilst the job was going rather badly wrong. The guy from the *Daily Mail* was being thrown into the gutter. There was an enormous punch up.'

Inside the Fillmore, Dave Robinson was attempting to delay the show, so that the press wouldn't miss the start of Brinsley Schwarz's performance. 'I was trying to hold the curtain,' says Robinson, 'and trying to stop Bill Graham chucking us off the bill. I had a huge argument with Graham where he spat all over me, but while that was going on I was happy, because the longer he was spitting, the longer the curtain was being held. I had somebody give me the nod – "They're here, they're here" – and at the precise moment the journalists entered the Fillmore, the Brinsleys were walking on stage.'

'The timing was uncanny,' says Alan Wright. 'As we made our way to our seats in the rear stalls, the group appeared.' Not all of the British contingent had made it into the theatre and one or two of those who had were not impressed. 'I was sitting next to the old boy from the *Jewish Chronicle*, who really didn't get it,' says Alan Marcuson. 'He said, "You mean they brought us all this way to come to a lousy theatre like this? Just look, the seats are all torn."'

At 8.20 p.m., Brinsley Schwarz walked nervously on to the Fillmore stage and played a 35-minute set comprising five original compositions: 'Indian Woman'; 'What Do You Suggest'; 'Rock And Roll Women'; 'Ballad Of A Has-Been Beauty Queen'; and their 'progressive dirge', 'Life Is Dead'. 'It was pleasant and well performed, but it didn't inspire me,' says Alan Wright. 'They sounded American – in fact, too American for the Americans.'

Charlie Gillett is even more harsh: 'Unfortunately, Brinsley Schwarz were totally unimpressive live. If the band had been as good as the build-up, it would have seemed like a wonderful stunt, but the gig was a disappointment.' Ricky Blears says, 'The boys were patently terrified, having never played a big venue before and the long and short of it was, they were crap! They did some of their Tunbridge Wells folk rock with subdued amplification and their knees shaking. It went downhill from there.'

Brinsley Schwarz left the stage to polite, muted applause. Many of the British contingent, who felt they had now fulfilled their obligations to Famepushers, strolled out on to the New York streets to sample the invigorating night life that the city had to offer. 'Some of the hardened journos were debating the relative merits, and safety to their persons, of going up to Harlem,' says Alan Wright. Others, like Wright and his girlfriend drifted back to the Royal Manhattan Hotel and checked in. The entire entourage occupied two floors. 'Jacqui and I were shocked by the number of locks and warnings on our room door,' continues Wright. 'This was all new. In 1970 there was a yawning gap between life in the USA and the UK.'

Back at the Fillmore, after a brief intermission, Brinsley Schwarz's disappointing performance was immediately put into context by the lethal professionalism of Van Morrison and his band, thoroughly road-drilled and musically dynamic. 'Van Morrison was a hero,' says Nick Lowe. '*Moondance* had just come out and he had the band that was on the record. I'd never seen anything as good as that, except maybe Cliff

Bennett And The Rebel Rousers some years earlier. I watched Van's show, or as much as I could stand because they were incredible and I had a mounting sense of dread that we'd made a terrible mistake.'

'Van Morrison was a revelation,' says Charlie Gillett. 'I remember being in the corridor and some guy said, "Van Morrison! Man, he's the greatest soul singer after Otis Redding!" The fact that he could put those two artists together was thought-provoking. I was still quite compartmentalised in my tastes and I would never have thought of Van Morrison as a soul singer, but I wasn't arguing. What an interesting way of seeing Van Morrison!'

A number of the journalists stayed on to see headliners Quicksilver Messenger Service and one or two of the more committed writers, including Pete Frame, even stuck around for the second house, which commenced at midnight. 'This was the last of our four shows,' recalls Brinsley Schwarz. 'The pressure was off and we gave a really good performance to a large responsive audience. People grooved. But the earlier set the press saw was not so good. We were too nervous.'

The following morning the hungover revellers awoke to a warm spring day with clear blue skies. Ideal weather, in fact, for a spot of sightseeing. For most, the Empire State Building, then the tallest structure in New York, was top of the list, followed by the Staten Island Ferry, the Rockefeller Center and the United Nations Headquarters.

Future Oscar-winning film director Jonathan Demme, who was the London correspondent for the Boston rock title *Fusion*, was sharing a room with Pete Frame and went record shopping on 42nd Street, purchasing a copy of John Phillips's newly released *Wolfking Of LA*. Frame himself went straight to Greenwich Village with Andrew Lauder and John Cowell. 'We had our photograph taken on the corner of Bleecker and MacDougall Streets,' recalls Frame, 'just like Fred Neil on the cover of his Elektra album.'

The more conscientious journalists then returned to the Royal Manhattan at 2 p.m. to attend the press conference that had been organised by Ricky Blears. 'It was very loose and had no apparent format,' remarks Alan Wright. 'Actually, it wasn't a press conference, it was a drinks party.' Ricky Blears says, 'The band, disappointed by their poor performance no doubt, had decided that the best way out for them was to get completely stoned and stagger about in a speechless state at the press reception, because they thought that's what pop groups did. I had great difficulty in getting them out of bed. The American press decided the whole thing was a shambles.

John Eichler and his crew were busy filming the proceedings. 'By this stage I was very concerned that we hadn't got enough film in the can,' says Eichler. 'I remember wandering around the hotel corridors encountering all these different scenes. In one room, members of the group were holding court with some journalists and in the next room the limousine drivers were sitting around a bed rolling one-skin joints for the drive back to the airport. The record company had a suite and were throwing a party. There were photographers everywhere. It was room service in excess and complete madness.'

By 7 p.m., the entire British party was gathering in the hotel lobby to leave for Kennedy Airport, again by limousine. Gradually, they filled the 24 cars that lined Eighth Avenue around 44th and 45th Streets, but before the motorcade would pull away there was one small matter to resolve. 'Strangely enough, Head Limousines wanted to be paid,' says Andrew Lauder, 'but Famepushers didn't have the money. It was the Sunday and in some magical way it became my problem, being a representative of the record label. In the pre-credit card era, my only recourse was to call somebody at United Artists in New York and ask for help. I said, "There's this large guy in my hotel room who's not gonna let me go home until he gets paid!" UA came through and I made it to the airport in one piece.'

Also there was the question of the hotel bill. 'Ricky Blears was the last person out the door,' says John Eichler. 'As he was just about to clamber into his limo, he was asked if he'd like to settle up.' Blears recalls, 'As I went to pay my respects to the hotel manager, two very large chaps in security uniforms grabbed me by each elbow and said, "You're not leaving this hotel until we get the $36,000 for the extras." The plane was warming up at JFK and I would not be on it unless I paid up.'

Eichler continues, 'Ricky said, "OK, I'll sort it out," and took out a chequebook. He then proceeded to write out a big cheque, which he signed Maxwell Joseph.' Amazingly, the hotel manager accepted the cheque, perhaps not realising that he was about to become the victim of a practical joke; Maxwell Joseph was the name of the Chairman of Grand Metropolitan, owners of the Royal Manhattan Hotel.

'I just wrote them a cheque, like you do,' says Blears. 'They accepted it. They must have thought that anyone who was a big enough operator to have hired a plane and flown 140 journalists to New York and hired 24 limos was some kind of big-time cookie.'

The return flight to London was a profound anticlimax. On board, the four members of Brinsley Schwarz sat sheepishly amongst the media folk, most of whom were nursing a giant hangover. There was little discussion about the show and throughout the flight the musicians generally kept their heads down. Even the usually effervescent Billy Rankin maintained a low profile. Bob Andrews sat talking with Jenny Fabian, co-author, with fellow traveller Johnny Byrne, of the recent sensationalist pop novel, *Groupie*, while Nick Lowe reflected on having achieved his ambition to visit 'the groupie club'. 'I hadn't wanted anything to interfere with that,' says Lowe, 'but in order to get down to the groupie club, which I'd heard so much about from Dave Robinson, I'd had to endure four shows. The club was called Nobodies and there I met the girl of my dreams. She followed me around all the next day, a real nuisance.'

Seated all around the group were the journalists, now split into two distinct camps – Fleet Street versus the music and underground press. 'You could almost put a chalk mark on the floor,' says George Darby, 'because when they allocated the seats, there was no point in putting the guy from the *Sunday Times* next to the editor of *Oz*.' What also distinguished these two opposing groups was their respective choice of stimulants. While the Fleet Street contingent got stuck into their drinks, many of the underground writers indulged in further drug-taking.

'I'm sure people were quietly getting stoned on cannabis,' says Darby, 'but you wouldn't have wanted to get out your test kit and walk down the aisle with it.' There was also the general necessity to consume all of the various illegal substances obtained in New York before encountering UK Customs & Excise officials. 'There was so much smoke on the plane,' says Jeremy Deedes, 'that I thought if the boys in blue were to be there when we arrived, they would have a field day.'

'The party was over,' says Ricky Blears. 'It was going to be Monday morning. We were travelling west to east which is always a bore, we'd lost one or two en route and we knew the journalists were going to file copy saying the whole thing was a shambles and the band weren't much cop anyway. It had been such a wonderful plan that went grotesquely wrong. Brinsley Schwarz got famous all right, famous for being rubbish. The one thing that I hadn't reckoned on, was that the band needed to be OK in those circumstances. I'd seen them do it in pubs and in colleges and they took the roof off. But on the night, when the crunch came, they died.'

As the 707 sped homewards there was also a growing mood amongst members of the establishment press that they would not, and could not, be bought. No matter how extravagant Famepushers' hospitality, they were under no obligation to say wonderful things about Brinsley Schwarz. Possibly the noisiest representative of the Fleet Street set was legendary *Daily Sketch* photographer Monty Fresco. 'He was a very good old-time photographer,' says Darby, 'never knowingly unvocal throughout his long and distinguished life. He was also the sort of bloke who was not going to take any crap.'

'Monty Fresco was so pissed,' says John Eichler, 'that he demanded that the captain arrest the underground journalists because they were all taking drugs.' The air hostesses were trying to explain to Monty that at 35,000 feet they weren't in a position to arrest anybody. 'I suppose I was in the respectable segment of the company,' says George Darby, 'but it was all so big that one was never quite sure who the hell was on the flight, except that over the years it's turned out that everyone and his brother was there. It was a pretty eclectic bunch.'

To conclude an American recording contract with Capitol, Dave Robinson had stayed on in New York, with his parting words – 'I foresee no problems' – ringing in the ears of the Brinsleys. But on Monday, 6 April at 7 a.m., as the Aer Lingus Boeing 707 made its descent to Heathrow through heavy cloud and driving rain to discharge its precious human cargo, the printing presses of Fleet Street and beyond were about to rattle with the story of one of the greatest public relations disasters in modern entertainment history.

8. BACKFIRING ON ALL CYLINDERS

'When we got off the plane there was a very strange feeling,' says John Eichler. 'I think the group had played under par. Brinsley was almost deaf and a number of things had gone against them. Had they been in better shape and had there not been the delays and had the journalists had a chance to go to the hotel first ... although I don't know how many of them you'd have got to the show if they had gone to the hotel first ... but things might have turned out differently.'

Brinsley Schwarz now faced the wrath of the press, including the music papers. 'The Schwarz Caper – Or How To Register A Name', blurted the *New Musical Express*. 'The Biggest Hype Of All Time', screamed *Melody Maker*. Even *Zigzag*'s Pete Frame was less then ecstatic, referring to *respectably performed but unmemorable numbers*, adding, 'I was sitting there making meticulous notes in the dark ... but there really wasn't anything to make notes about ... they were totally mediocre.'

Nick Lowe recalls the humiliation:

They say pride comes before a fall. I remember a week before we went. I was lording it in front of my contemporaries, saying, 'Of course we're going to "the States" next week ... and when we come back from "the States" ... We reconvened in Wardour Street to watch the rushes of the film and as we walked into the viewing suite, all heads turned. Everyone was holding the *NME* and *Melody Maker*. To make matters worse, the film seemed to consist of hours of blurred footage of a drunken Billy Rankin touching up air hostesses. We were a laughing stock. Dave Robinson was very positive, though. He didn't see the bad press as bad. 'They don't mean that', he would say. 'What they really mean is, you guys were great!'

'They wrote more about the event than the band,' observes Dai Davies, then a columnist on *Top Pops and Music Now*. 'It was a fabulous opportunity for a writer to get his teeth into. It was a time when writers were influenced by *Rolling Stone* – music business excess more than music and consequently the Brinsleys were diminished by the whole thing.'

This approach to reporting the event was adopted by George Darby, who wrote one of the most lucid assessments of the Fillmore debacle in the *Sunday Times*.

The trip itself was a phenomenon [Darby says today, explaining his angle]. Instead of just giving people tickets or a drink afterwards, that sort of petty payola, this was a major promotional event and so one was writing about it for a mainstream audience who might not have read too much about that sort of procedure to launch a band. The absurdities, the excesses, whatever one found . . . rather than write about the band and whether it was any good or not. Because, who could tell at that stage?

I think that the danger wasn't so much in the hype for its own sake. The danger lay in the sheer scale of the chutzpah and the ambition. If you're going to stake everything on appearing at the Fillmore East and crash land in cutting-edge New York, shouting, 'Here we are, we're going to knock your socks off!', that was pretty ambitious stuff. People were bound to say, 'OK, we'll take you at face value', not 'they were quite good actually' . . . 'You said you were going to be really hot, well take it from me buddy, you weren't.' In other words, they were deemed to have failed because they didn't live up to their own billing. Brinsley Schwarz were just gonna parachute in as Britain's hottest band for the 70s! That was why they were likely to have failed. It was all or nothing. They were staking everything on that one public appearance. It was a very big throw of the dice.

But whatever the fate of Brinsley Schwarz, the whole episode left an indelible mark on all who participated. 'After the trip we talked about it like we'd never talked about anything else for ages,' says Jeremy Deedes. 'People would often pull PR tricks, but there was never anything like it before, or since. It was so outrageous, the enormity of it, that I can remember it like nothing else in the 70s. It was a fantastic stunt. I still remember Brinsley Schwarz; everybody does.'

For the foreseeable future, Brinsley Schwarz were out in the cold, but a number of positive factors did emerge from the trip.

In America, press reviews of the Fillmore shows had been less harsh, because the writers were only reporting on a single show, rather than a wild weekend. 'In America they carried the story on the wire,' says Dave Robinson. '*Variety* and *Billboard* had their abbreviated headlines like "Brit Group Debut Fillmore East". It looked great in shorthand.'

In England, Brinsley Schwarz's agent, Tony Howard, now had an easier job on his hands. 'Everyone slammed the group,' says Howard, 'but with all that publicity, a lot of people wanted gigs.' With public curiosity aroused, Brinsley Schwarz was able to undertake a busy schedule of live appearances.

Billy Rankin says, 'It turned us from a local £60 a night group into a £200 name group, playing all over the country. It opened it all up. If the trip had gone incredibly well, we wouldn't have had so much press and we might not have carried on.'

On the record front, Dave Robinson was able to secure a contract with Capitol Records for the USA. 'I made the deal with Al Bennett and Artie Mogull,' says Robinson. 'I gave them very little time to make a decision. I learnt very early on to make a big noise about the fact I had very little time – "If you want it, make the decision quickly, like NOW! While I'm in the room." It also had to be firm for three albums. Al fell for it. A couple of his A&R men were a bit iffy, but Al loved the fact there were a hundred journalists in New York and we'd made a film.'

Most importantly – and most ironically – having been shunned by the media, Brinsley Schwarz turned their back on the whole showbiz ethos and threw themselves into their music. In the aftermath of, perhaps, the greatest hype in pop history, Brinsley Schwarz, through sheer dedication, would turn their name around and become a symbol for anti-hype.

* * *

Brinsley Schwarz, the group's eponymous debut LP, was released on 17 April 1970. It contains seven songs, six of which were Nick Lowe compositions, undoubtedly influenced by the sound of Crosby, Stills & Nash. 'Lady Constant', for example, draws heavily on the melody of Graham Nash's 'Lady Of The Island', demonstrating how easily Lowe could approximate an existing song and ring the 'Where have I heard that before' bell. Perhaps predictably, in the wake of the Fillmore fiasco and despite its warm melodies and classy Barney Bubbles packaging, the LP received a lukewarm response from the press and enjoyed only negligible sales.

It was now time for Dave Robinson to secure a publishing contract for Brinsley Schwarz and the other acts in the Famepushers stable – Help Yourself and Ernie Graham. Robinson returned to New York and negotiated with a company called Chartwell. While in New York, Robinson was hounded by various parties for the payment of outstanding debts relating to the Fillmore trip. To raise further funds, Robinson entered into a complex deal involving a loan against future publishing rights offered by Jerry Parencio and a company called Crapshoot, in which the singer Andy Williams was involved.

I was looking for $50,000 or thereabouts [says Dave Robinson]. Parencio wouldn't put up that sort of money, so he set up Crapshoot, got a few friends together and they each put in five or ten thousand bucks and I think they gave us $30,000. It was used to pay off the immediate debts. We needed to pay the people who were threatening to sue the group, as opposed to Famepushers. The group wanted to go on rather than just implode, which would have been the obvious thing to happen at the time. That's where the money came in.

In May 1970, Brinsley Schwarz were introduced to the music of Jim Ford. 'Dave was in the States on one of his money-raising exercises,' says Nick Lowe. 'He heard about Jim Ford from Sy Waronker, the boss of Liberty Records. Sy said, "I'll invest in your group but in return I want the group to

work with Jim Ford. He's a wayward genius, but you've got long hair so you'll be able to communicate with him." '
Robinson agreed and plans were made to bring Ford to London for a session with Brinsley Schwarz at Olympic Studios.

John Eichler went to pick Jim up from the airport [says Lowe]. Jim arrived with a big Stetson on, rose-tinted shades, jeans with creases in and round-toed cowboy boots. I thought cowboy boots had to be pointed, but real cowboys wear the round-toed comfortable variety and they put creases in their jeans, because it's smart. Ford was the real thing, or as near to the real thing as I'd ever encountered. He was other-worldly and very charismatic. He turned up with a $3,000 guitar, an astronomical sum for 1970, but it seemed he could barely play it, and yet it was so mean, the way he hit the thing. I'd never heard anybody who played like Jim Ford.
He was totally unimpressed by us, but he was making the best of a bad job, I suppose. 'Ju Ju Man' may have been one of the ones we recorded with him, plus '36 Inches High', 'I'm Ahead If I Can Quit While I'm Behind' and 'Harry The Hippie'. He told a lot of terrible stories and he used to bend the truth a bit, but this one I believe. He told us he used to live with Bobbie Gentry when she was a telephonist with RCA and she stole 'Ode To Billie Joe' off him. It is a typical Jim Ford-type song and in the light of what Bobbie Gentry has done since, it makes sense. He was a blues guy, but he'd stick extra bars in. We were very conventional young kids and we knew it went verse, chorus, verse, chorus, a little solo, and we said, 'Er, Jim, last time you played that little bridge bit it went like this . . . now how does it go?' But Jim Ford's songs made a tremendous impact on me. Along with guys like Dan Penn, Spooner Oldham, Joe South . . . he's the last piece of the jigsaw.

Another artist that Brinsley Schwarz were asked to record with during this period was the legendary P. J. Proby. Proby, who had failed to achieve any substantial UK chart success since 1965, was managed by United Artists boss, Martin Davies. Nick Lowe recalls:

Martin said, 'Look, it's sort of all over for P.J. Proby, but I think he's a great artist. Before we do anything hasty, we should get him in the studio and see if he can come up with something new. I envisage a sort of country rock sound. You guys are the country rock blokes, so how about it?' We were knocked out because Proby was the nearest thing to a bona fide pop star that we'd ever met. We told Martin we'd been working with Jim Ford and suggested that we try some of Ford's material. We weren't really aware that Proby had already done 'Niki Hoeke'. It turned out that Proby and Ford knew each other. They are, in fact, very similar.

We sent Proby a selection of Jim Ford tunes that we'd learnt up. We were assured that he would be *au fait* with the songs when it came to cutting time. The day came and we waited for Proby to turn up. We were on evening sessions at Olympic. First of all, a roadie arrived with tons of guitars, all belonging to Proby. Every type of guitar you could imagine, plus boxes of percussion instruments. We thought, 'Bloody hell, he's taking this very seriously.' About two hours later the great man arrived, wearing a cowboy hat. On his arm was the extremely attractive actress, Angharad Rees. It seemed that she was absolutely less than happy to be there.

Proby had immense charm and charisma and had probably told Angharad something like, 'I've just gotta drop some stuff off at the studio, honey.' The next thing that emerged was that Proby had obviously not listened to the songs at all and, to make matters worse, they were difficult songs with irregular bars and intervals. Typical Jim Ford songs. We knew them inside out, we'd learnt every nuance, but it was hopeless to expect Proby just to dive in and start getting them straight away. He had no idea, but he pretended he did.

The first thing we did was 'Ju Ju Man'. The lyric goes, 'I was just sixteen years old, Maggie's hair was as black as coal, and this old heart of mine goes slipping away.' The first thing that Proby did was to sit down and rewrite it. Then he read it out, 'I was just sixteen years old' – and by this stage he was getting tearful and saying to Angharad, 'Honey, I'm gonna show you what I can do for you . . .' Angharad was yawning at the back. He carried on, 'I was just sixteen years old . . . Angharad's hair was flaxen gold!' Proby rewrote the whole song, substituting Angharad. It's a beautiful name but, let's face it, it doesn't exactly roll off the tongue like Maggie, does it?

Meanwhile, Stephen Warwick began making plans to complete his film of the Fillmore Trip. With editor Graham Bunn, Warwick laboured over hours of footage, much of which was of little use. Although there was no footage of the group's performance at the Fillmore, Warwick managed to produce a short feature. Despite a preview at a cinema in Scotland, full commercial distribution of the film was not possible. Says producer Jodi Routh:

> It was banned by the ACTT [Association of Cinematic and Television Technicians]. The American Union had complained that we'd made a film in America without telling them and they wanted £5,000 as a pay-off. I received a letter from the ACTT saying, 'No further production work involving Jodi Routh Entertainments Ltd may be carried out until further negotiations have taken place.' This meant that no British projectionist who was a member of the ACTT was allowed to handle the film because it belonged to my company.
>
> Everything broke down. I realised that I was going bankrupt and did a bunk. Quite simply, I got some of the staff together, including John Eichler and Les Young, and we ransacked our own office, getting our equipment out – the stereo, the electric typewriter and a lot of film stock as compensation to Les Young and his crew, who would otherwise not have been paid. It ended my career in the industry in Britain and I felt very bitter. It was my own fault of course, to allow myself to be caught up with Molton and Warwick.

I remember that Stephen Warwick was getting something done on his teeth. It was quite expensive and he seemed to be doing it with my money. I remember asking, 'Why is production money being spent on Stephen Warwick's teeth?' Edward Molton was more of a hard nut. I don't know if he'd been a mercenary, but he had the look of someone who could keep his cool in any situation. Once I drove him somewhere and I was going too fast and I almost crashed. Molton sat very calmly next to me. I asked him if he'd been frightened and he replied, 'No, I've had so many nasty accidents and catastrophes in my life, nothing would worry me any more.

'Molton was an egomaniac,' says Bob Andrews. 'He was completely in charge of himself and usually acting jolly. Everything was "Blah Blah Blah." We were so naïve. I remember going in there and saying, "Hello Eddie, how's it going?" and he'd say, "Here's fifty quid Bob. Go and have a good time!" It looked like they had something. Nothing was too much for them.'

Ricky Blears remarks, 'If you wanted some money, you asked Eddie and he gave you some. He would return to the office after piecing some deal together, brimming with self-congratulation and grinning for England.'

Despite Molton's confidence, cracks were beginning to appear in the Motherburger organisation. First to feel the pressure was Barney Bubbles, a sensitive soul whose business arrangements with the hard-nosed Molton had been a disaster. As the unwitting catalyst in bringing together many of the leading players in Molton's crumbling empire, Bubbles was now wracked with guilt.

In a last-minute bid to salvage his business relationship with Molton, Bubbles summoned up the courage to call a meeting. Molton obliged, but before Bubbles could bring up the matter of his beleaguered finances, Molton suddenly stated that he had a serious heart condition and only six months to live. Bubbles and his design colleague, John Muggeridge, were initially taken in and the question of money was respectfully dropped, but Bubbles was now desperate to depart 307 Portobello Road. In June 1970, he placed the following small ad in *Friends* magazine:

> Boss penciller Barney Bubbles, Bumper Bundle Bonus of fun, poor but honest, urgently requires unfurnished pad in Gate or Grove area, lousy with smiles, phone 969 7683.

'Barney was very sad to leave Portobello,' recalls his girlfriend, Giana Cioffi. 'He was heartbroken because it was his project, his studio, and he couldn't afford to stay there any more. Everybody moved out when Barney left. A friend of ours, an American girl called Kathy Moon, had managed to get hold of a council flat in Octavia House, Ladbroke Grove and asked us to move in with her.'

Molton and Warwick were now in dire financial straits. 'Money was starting to become a real problem,' says press assistant Christie Sutton. 'We always had to be careful how we paid bills. We had to calculate the last possible moment cheques could be posted and we were told to send certain cheques in the late post. When it got really bad, Ted and I would drive around London to all the different branches of the bank and, at each one, cash a cheque for thirty pounds – the maximum we could get against our guarantee card. We were in a limousine though. Ted liked a bit of style.'

Although the Pleasuredome had been abandoned and *Bridge-O-Rama* remained unfinished and therefore unsaleable, Molton continued to convey a confident air to his clients and associates. 'When he spoke to you, it was as if he'd been your friend forever,' recalls Dave Robinson, 'but I was beginning to have my doubts.'

Despite Molton's predicament, Dave Robinson and the members of Brinsley Schwarz felt they were financially secure, having banked the proceeds of the Capitol deal and their recently signed publishing contract with Chartwell Music. Live work was abundant and Robinson was happily writing out cheques on the group's behalf to cover various touring costs. A visit to Hamburg was imminent, where the Brinsleys were booked to perform three songs on the German TV show *Beat Club*. Robinson went to the Olympia branch of his bank to withdraw some petty cash for the trip. 'I had a rough idea how much was supposed to be in the account,' says Robinson, 'so when they refused to cash the cheque I asked to see the manager. He told me that our money had been moved.'

It looked to Robinson as if Molton was still in the habit of shifting funds between his various bank accounts to bail out whichever of his companies needed it most. The Brinsley Schwarz account, however, was governed by a mandate that required Robinson's counter-signature on all transactions, a precaution that Robinson had taken some months previously. It was evident that the bank had acted improperly by releasing funds on the sole instruction of Famepusher-in-chief Edward Molton. 'I called my lawyer,' says Robinson, 'and then I decided to look a little deeper into the affairs of Edward Molton.'

At this point, former Red Sands caretaker Malcolm Addison was hanging around the Famepushers office, ready for any odd jobs that needed doing. Recalling Addison's credentials as a private investigator, Robinson asked him if he would mind investigating Molton. 'Dave took me to one side,' recalls Addison. 'He said, "Would you have a sniff around Ted for me?", which I agreed to do.'

Help Yourself guitarist Richard Treece recalls, 'We were out with John Eichler one night. Crossing Waterloo Bridge, we bumped into Malcolm Addison. He was shadowing Molton. At one point, Paul Burton and myself burst into the Famepushers office with a camera to try and get a photograph of Molton, because he was about to disappear.' Ricky Blears says, 'Molton was absolutely paranoid about not getting his photograph taken at various functions. We should have known.'

'I spent two days gathering information on Molton,' says Addison. 'I still had some contacts in the police – and I discovered that Molton operated under several aliases. Not surprisingly, Molton was not his real name. My contact at the Criminal Records Office said, "Don't do business with this guy." '

But Addison was feeling a sense of guilt about shopping Molton to Robinson. It was Molton, after all, who had rescued Addison from the gutter and given him a job at the fort. 'I liked Ted and Dave equally at that time,' says Addison. 'Molton was "a robbing Peter to pay Paul" sort of guy. He wasn't a nasty person. Deep down he was probably very genuine, but he just couldn't handle it.' That night Addison wrestled with his conscience and decided to let fate take its course.

'I had Ted's home number and I had Dave's,' recalls Addison. 'I liked Ted and I tried to warn him first that I had this information on him. I made several attempts during the night to phone Ted, but there was no answer. I couldn't get a reply from Dave Robinson's phone either, so I decided that when I went into the office the next morning, I would talk to whichever one of them was there first. It just happened to be Robinson. I gave Dave all the information I'd got on Ted Molton.'

Robinson confronted Molton immediately. 'He tried to bluff his way out of it,' recalls Robinson. 'He said he was on the board of Famepushers. He was this; he was that. Maybe his plot was to row me out, but I never had the inclination to probe any further.' As a result of what Robinson saw as a betrayal, he promptly vacated the Famepushers office with what little cash there was left in the kitty and drew up a survival plan for Brinsley Schwarz.

It was decided that the group would find a large house and adopt a communal lifestyle. With around £800 a week coming in from college dates, their business and domestic overheads would be met and everything in the refrigerator would be shared. 'Dave asked me to look around and find the group somewhere to live,' recalls Malcolm Addison. 'They needed a big place with a garage, so I phoned round the estate agents and found a house in Northwood, Middlesex, for £40 a week. I told Dave it was the ideal place, so he came out and saw it.'

'I hired a car for the day, because the people who owned the house needed a bit of convincing,' says Robinson. 'They were looking for a family with three kids and they wanted references. I put a suit on and went and did a bit of a job on them.' The following week, Brinsley Schwarz vacated their lodgings at the Red Lion and moved into 10 Carew Road, Northwood, Middlesex.

The house was the ideal place for Brinsley Schwarz. It had previously been an annexe to a private girls school and contained enough space to accommodate Dave Robinson and all of the group including Brinsley's family, plus a rehearsal room, sleeping quarters for the roadies, kennels for the dogs, and a small office space. Addison, who had some typing skills, was retained to handle paperwork and would become the group's road manager. Initially Robinson rented the property for three months and would later sign the lease a year at a time. As he recalls:

Northwood was a very conservative area. We had a dog called Poacher that attacked the wife of a local justice of the peace. Amazingly, the local police were very helpful and appeared to be on our side. Carew Road was also nicely located for the M1. We got all the gigs that other bands couldn't make. We had a reputation for being the band that lived under one roof and was ready to boogie at a moment's notice. Having recovered a bit of money from the bank, I wasn't unhappy to be out of Famepushers. My attitude was, 'This group is quite good and now we're gonna undo all the bad press.' I had a bit of a downer on the journalists because they never reviewed the group's music at the Fillmore. I thought, 'Right, we'll show these bastards.' Everyone had turned against the promotion angle, so we went the opposite way and turned to the music angle.

Following Dave Robinson's showdown with Edward Molton, the self-styled 'financial consultant' suddenly disappeared. 'We had begun to see less and less of Ted,' recalls Christie Sutton. 'For a while he hid away in an apartment in Hanover Gate Mansions, almost opposite our office in Park Road, but eventually, he had to disappear. Rosalind Pearce stayed with him until the bitter end.'

On 4 August, Molton made one last desperate attempt to salvage Famepushers and his own relationship with Brinsley Schwarz.

From 28 Hanover Gate Mansions, in a letter to Nick Lowe's parents, Molton wrote:

> *It is an irretrievable fact that the group Brinsley Schwarz, of which your son is a member, have broken their contract with Famepushers Limited . . . this has allowed Dave Robinson, who as the managing director was always in very close contact with the band, to take over the management of Brinsley Schwarz . . . we obviously have your son under both a management contract, a production contract and a publishing contract, and I want to apologise in advance for any problems I may cause in trying to assert our legal rights . . .*

Nick Lowe's parents did not reply to Molton's letter.

The collapse of the Motherbuger empire resulted in many casualties, not least of all the bank manager, who reportedly lost his job and Messagemakers head, Ricky Blears, who lost his house. Blears reflects on his disaster:

I suffered ruination. All the promises I had made to my own bank ended up being worthless. I had a wife and children, other people had houses, flats and lives to lead. A lot of people had been bowled along by Molton's enthusiasm, Dave Robinson's enthusiasm and my enthusiasm. We were all in our late twenties and it was all terribly exciting, this stuff. Minicabs flying everywhere, bottles of champagne, huddling in corners smoking pot. We were all having the time of our lives.

I took the work I did extremely seriously and I'd put a huge amount of time and energy and effort into this enterprise. Our intention was to build this conglomerate of media businesses out of which people were going to do terribly well. People had taken out loans, risked their livelihoods, and committed themselves to it. There was almost an evangelical fervour about the whole thing. We were tearing up the social fabric and putting a different kind of social fabric in its place. It was where all the smart money was and all the smart brains were. That's what the 60s was all about. We thought we were building another Apple.

Stephen Warwick deluded himself. I think he thought he was in collusion with Molton, but Warwick discovered the collusion was a one-sided affair. Eddie split and Stephen Warwick missed having a Machiavellian cohort more than anything else. None of the other jokers would do. He pined for Eddie like a dog. In a strange asexual way, they loved each other. That was the bit that fooled everyone. They did the whole thing as part of a manic courtship. Stephen was given to wild fits of over-confidence and, although he somehow managed to convince people, beneath the surface he was fighting despair.

After the disappearance of Molton, Stephen Warwick was left to pick up the pieces. His priority now was to raise cash for Grand Slam Productions so that *Bridge-O-Rama* could be completed. But Warwick, who professed an interest in Eastern religions, was also becoming deeply involved with the Divine Light Mission and the teachings of the Guru Maharaj Ji, the twelve-year-old son of the movement's late founder.

In November 1970, the *Sunday Times* published an exposé of Molton and Warwick in its 'Insight' column. 'It was a well-researched piece by a very hot team,' says Ricky Blears. 'I remember letting them into the office at Hanover Gate Mansions with their spy cameras to raid the files. It was real James Bond stuff.'

To defend his position, Molton suddenly reappeared and agreed to be interviewed, boasting that he and Warwick had enjoyed 'a wonderful year'. The article reported a number of bad debts and unpaid bills run up by Molton and Warwick and the fact that in June 1970 they had drawn up a list of 75 stopped or returned cheques totalling £10,531, with 'individual debts ranging from 12 shillings to the station master at Paddington to £2,000 to a fashion boutique'.

Warwick explained why *Bridge-O-Rama* had not been completed. 'The TV series may emerge, if somebody produces £8,000 to edit the material ... we in the film world never like to comment until the programme is sold ...' Molton, clearly a man who believed that something would always turn up, added, 'My percentage will be enough to pay off everything and still leave me in pocket.'

Also reported was Molton and Warwick's involvement with *Friends* magazine; the Forbidden Fruit episode; and certain financial dealings with one George Dawson, who was described as 'One of the more colourful characters on the postwar commercial scene – with a series of deals involving white fish, orange juice and buses.' George Dawson was an undischarged bankrupt for whom Molton and Warwick agreed to do business, including the sale of a conveyor belt to a customer in the Sahara.

The *Sunday Times* went on to report the disastrous launch of Brinsley Schwarz, succinctly informing its readers that: ' "Hype" is the superlative sales promotion of a mediocre product.' Famepushers, it continued, 'paid no major bill – the debts of the trip added up to almost £13,000. It has been left to the group to pay off these as they can, yet the group had turned over earnings of almost £25,000 to Famepushers. What has happened to this is unclear.' The closing quote in the *Sunday Times* is from Molton and exudes optimism: 'If creditors will be patient, they will be paid.'

'Con men like Molton are not fundamentally evil,' remarks John Eichler. 'They are dreamers who hope that the big deal will come through and allow them to pay everything off. Molton liked a bit of luxury and he was going to get it any way he could.'

9. PISTOLS AT DAWN

In September 1970, Robinson registered a new company called Dave Robinson And Dot Burn-Forti Ltd, but after the move to Northwood, Dot had less involvement with Brinsley Schwarz and eventually handed over the reins completely to Robinson.

Comfortably ensconced at Carew Road, it was now time for Brinsley Schwarz to record their second LP, to be entitled, perhaps appropriately, *Despite It All*. Again, Olympic Studios were used, with Dave Robinson in the co-production chair. The opening cut, 'Country Girl', reflected the group's new-found confidence, and would become a stage favourite. Elsewhere, the 'Crosby, Stills & Nash sound', which had dominated their debut, was now largely replaced by the 'Van Morrison sound', particularly on cuts such as 'The Slow One' and 'Funk Angel'.

Guitarist Schwarz had overdubbed many of his parts on the LP, to fill out the group's sound. In order to emulate the sound of the record on stage it was decided that the group needed an additional musician, so an advertisement was placed in the venerable *Melody Maker*. 'We got lots of replies,' recalls Nick Lowe, 'and we kept a note of all the applicants. Those who answered the phone were instructed to write in a book what their first impressions of the applicant were. Brinsley's wife Bernice answered when a chap called Ian Gomm phoned. It was noted that he liked a lot of the artists that we liked, that he could sing and he had the right kind of guitar.'

Ian Gomm says, 'I was into James Taylor, "Fire And Rain", American stuff. I used to read the *Melody Maker* adverts avidly, in search of a full-time musical career. Reading those adverts is an art form. It's a learning curve. After you've been on the tube and gone to some weirdo's bedsit in North London, you start reading them more carefully. The way the Brinsleys' ad was worded, I thought, "This is me." It didn't say "Professional Group." When you see that, you know they're not.'

The Brinsleys' advert in fact read: 'NAME BAND require rhythm/lead guitarist with vocal ability to sing, write and play any other instruments. Interested, or into country flavoured music 01 876 5345'.

Gomm was invited to audition along with eight other hopefuls. Lowe recalls:

We decided that as well as playing with them, we would have a little talk with them as well. The night before the auditions, Billy Rankin and I had stayed up tripping. We had a very nice time. The next morning, as we were coming down, the guitarists started arriving. They all turned into various farm animals as far as I was concerned. There was a goat and a pig and a turkey before Ian Gomm. When Ian arrived, he had red hair. Nobody thought he would have red hair, plus a sort of car coat and suedette shoes, an extremely normal look. He sang a couple of tunes and I said, 'Right, you're in, you've got the job.' Brinsley hit the roof.

Lowe's impulsive declaration had, for the first time, shaken the group's democratic foundation. Schwarz objected to the fact that Gomm's appointment hadn't been put to the vote. 'I said, "We haven't talked about this," recalls Schwarz, but Nick kept saying, "No, he's definitely the guy." I turned to Dave Robinson and said, "You're gonna have to tell him there's been a mistake; he's not in the group," but Dave wouldn't have it. "Nothing to do with me. You tell him!" I was horrified, but musically Ian was the only one who had remotely the same ideas as us.'

'He also had a very dry sense of humour,' recalls Lowe. 'Although he looked completely wrong. I guess we were looking for a laid-back guy with cowboy boots, been places, done things, would know a couple of semi-famous American singer-songwriters, maybe had something to do with John Sebastian or knew one of the guys in NRBQ. I thought Ian Gomm was completely right, but Brinsley and Bob didn't see it at first. They hadn't been up all night like Billy and me. Then I suddenly thought I may have made a horrible mistake, but it was too late, he was in.'

Ian Robert Gomm joined Brinsley Schwarz in September 1970 and brought to the group a deep knowledge of pop, combined with practical and electronic skills, having previously worked as a draftsman for EMI and latterly, Addo Electronics. 'Ian would practise all day and build a p.a. cabinet at night,' recalls Dave Robinson. 'He would also be happy to spend endless hours customising the group's equipment, some of which we had permanently set up in the rehearsal room at Northwood. Ian also had a lot of musical ideas. He had a Fender Telecaster and all the right gear. He had sat at home with his records learning every Tamla song, every Beatle song and came with a whole knowledge of pop that the others didn't really have. Everyone thought he was pretty damn good pretty damn quick.'

Gomm also broadened the group's sound out, and provided Nick Lowe with some songwriting competition. 'I didn't think his songs were as good as mine,' says Lowe, 'but I was very pleased to have another writer in the group.'

After their early country rock phase, the group became infatuated with obscure rhythm and blues as a result of investigating the musical roots of their heroes, The Band. All forms of popular music were explored deeply and, to help with these investigations, Robinson would be dispatched to London to locate various imported records. 'The record player, of which there was one, was the main source of research for the group,' says Robinson. 'It was the focal point and whatever got played, got played a lot.'

'Dave used to feed us stuff,' recalls Lowe. 'Tracey Nelson, Area Code 615, Clover . . . He used to give us records he'd brought back from America, like the first Little Feat record, and say, "Everyone's talking about this, although I haven't heard it myself . . ." I owe Dave a lot, he turned me on to a lot of stuff. He had his ear to the ground. He knew a lot of hip people and he had very fertile ground to put his seeds in. I can't minimise his contribution.'

Shortly after Ian Gomm joined Brinsley Schwarz, the group flew out to Essen in Germany to appear at a rock festival, downbill to Deep Purple and Ginger Baker's Airforce. Brinsley Schwarz recalls, 'No one knew who we were. German

National TV came down to film Ginger Baker, but he threw a wobbler because he didn't like the lights. Someone said, "Ginger, it's German television. They've come down to film you." Ginger said, "I don't fucking give a fuck. Tell them to fucking fuck off." They were without anyone to film. Then they saw us down the other end of the place and said, "They'll do." We were on German TV, described as "British super-group, Brinsley Schwarz!" '

Before long, Germany was beckoning and Brinsley Schwarz undertook a three-night stint at Frankfurt's Zoom Club. Roadie Mick Hince took the equipment in his converted rag-trade van and Dave Robinson drove the group in his new car, a Daimler Majestic Major, affectionately dubbed 'the Daimlerooni'. Nick Lowe relieved the tedium of the journey with a strong dose of LSD, but his acid trip was far from pleasant. 'I fell asleep in the back of the Daimlerooni,' recalls Lowe. 'I woke up feeling paralysed. I couldn't speak and I couldn't move and I remember feeling very panicky.'

In Frankfurt, the Daimler broke down. 'Dave had forgotten to put antifreeze in it,' says Ian Gomm. 'We had to tow it back. We were near a US airbase and one of the pilots gave us the webbing from his parachute. We tied the Daimler to the back of Mick Hince's van and he towed us through the night, from Frankfurt to the Hook of Holland. It was pissing down with rain and the webbing kept snapping, so we'd stop and tie it up again. The webbing was getting shorter and shorter and the Daimler was getting closer and closer to the back of the van. We nearly killed ourselves.'

The five-piece Brinsley Schwarz were now living their music 24 hours a day and beginning to develop a unique stance. Whereas nearly every other group in the UK was using massive banks of amplifiers and playing at ear-splitting volume, Brinsley Schwarz acquired the smallest amplifiers they could find and turned the volume down.

Billy Rankin says, 'The small amps and playing quietly originated, I think, from the Fillmore. Drums were the only acoustic instrument on stage. The rest of the group had to hear them. I was always telling the guys to turn down so they could hear me. I wanted to swing so much that people would dance. That was my objective.'

The Brinsleys' approach to their live sound was the subject of two readers' letters to the 'Any Questions' section of *Melody Maker* in April 1971, to which Schwarz replied: 'We had large, heavy 100 watt stacks. They make one type of distorted sound which is very English and very suitable for loud bands, but unfortunately you can't turn it down successfully. To communicate, we have to have a clear sound . . . We don't want to be the world's loudest band.'

Much of the Brinsleys' equipment set-up was customised by Ian Gomm. 'The group used to call me Bicycle Repair Man,' says Gomm. 'I always had my soldering iron out. We used to use two separate p.a. systems, one for vocals and other for the backing. On club dates we'd use just the vocal p.a., with open-back cabinets, so we didn't need monitors. We didn't want to play loud on stage. We had to be able to hear each other.'

'The Brinsleys were the quietest band I'd ever heard in my life,' says Martin Belmont, who would soon replace Mick Hince as the group's roadie. 'That was their whole thing. They took a perverse pride in it. The Brinsleys were the complete antithesis of what was going on elsewhere, with quiet simple songs with great lyrics, mostly written by Nick. But no one person was more important than the whole.'

Andrew Lauder says, 'Within a year of the Fillmore trip, Brinsley Schwarz didn't look like the same band. They had completely reacted against the hype and now it was all lumberjack shirts, crew-cuts and free concerts. When a promoter lost money, the Brinsleys would say, "No, we don't want paying. You've probably not made enough." '

As the group became more introverted, rejecting ambition and volume for volume's sake, the pressure was now on Nick Lowe, the group's creative linchpin, to conjure up new songs appropriate to this low-key approach. In Lowe's mind, nothing flashy or overtly commercial would fit the bill and he struggled to write within this tight, self-imposed framework. Crumbling under the weight of his introspection and pummelled by liberal doses of psychedelic drugs, Lowe felt the first tremors of an impending nervous breakdown. 'Although I was singing and writing and standing in the middle,' recalls Lowe, 'I was also the most irresponsible and out of control.

'They'd take me to gigs and I would sit in the dressing room after the show,' continues Lowe. 'I couldn't help with the gear. As we were about to leave, I would hear someone say, "Who's got Nick?" Then they'd put me in the van. I was as good as gold but I had nothing to say. I was completely gone. Ian Gomm didn't really understand what had happened to me and it was lovely having a really sensible person like him in the group.'

Brinsley Schwarz remembers Gomm's relative naïveté. 'Ian kept asking, "What's wrong with Nick?" The rest of us sort of knew. If Nick talked at all, it would be about the meaning of life, knowing the truth, having the answer, and his own insignificance in the scheme of things.'

When Lowe's unpredictable behaviour began to affect his on-stage performances, his colleagues became even more concerned. Some nights, Lowe would suddenly change a song halfway through, or sometimes he would cease playing altogether. 'We'd be playing along and everything would suddenly go high and clicky,' recalls Schwarz. 'We'd look round and Nick would have his hands in the air, no bass. We'd shout out, "Nick! Play!" He'd say, "No man, it sounds great without me!" '

'It was at a naval establishment in Plymouth,' says Lowe. 'There were all these officer cadets dressed up in uniform. The ladies were in ball gowns. I really thought we were playing on the deck of *The Victory* and it was the Napoleonic Wars. I was hallucinating like mad. Billy Rankin was in the same state as me, but when he tried to stop playing his drums it did get a little thin. But they loved it. We went back a year later and played a sensible show. We were good the second time, but I remember the guy saying, "Frankly, we were rather disappointed this year. Last year you were much better!" '

On one occasion during this period, Lowe was simply incapable of taking the stage. 'It was at St Albans Civic Hall,' says Bob Andrews. 'I played the bass and sang some of the songs from *Despite It All*. Ian sang some of his songs and Brinsley did a couple. We got through it.'

With everyone covering for Lowe, the group was able to muddle through. 'Nick was certainly physically unwell,' continues Bob Andrews. 'As a group we were very insular. With most groups it's "Us Against the World", but we were even more so, hardly acknowledging "the World" at all. Nick had a very large imagination, but he was poorly and very fragile. He didn't get out of bed for a couple of days. There was a period when it got very black and existential. He had nothing to say.'

Following the previous year's sessions with Jim Ford, this American artist had become one of Lowe's favourite song-writers and '36 Inches High' his favourite Ford song.

Once I was a soldier . . . I rode on a big white horse . . .
Silver pistols at my side . . . carrying the flags of war . . .
I lost track of the men who fell, in the cannon's roar . . .
I never got over – being a soldier . . .

'It was the terrible bad trip song,' says Lowe. 'Panic . . . third eye . . . I was having a very bad time on acid.' Ford's imagery had a profound effect on Lowe's ravaged brain and Lowe adopted the term 'Silver Pistoling' to describe the LSD experience. 'It became the group's phrase for going through the acid awakening,' says Martin Belmont. 'They thought they'd found themselves.' Malcolm Addison adds, 'Nick used to holds his fingers to his head, like a gun and sing, "Silver pistol to blow my brain." He used to do that a lot.'

Despite Lowe's problems, the work continued to flow in, including a return trip to Germany, where the group had secured a week's residency at the Blow Up club in Munich. On the way to Harwich, where the group were due to catch their ferry, Robinson crashed the Daimler. Ian Gomm recalls, 'We'd been delayed at a petrol station and Dave had to step on the gas. He lost it on a curve and we ended up in an old lady's garden. The car was on its side, a write-off. We would have been killed had it not been such a well-built car. I climbed out of the wreckage and was just about to jump off the car and the old lady said, "Don't jump there. Those are my rhododendrons." We hitched a lift to Harwich and had to get a train to Munich.'

* * *

Following the Munich trip, Brinsley Schwarz recruited Martin Belmont as their new roadie, to work alongside Malcolm Addison. Belmont was an aspiring musician who had first picked up a guitar when he was 13 years old, influenced, like many others, by Hank Marvin. Attending art college in Bournemouth during the late 60s, he'd had a go at playing in groups but decided he wasn't proficient enough. Belmont recalls:

> I joined one group as the singer, which shows you they didn't know what they were doing if they took me on as the singer! I also did a lot of acoustic playing in folk clubs, Bob Dylan songs.
>
> I met the Brinsleys through a fellow pupil at art college, Chris Gabrin. He introduced me to John Eichler who introduced me to Dave Robinson. There were certain qualifications required for the roadie job: mainly you didn't expect to earn any money, but you got somewhere to live and everything was provided – food, cigarettes, hash. What more do you want? I felt sorry for the girls – Brinsley's wife Bernice and Ian's wife Karen, because they did the cooking for about twelve people. Plus Brinsley and Bernice had a little girl, Katie, who was around three or four. They were a family within a larger family. It was good for the band. They could rehearse, there was a huge garden, lots of dogs, lots of bedrooms – it was a huge place.

On the first day in his new job, Belmont was dispatched to Glasgow to set up for a show at Paisley Polytechnic College. 'I was in the rag-trade van with the gear and the group followed in the van that had a sofa in it,' Belmont says. 'Dave did the sound. The work pattern was three or four gigs a week: mostly colleges, the odd club, May balls. Some of the other groups around were Quiver, Patto, Terry Reid, Procol Harum. We did one gig with Hardin & York, who each turned up in his own Rolls Royce.'

A tour of Holland followed, during which Belmont was given his most challenging driving job. During the group's recent visit to Munich, their van had broken down and was replaced with a hire vehicle, which the group had used to transport themselves back to the Hook of Holland. At the end of the trip the hire van was left at the Hook, while the group's own van had been abandoned in Munich. Belmont was charged with the task of reversing the location of each vehicle.

'First, we had to get the Brinsley's van from Munich,' says Belmont. 'So after each Dutch gig, Dave Robinson and myself would drive into Germany in the middle of the night, find the van and tow it a bit further north. This took several nights. Dave was in front and I was the towee, passing the time listening to 'Peaches En Regalia' from Frank Zappa's *Hot Rats*. Then I had to drive the hire van back to Munich.'

Brinsley Schwarz would return to Germany later in the year. During the course of these visits, in addition to the transport mishaps, a number of strange, almost surreal incidents deeply affected the group and Nick Lowe in particular. Lowe's expression 'Silver Pistoling' was in constant use throughout the year.

In Munich, after one of the shows at the Blow Up, Nick Lowe and Bob Andrews had been invited to the house of a member of the German progressive group, Amon Duul II. It was deep in Bavaria and sparsely furnished. After conversing with the German musicians, Lowe decided to take a look around and went wandering off on his own, through long corridors and huge empty rooms. Eventually Lowe came to the last room and entered. Inside he found a glass ornament case and in the case lay two silver pistols. Schwarz takes up the story:

It did him in. I think Nick was already verging on insanity. Now he really went in on himself. Those German tours were a nightmare. We were at the height of our minimalist phase. We wouldn't even use reverb. We were also getting involved with the music of Redbone, Jim Ford, Louisiana swamp stuff, but the Germans saw us as being an out-and-out pop group and we'd get fruit thrown at us. We played an ice rink with the Edgar Broughton Band. We'd gone down incredibly badly and we were watching Edgar throwing his guitar down, but it would always stop within an inch of the ground. Edgar shouted, 'Freedom!' and about 7,000 Germans shouted back, 'Freedom!'

Then, in the Black Forest, a promoter asked us back to his family's house. His mother cooked us pea soup in the middle of the night. They were really nice, but they couldn't speak English very well. They would say, 'You vill enjoy yar pea soup, ya?' It was horrible and it got worse. At a university in Heidelberg we walked through some big ornate doors and there was a huge eagle and red leather chairs. Left-over Nazi regalia. It made us more and more introverted.

At the end of their final German visit, the group made for home via Frankfurt where they played once more at the Zoom Club. 'We said, "Enough is enough", and played our Shadows-style instrumental, "Rockin' Chair",' recalls Schwarz. 'It was an anti-encore, and then we did "Niki Hoeke", jamming for forty minutes in a Redbone-cum-James-Brown groove. Everyone found a pocket and then sat in it for as long as it felt good. Then one of us would move up a gear, and we'd sit on that for a bit. Heads down. When we stopped playing, the audience went berserk. We discovered they were all US Air Force men. They loved it.'

'Then we drove home via Dover,' continues Schwarz. 'I remember Nick and myself were in the front of the van, completely wasted and mentally exhausted. I was driving and the others were asleep. I said to Nick, "I've really had it, I don't know how much more of this I can take." And Nick replied, "Me neither. Why don't you drive into a tree?" For a brief moment I contemplated it, to get it over with.'

PART III
LET IT ROLL

10. GIVE US YOUR WORST NIGHT

While Brinsley Schwarz had been suffering their doom-laden tours of Germany, which were exacerbated by Nick Lowe's hallucinogenic excess, they weren't to know that their lives would soon be altered by an American group called Eggs Over Easy, who had arrived in London just seven months after the Fillmore fiasco.

The purpose of their visit was to make a record with ex-Animal and former manager of Jimi Hendrix, Chas Chandler. This arrangement had been proposed by the group's manager Peter Kauff, a former American agent for the Beatles. Kauff had been hired by Cannon Films, who were about to set up a music division and were looking around for a suitable group to sign.

Chas Chandler wasn't the group's original choice of producer – they'd also approached Jerry Ragavoy and David Bromberg – but Chandler's connection with the recently deceased Jimi Hendrix, was the deciding factor. Group member Austin de Lone remembers their reaction to Kauff's proposal. 'We thought, "Hey! Chandler – Hendrix – Eggs Over Easy – Cool!" '

Eggs Over Easy wanted Cannon to insert a special clause in the contract that would allow the group to terminate their contract if Kauff was ever fired by Cannon, but this idea was dropped. 'We signed with Cannon the day before we left for England,' says de Lone. 'They took out our key man clause relating to Peter Kauff, but we still signed it because we trusted Kauff and we were primed to come to England. It would be our first time over.'

Jack O'Hara, Brien Hopkins and the aforementioned de Lone comprised the group. All were multi-instrumentalists and accomplished singers. On meeting Chandler, still grieved by the recent death of his protégé, Jimi Hendrix, the Eggs were introduced to former Animals drummer John Steel, then working with Chandler as a production assistant. As well as playing drums on some of the Eggs Over Easy sessions, it was also Steel's job to make sure the group reached the studio on time each day. 'We used to stay at the Grantly Hotel on Shepherds Bush Green,' recalls de Lone. Slade also stayed there, and Freddie King. John Steel would pick us up in a van every day and take us to Olympic Studios.'

The early sessions at Olympic went according to plan and after a photo session with Gered Mankowitz on 21 December, the group flew home to the States for Christmas, returning in January 1971 to complete the recording. But back in the States, Kauff was running into contractual difficulties with Cannon. 'The shit had hit the fan,' says de Lone. 'Kauff had done a deal with Mercury Records for Cannon to have their own label and we were spearheading the deal. But Kauff was beginning to think we could do better and recommended that we try to get out of the deal.'

Kauff's strategy was to advise Eggs Over Easy to stay in London until things cooled down. 'It was a tactic,' says Jack O'Hara. 'By staying in London we would be diminishing our worth in the eyes of Cannon by not moving forward. The whole reason we were in London was that we were laying low until the problem was resolved.' Although some money was still dribbling in from the Cannon deal, the group needed to work.

'Chas was working in association with Robert Stigwood,' says de Lone, 'so there was never a problem with work permits. Also, Brien had a friend whose father was working at the American Embassy in the US Information Service. He got us on some American cultural shows. There were poetry readings at the US Embassy and we got added to some of these shows as a musical interlude.'

'We also played at colleges in Manchester and Birmingham,' recalls de Lone, 'with a drummer called Les, who maybe did some work with Noel Redding. He was also a plumber.' Then, through their contact at the US Embassy, Eggs Over Easy found somewhere to live. 'It was a house in Alma Street, Kentish Town. The owners also had a house in the country and were spending all their time there, so it was vacant. The three of us rented the place. It was a two-storey house with three bedrooms and a piano. Cannon still had us on a salary, so we got $100 a week to drink beer.'

Through the owners of the house the Eggs learned that there was a jazz pub nearby called the Tally Ho. One Sunday evening Jack O'Hara wandered up to the pub to find a jazz quartet playing quietly in the corner for the benefit of a small number of customers. At this time, a typical week's line-up at the Tally Ho looked like this:

Monday	Alan West Trio
Tuesday	Denny Ogden Quartet
Wednesday	Robin Jones Quintet
Thursday	New Tuxedo Jazz Band
Friday and Saturday	Phil Seaman/Brian Lemon/
	Kenny Baldock
Sunday	Tally Ho All Stars

When O'Hara enquired about the possibility of some work for his own group, he emphasised the 'fun' element of the Eggs' music and, sensing that the landlord was still unsure, quickly added, 'Sure we play jazz.' The truth was that the Eggs were homesick for the club work on which they thrived in New York's Greenwich Village. 'We used to play the Village bars and folk clubs,' recalls de Lone, 'the Underground, managed by Betty Smyth, mother of Patti Smyth, the Feenjon on MacDougall Street, the Gaslight, the Au Go Go, Gerdes . . . plus occasional gigs that Kauff would get us on Long Island.'

'We didn't care about getting paid,' says Jack O'Hara. 'The barman told me he would have to speak to Lillian, who was the boss. He went upstairs, came back in ten minutes and said, "Sure, come on in." '

Dave Robinson sums its up, 'The Eggs did what any American band would do. They went to their nearest bar and said "Give us your worst night." '

On 3 May 1971, Eggs Over Easy commenced a Monday night residency at the Tally Ho. 'It was dead quiet the first night,' recalls O'Hara, 'but the people there were enthused. About fifteen people actually, including a group of Canadian squatters who loved it.' The pub's proprietors, Jim and Lillian Delaney were pleased with the increased business the Eggs brought in and, over the next five months, the group's residency would grow to four sessions a week, by which point the Tally Ho would be presenting only one night of jazz.

'We were basically a trio,' says Austin de Lone, 'with myself on piano, guitar and vocals, Jack O'Hara on guitar, bass and vocals, and Brian Hopkins on piano, guitar, bass and vocals. Consequently, we could swap instruments on stage, a bit like The Band. I guess you could say we were a loose rockin' unit, with a countryish twinge.' The trio was now augmented by drummer John Steel and their repertoire consisted of original songs, plus numerous covers. 'We'd recorded with John Steel and so we wanted him when we started at the Tally Ho. He also had the van! He was the perfect guy, a sensitive drummer.

'We'd managed to buy a WEM p.a. system out of Cannon money,' recalls de Lone. 'Eight column speakers, three amps and a six-channel mixer. That was a lot. We could only use some of it at the Tally Ho.' By the end of May, the group was asked to add a second night, namely Wednesdays and on 13 June expanded to three sessions a week by stealing the coveted Sunday lunchtime slot from the dwindling jazz fraternity. The audiences at the Tally Ho were growing in size and the group soon started to appear at other venues in the capital.

On 15 June, Eggs Over Easy appeared at the Marquee as an acoustic trio, opening for progressive organ and drums duo Hardin & York. This date had been organised by Chas Chandler. 'I particularly remember Hardin & York,' says de Lone. 'They wore suede jeans on stage and after their performance changed into slacks and sports jackets!' Dave Robinson happened to be at the Marquee that evening, hustling dates for Brinsley Schwarz. While standing at the bar, he caught sight of Eggs Over Easy through the double-glazed window that separated the bar from the main room. It was the Eggs' slightly unusual appearance that first intrigued Robinson, who walked through into the club for a closer inspection. The Eggs' music, thought Robinson, was reminiscent of the Californian group Clover, whose debut album was a popular turntable item back at Northwood.

As soon as Eggs Over Easy had finished their set, Robinson burst into the Marquee dressing room and introduced himself. 'Dave told us we reminded him of Clover,' recalls

Jack O'Hara. 'We were pretty laid back. At that time, "laid back" was the cutting edge. Dave told us that he managed a group called Brinsley Schwarz, who were big Clover fans, and said we ought to meet them. He bundled us into his car and we set off into the night.' 'We were up for anything,' adds Eggs pianist Austin de Lone, 'and we reached Carew Road around eleven o'clock.'

The arrival of Eggs Over Easy at Northwood that night marked an important turning point in the Brinsley Schwarz story. 'Some of the Brinsleys had retired for the night,' says de Lone, 'and others were sitting around strumming guitars. We stood back and watched and after a while picked up some instruments and joined in.' Nick Lowe elaborates: 'At that time we used to get on a riff and hammer it out for an hour until everyone got exhausted. The Eggs began to realise the session was going nowhere and asked if we knew "One More Heartache".'

The Brinsleys were certainly familiar with the Marvin Gaye song but it would never have occurred to them to play it at an informal session. 'That was a brand new concept for us,' continues Lowe. 'Prior to that, if we were gonna do a cover, we'd learn it up for the stage, but this was playing covers for the pure enjoyment. In a way they were the first American musicians we met, great players, who played in the style we aspired to play in – that very loose R&B style we liked so much that seemed to come very easily to Americans.'

'Nick was kind of embarrassed,' says Dave Robinson, 'because the Eggs showed him a song, probably "The Factory", which they all played and afterwards they said, "Let's play one of yours." It was at this point Nick realised he didn't have anything as good and there was a long period of silence.' During this respite in the proceedings, Eggs Over Easy told the Brinsleys that they had been playing in a pub in North London, called the Tally Ho.

Kentish Town was a wild neighbourhood [recalls Nick Lowe], not the chi-chi spot it is now. We girded our loins, me and Billy Rankin, being the unattached ones, and went to the Tally Ho the following night. There was quite a small audience, but Eggs Over Easy were really great. At first it was a groovy little thing, rather Hogarthian, with snotty-nosed urchins hanging round the door and a Sikh bus driver doing a wild frug-a-gogo routine. But within a few weeks it was getting discovered by the clique, the beautiful people.

Eggs Over Easy played very quietly. They also had small amps, which was quite unusual then. Coincidentally, we'd recently adopted a similar approach and seeing the Eggs doing it was a kind of confirmation that it was the right thing to do. They also performed covers effortlessly, like 'Brown Sugar'. It seemed unbelievable to do a song that had just been in the charts. So hip. They had a very good look as well – like trainee novice monks.

'We weren't loud,' confirms de Lone. 'In fact we were pretty quiet, playing as a combo, trying to listen to each other . . . jazz sensibilities. We had that kind of telepathy. The songs were fairly well worked out in the parts department but I would say you would never hear a song played the same way twice. The Ray Charles stuff depended on if we had a piano or not. We'd do some Band songs maybe, blues stuff. We did these songs because we loved them. We had loads of material, although we had no sense of how to sell ourselves.'

Dai Davies, now a permanent fixture in the Brinsleys' entourage following his interview with the group for *Top Pops And Music Now*, recalls Lowe's reaction to discovering Eggs Over Easy. 'I remember Nick telling me in awe that the Eggs could call on over a hundred songs – fifty originals and fifty unashamed covers. This impressed Nick no end. People would call out for songs and the Eggs would respond. They were remarkable – a living jukebox!'

'Well, we used to do some Ray Charles and some Jimmy Reed,' says de Lone. In response to the living jukebox tag, de Lone adds, 'We did songs like "Brown Sugar", "All Along The Watchtower", "Please Please Me", "The Night They Drove Old Dixie Down" and an obscure Band song called "Get Up Jake"; plus our own numbers, like "I'm Funky But I'm Clean". Also, we would do a song only once. Learn it up, do it, not do it again . . . "Honky Tonk Women", "The Last Time", "Like A Rolling Stone", "Just Like Tom Thumb's Blues".'

Dave Robinson says, 'I said to the Brinsleys, "This is obviously what you do. You learn a lot of material, then you can play several sets. This is what The Band are about." Nick got it straight away and started writing in that mould. He was the brains. The whole group bought it in the end.'

Sensing that this scene could be the beginning of something worthwhile, Dave Robinson commenced a telephone campaign to get more people along to the Tally Ho. 'Everybody started trouping up there to see the Eggs,' says Dai Davies. 'Initially, it was the elite few people, then it gradually built up,' adds scenemaker Ted Carroll. 'And don't forget this wasn't long after the era when all those Vertigo-type groups would play to three men and a dog in obscure pubs in Upton Park.'

'The Brinsleys immediately decided they too would do pubs,' says Dai Davies. 'Nick, abetted by Dave Robinson, had made the decision and the rest of the band fell in, probably thinking it was a democratic process.' There were, after all, plenty of free slots on the Brinsleys' date sheet and regular pub dates would help to pad out the schedule. At this point the group were on the college circuit earning between £200 and £300 per show, of which there would be three in a typical week.

Dai Davies says, 'The wisdom in those days was that if you went out for £300, you couldn't possibly drop below that because it would compromise your status. But by doing pubs you could have a parallel career, getting only £30 a night, because at that stage, pubs didn't count.'

Furthermore, playing in pubs fitted in perfectly with the group's reaction to the Fillmore stunt, although it would be some months before Brinsley Schwarz had built an extensive enough repertoire to take the plunge. 'It was Nick Lowe and Dave Robinson who were fanatical about the anti-hype approach,' continues Davies. 'The adjective "real" was banded about a lot. It was an us-and-them-philosophy.'

While building their repertoire, the Brinsleys continued to check out Eggs Over Easy at the Tally Ho. Occasionally, other musicians would sit in with the Eggs. The first of these was George Gerdes, who had released an LP on United Artists called *Obituary*. 'He called it *Obituary*,' says de Lone, 'so that he could call the follow-up *Son Of Obituary*.' Gerdes was a friend of Eggs Over Easy and had been at university with Loudon Wainwright III, who in 1971 was being hailed in the press as 'the new Bob Dylan'. 'When Loudon came over to England in the summer of 1971, we met him and he too came and sat in several times,' recalls de Lone. 'We did "Dead Skunk" with him. He was getting into rock 'n' roll. Then various Brinsleys would sit in, Frankie Miller also. Ben Webster, the jazz player, came along one night. That was pretty cool.'

Dave Robinson says, 'I remember finding Frankie Miller down at the Tally Ho. It was a really packed night. The Eggs were playing and I was standing at the bar. I suddenly heard this incredible soul voice. I knew it wasn't one of the Eggs singing. I turned round and there was nobody at the microphone. I turned back to get my pint and the voice started again. I swung round and again there was nobody at the microphone. It turned out to be Frankie Miller. He was so pissed he kept falling down, but he had an extraordinary voice for London at that time.'

On 2 June, The Band had played the Royal Albert Hall. It was a momentous occasion for fans of American roots-rock and many musicians, including members of Brinsley Schwarz, had attended. The Band's influence could certainly be detected in the new songs of Nick Lowe and Ian Gomm, who were both preparing new material for the Brinsleys' forthcoming LP, *Silver Pistol*, to be recorded in the group's house at North-wood. Ian Gomm's electronic skills had been put to good use building a home studio, with eggboxes and asbestos lining the walls for soundproofing.

On 21 June, Brinsley Schwarz played at the Glastonbury Fayre, sandwiched between appearances by Skin Alley and Quintessence. Ian Gomm recalls, 'It was the first Glastonbury festival. There wasn't enough p.a equipment, so we loaned them some of ours. It was brilliant when we went on. It was just starting to get dark. It sounded great and we were playing great. Suddenly, I became aware of the presence of these people with robes on.'

As the Brinsleys continued their performance, the musicians were suddenly distracted by a shower of coins and pebbles being hurled at them from all sides. They looked up from their instruments to see a procession approaching the stage. The Brinsleys were about to be interrupted to make way for the Guru Maharaj Ji and the followers of his Divine Light Mission, four of whom were carrying the teenage guru on a dais. Trailing the procession and directing the accompanying film crew was former Famepusher, Stephen Warwick.

'Warwick had become a head honcho with Divine Light,' says Help Yourself's Richard Treece. 'They had so much bad publicity. The Guru Maharaj Ji had bodyguards. His followers were throwing the coins to get the Brinsleys offstage so that the Guru could get his message to the people. Stephen Warwick was filming it all.'

Ian Gomm recalls, 'The stage manager told us we had to stop. We refused and they pulled the power. A throne was put on the stage and buckets of white rose petals. They had the nerve to use one of our mic stands. The guru started his speech but the mic wasn't switched on. He didn't realise. One of his minders had to tell him the mic wasn't on. By the time they got the mic going, Robbo was shouting, "Strip the p.a. down! We're having it back!" Dave was hopping mad. The guru was saying to the audience, "In order for me to carry on my work, I need your money." We had to stop the most perfect set we had ever done for this little twerp to come on and ask for money.'

During the Eggs' five-month residency at the Tally Ho, there was no admission charge, although a small amount was put on the price of the drinks to allow the landlord to pay the group a modest fee, which by October 1971 had risen to £25 per two-hour session. Austin de Lone recalls:

At one point we did an Inde Coope pub tour, in and around London. It had been organised by Chas Chandler and John Steel. Chas would come along and bring record company people, but it didn't feel right. Then we had to leave the country to get our work visas straightened out. I went to Paris whilst Jack and his girlfriend went to the south of France. Jack came back ahead of me and, unbeknown to me, encountered some trouble with Customs at Dover. The next day, the Customs officer at Dover said to me, 'Do you know Jack O'Hara?' 'Sure,' I replied innocently. 'Search him!' they shouted.

In September 1971 Eggs Over Easy were offered the support slot to John Mayall on a 12-date tour of major UK venues. Drummer John Steel was unavailable for the tour so the Eggs recruited George Butler to take his place. The tour commenced on 23 September at Portsmouth Guildhall and played ten further cities, concluding at Birmingham Town Hall on 5 October. Meanwhile, the Brinsleys were still busy expanding their repertoire to meet the requirements of a Tally Ho residency and completing the recording of *Silver Pistol*, but during the Eggs' brief absence, another group, this time Anglo-Irish, was also making plans to appear at the venue.

One of the jazz musicians who had regularly played at the Tally Ho was string bassist Barry Richardson, who had been in several Irish showbands while he was also a student at Dublin's Trinity College and was now playing jazz as a member of the Brian Lemon Trio. Richardson had a wide appreciation of musical styles, particularly R&B and country rock and, with his ear to the ground, had also learnt about Eggs Over Easy and their Monday night appearances.

'Eggs Over Easy were an astonishing band,' confirms Richardson. 'And a tremendous inspiration.' At that point, Richardson was also playing in a country group called Jan And The Southerners, and had persuaded some of his former musical colleagues from Dublin to come and see the Eggs, including multi-instrumentalist Ruan O'Lochlainn and guitarists Mick Molloy and Deke O'Brien, all of whom became members of Richardson's new group. Through his longstanding association with the Tally Ho, Richardson was able to secure some dates, although at first the landlord was nervous. 'I had "The In",' says Richardson, but I think if anybody else had gone along and said, "Right, we're a rock 'n' roll band, give us a gig", the governor would have told them to fuck off.'

'I came over from Dublin to see Eggs Over Easy,' says Deke O'Brien. 'I joined up with Barry's group, which at first did not have a name. We used the Tally Ho to exploit it, to see if the songs worked. We played Wednesdays and Sunday mornings; that ran in parallel with the Eggs for months. I remember Jack O'Hara sitting in on drums, but you have to remember at the time there was a total narcotic haze. We had to get a name and eventually Ruan's wife came up with Bees Make Honey.'

Bees Make Honey were rooted in the Irish showband circuit of the 60s, on which guitarists Molloy and O'Brien had also cut their musical teeth. With Richardson, they had been members of the Alpine Seven.

We had a successful time, travelling all over Ireland [says Richardson]. We came into contact with Ian Whitcomb and when he joined we became Bluesville. Whitcomb took a holiday in Seattle and took over a demo we'd done in Dublin. He persuaded Tower Records to release it and it became a local hit. Ian later recorded another song with Bluesville called 'You Turn Me On'. It was a national hit in the States.

Because we all had showband training, it was a very well-drilled machine. We were jamming it full on Sunday mornings. The key thing that turned it all round was making contact with Charlie Gillett. I sent Charlie a tape and that evening, just as we were getting ready for the gig, this extremely sweaty person turned up. It was Charlie who'd run all the way from Clapham to Kentish Town to see us.

Mick Molloy says, 'One of the qualities that the band had was that we could produce that kick in the home straight. Whatever way the gig was going, we could lift our game over the last fifteen minutes and turn it round. We knew we could deliver the knock-out blow at the end of the evening.'

Above left: Burford Villa, Barnes: 'the epicentre of creativity' (courtesy: Richard Treece)

Above right: Dave Robinson, pre-Famepushers (courtesy: Ian Gomm)

Right: Brinsley Schwarz at Northwood, post-Fillmore fiasco (left-to-right: Nick Lowe, Bob Andrews, Brinsley Schwarz, Billy Rankin, Poacher the Dog) (courtesy: Chris Gabrin)

Above: Brinsley Schwarz and Help Yourself (left-to-right: Richard Treece, Brinsley Schwarz, Dave Charles, Malcolm Morley, Ernie Graham, Dave Robinson, Billy Rankin, Ken Whaley, John Eichler, Nick Lowe, Bob Andrews, Ian Gomm) (courtesy: Chris Gabrin)

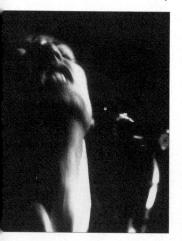

Barry Richardson of Bees Make Honey in full flight (courtesy: Barry Richardson)

Eggs Over Easy (left-to-right: Austin de Lone, Brien Hopkins, Jack O'Hara) (Gered Mankowitz)

Above: Nick Lowe in Lyceum dressing room. John Eichler looks on (courtesy: Chris Gabrin)

Below: 'The Kilburns' (left-to-right: Keith Lucas, Ian Dury, Davey Payne), The Kensington, 1973 (Mick Gold/Redferns)

Left: The late, great Barney Bubbles (© Phil Franks)

Below: Bees Make Honey; The Kensington landlord Matt Farley edges in (left-to-right: Bob Seebenberg, Matt Farley, Deke O'Brien, Ruan O'Lauchlinn, Barry Rihardson, Mick Molloy (courtesy: Deke O'Brien)

Right: Dr Feelgood's onstage tension (courtesy: Phil Smee)

Below: 'We had to travel on Paul's coach'; Brinsley Schwarz on tour with Wings, 1973 (courtesy: Malcolm Addison)

Right: Barry Masters leads the Hot Rods (Keith Morris/Redferns)

Above: Ducks Deluxe (left-to-right: Andy McMasters, Nick Garvey, Tim Roper, Martin Belmont, Sean Tyla) (Glen A Baker Archives/Redferns)

Right: Nick Lowe with fleeting Ramones barnet. Note bizarre jacket stain (Pennie Smith)

Below: Kursaal Flyers contemplate the pub rock circuit, 1974 (left-to-right: Dave Hatfield, Vic Collins, Paul Shuttleworth, Will Birch, Richie Bull, Graeme Douglas)

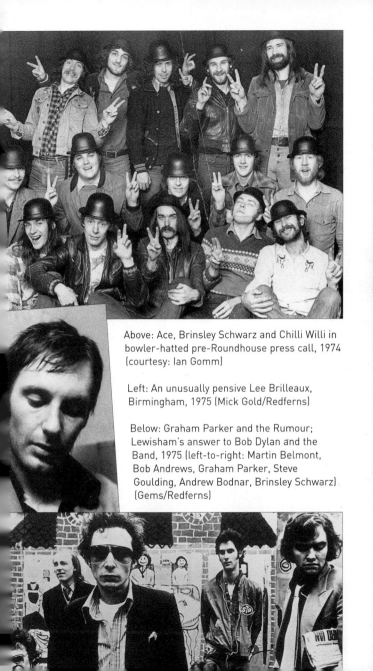

Above: Ace, Brinsley Schwarz and Chilli Willi in bowler-hatted pre-Roundhouse press call, 1974 (courtesy: Ian Gomm)

Left: An unusually pensive Lee Brilleaux, Birmingham, 1975 (Mick Gold/Redferns)

Below: Graham Parker and the Rumour; Lewisham's answer to Bob Dylan and the Band, 1975 (left-to-right: Martin Belmont, Bob Andrews, Graham Parker, Steve Goulding, Andrew Bodnar, Brinsley Schwarz) (Gems/Redferns)

Above: Ian Dury spills his pint (Alain Lekim)

Right: Elvis Costello plays Dingwalls, 1977 (Ian Dickson/Redferns)

Below: The human dynamo: Jake Riviera (Keith Morris/Redferns)

'It was down to our showband experience,' Richardson adds. 'Over the years, Mick, myself and Deke had learnt to read a crowd and turn it on. You watched the mood of an audience; you could see when they were twitching and ready to dance. You were confident enough to know you had the numbers up your sleeve, and you kept them up your sleeve until they were needed. I used to watch the crowd from the first song to the last song.'

The Irish showband circuit is fondly remembered by Ted Carroll and Roger Armstrong, who says, 'In the 60s the Irish spent more on entertainment than any other country in the world. There was a huge number of venues. Albert Reynolds and his brother built all those ballrooms. They sat down with a map of Ireland and they'd pick a crossroads between two nearby towns. Then they'd buy a field, build a hall and have it up and running in a month. There were about 20 brilliant showbands: The Clippers, The Royal Showband, the Johnny Quigley All Stars, The Black Aces. Johnny Quigley was the one. If you met a girl and she said she liked Johnny Quigley, you soon realised you were on to a winner.'

'The showbands were great,' adds Carroll. 'A lot of money was made on that Albert Reynolds circuit. At his peak he had over a dozen venues. Backstage, you'd see the promoters and the bands' managers skimming the figures. They all worked on percentages. They'd go in an hour before the end of the dance and the promoter would say to the band manager, "How many in tonight?" There would have been, say, 1,200. The manager would say, "Oh, about 800, or 840." That became the official figure. The rest wasn't on the books.'

The embryonic Bees Make Honey were ensconced at the Tally Ho when Eggs Over Easy returned from the John Mayall tour. 'I don't specifically remember seeing the Bees,' says Austin de Lone, 'but they came in while we were there and by now the Tally Ho had only one night of jazz. The rest of the week was all rock 'n' roll. We were doing three nights and a Sunday – four sessions a week.'

But, by now, the Eggs were getting phone calls from their manager in America. Austin de Lone recalls, 'Peter Kauff was saying he couldn't manage us from 5,000 miles away and we should come back to the States. Chas Chandler was saying, "Stick around guys," but I think the visas were becoming a problem as well.'

On 7 November 1971, Eggs Over Easy made their final appearance at the Tally Ho and returned to the USA with an unreleased album in the can and the legendary status of having initiated a scene that, for better or worse, was about to become known as Pub Rock.

Nick Lowe had derived much inspiration from Eggs Over Easy and was about to become a central figure in the emerging pub scene. But although Lowe enjoyed a return to his musical roots in the Guinness-fuelled atmosphere of the Tally Ho, he was still suffering from self-neglect and an over-exposure to psychedelic drugs. 'I finally lost my mind through taking LSD,' Lowe confesses. 'I had to be literally led around for nine months. I was also in a terrible state. I was covered in lice and I had gonorrhoea. I was a horrible hippie case and my mind had really gone. I certainly thought I was never going to be mentally well again, and as a matter of fact, I don't think I'll ever recover from it.'

With some gentle prodding from Dave Robinson, Lowe sought medical help, visiting Dr Sam Hutt at his surgery in Exhibition Road, close to the Royal Albert Hall. Hutt, who shared a flat with Roger Chapman of Family and *Groupie* author Jenny Fabian, had been on the Fillmore trip and was well acquainted with the lifestyles of musicians. Lowe recalls:

Sam Hutt had Indian drapes in his waiting room and was playing *Workingman's Dead*. Basically, I went to see him because I had the clap. He examined me and asked, 'What's that in your hair?' I said, 'You may as well have a good look at me because I'm alive with shit. You might have to fumigate your surgery afterwards.'

Sam asked me what was wrong. I blurted it out. I told him I felt like I was looking at myself doing stuff and that I couldn't seem to drop back into my own self. He knew I'd been tripping. He mixed up a powder with a pestle and mortar and put it into little packets. I don't know whether it was a placebo or not, but I felt better. Sam Hutt got me good. Then I discovered alcohol. I hadn't been really interested in alcohol although in New York I'd had several drinks of the Southern Comfort and Coke variety. But like a lot of people who'd been through the same experience as me, a drink was a good antidote.

Now lice-free and with newly shorn hair, Nick Lowe confidently fronted Brinsley Schwarz for the group's first appearance at the Tally Ho on 19 January 1972. The Brinsleys slipped into the groove with ease, although Bob Andrews nearly didn't make this auspicious occasion. 'I'd broken my arm,' recalls Andrews. 'I wasn't going to play and they all went down without me, but I said "I can't miss this", so I went down to Kentish Town on the tube and I played that rickety old piano with my left hand, while my right arm was in a sling.'

Following their Tally Ho debut, the group went to Ireland on 26 January to play shows in Dublin, Cork, Londonderry and Belfast. 'Dai Davies came with us,' recalls Andrews, 'and I remember being stopped at a checkpoint in Londonderry and I had the broken arm and Dai said to me, "Why didn't he look in your arm? You could have had a gun in there."'

On 2 February, the Brinsleys returned to the Tally Ho and commenced a run of 12 consecutive Wednesday nights. 'The Brinsleys played every week because the whole idea of residencies became part of their philosophy,' says Andrew Lauder. 'Their show became pretty snappy with not much screwing around between numbers and other musicians started sitting in, like Frankie Miller and Cyril Jordan from the Flamin' Groovies.'

'We were such outcasts,' says Lowe, 'but when we started playing this funny pub, a bit of credibility started to come our way.' After the trauma of living down The Hype, playing in a pub came as a relief, although group member Schwarz recalls, 'It was a terrifying experience – the audience was in our face. The atmosphere was good but we were really aware of people scrutinising us. That contact is great, but if you're not happening, you can't conceal it.' Nevertheless, the Brinsleys obviously were happening, as the Tally Ho soon became packed to capacity.

Bees Make Honey also stepped up their Tally Ho sessions, often making three appearances on weekends, having first been billed under their new name on 21 January. Jazz had disappeared, so to fill the Tally Ho's rock 'n' roll date sheet it became necessary for Jim and Lillian Delaney to book various obscure rock groups that were all outside of the Pub Rock mould. These included groups named Wine, Wool Thumper, Sun's Anvil and Gnome Sweet Gnome. It would be another six months before the next authentic Pub Rock group appeared, in the form of Ducks Deluxe.

In February 1972, Brinsley Schwarz released their third LP, *Silver Pistol*. It had been Ian Gomm's first opportunity to have some of own songs recorded and the LP contained four of his compositions, including the opening cut, 'Dry Land', a three-quarter time, Band-like, sing-along. There are also two Jim Ford covers, 'Niki Hoeke Speedway' and 'Juju Man'. The LP has a naïve charm, with a deliberate down-home feel and DIY quality. The Brinsleys even recorded in the garden and on one track, 'Egypt', the group's dog, Poacher, can be heard barking in the background.

Guitar solos and overdubs are kept to a minimum throughout, enhancing the low-fi listening experience. After the closing instrumental, 'Rockin' Chair', in which the Brinsleys pay tribute to the Shadows, a snippet of studio banter is heard. This gimmick, of retaining count-ins and comments between the studio floor and the control room, was much in vogue at the time, initiated by Bob Dylan's enquiry, 'Is it rolling, Bob?', on 1969's *Nashville Skyline*.

The influence of The Band permeates every track on *Silver Pistol*. From Brinsley Schwarz's approximation of the Robbie Robertson guitar sound on the title track, to Nick Lowe's Dylanesque warbling on 'The Last Time I Was Fooled', we hear the sound of wet-behind-the-ears Englishmen earnestly trying to emulate the sound of seen-it-all-done-it-all veterans from the North American continent, although, ironically, The Band themselves were reckoned, by eminent rock critic Paul

Williams, to have been influenced by an English group — Procol Harum.

Very few British musicians were this deeply immersed in Americana. The Band's influence can be detected in just a handful of British records from this period. Albert Lee's Heads Hands & Feet, whose eponymous debut LP was recorded a year earlier than *Silver Pistol*, is probably the best-known example. Another, less well-known, record is *First Album* by Roger Morris on the Regal Zonophone label. Recorded in London at precisely the same time as *Silver Pistol* and also released in 1972, Morris's record is an eerie second cousin to the Brinsleys' release. Morris, a native of Upminster, Essex, managed to assemble a sympathetic session ensemble including John Weider and Glen 'Fernando' Campbell for his lone LP, which was co-produced, coincidentally, by Keith West of 'Excerpt From A Teenage Opera' fame — West's producer, Mark Wirtz, had produced Kippington Lodge.

By the time Silver Pistol appeared in the shops, Brinsley Schwarz had moved on. In the lengthy gap between the recording and the release of the LP, the Brinsleys' music veered closer towards the roots of rock 'n' roll and rhythm and blues, reflecting the group's new status as leaders of the bar-room revolution. 'I guess it was because of the Eggs that we got more rock 'n' rolly,' says Bob Andrews. 'They were a big influence, along with Clover, but I remember being one of the few people that was against this change in direction.'

In April 1972, Brinsley Schwarz commenced the recording of *Nervous On The Road* at Rockfield Studios, where they ran into the Welsh rocker and reclusive record producer Dave Edmunds. 'I thought Edmunds was really cool,' says Nick Lowe. 'He used to turn up at the studio just as we were packing up. He would arrive from the pub to start work late in the evening, with a bottle of whisky, and spend the night recording or mixing at earsplitting volume. Then, around breakfast time, he'd drive away in his Jag, in whatever state he was in. I thought I ought to try and meet him, but he was very secretive, like a hermit.'

'There were more myths about Edmunds than was humanly possible,' says Brinsleys' roadie Martin Belmont. 'He had a big house in Monmouth . . . his chemical intake was massive . . . he would drive his Jaguar at 90 miles an hour through country lanes on Mandrax and whisky with his vintage Gibson 335, out of its case, on the back seat. We thought this was perfect. In the studio, he would listen to playbacks at deafening volumes and squeeze the EQ up so far that peoples' trousers would rustle.'

Eventually, Edmunds dropped in on a Brinsleys session with engineer Kingsley Ward. Nick Lowe recalls:

Edmunds listened to one of our recordings and asked us if he could have a tinker with it. Dave Robinson, who was our producer, looked a bit tense, but we all thought it was a good idea. Our recording was very tiresome, but Edmunds got a few Revoxes going, patched in some echo effects and suddenly the thing was jumping. In next to no time, he had transformed our leaden sound into an all-singing, all-dancing groove. We were a bit slack-jawed and saucer-eyed at this, although Dave Robinson got a bit cross. After Edmunds and Kingsley Ward left the room, Robbo said, 'You can't have that, it's not real!' 'Real' was the word we bandied about! But I'm not blaming Robbo; we were all learning.

Nervous On The Road was released in September 1972. The LP opens with a breezy power pop gem from the pen of Ian Gomm entitled 'It's Been So Long', followed by the Bob Andrews/Nick Lowe collaboration 'Happy Doing What We're Doing', a succinct mission statement reminiscent of the Lovin' Spoonful's 'Jug Band Music', with a superb minimalist guitar 'solo'.

'We went over the top with our minimalist approach.' says Lowe. 'It was aggressive. Solos had to be really, really pathetic. It could never be thin enough.' Three strong Lowe compositions follow: 'Surrender To The Rhythm', 'Don't Lose Your Grip On Love' and the title track, 'Nervous On The Road'. The sound throughout is basic, but the songs are strong enough to withstand any amount of under-production.

* * *

It was now two years since the Fillmore debacle and the Brinsleys' Tally Ho residency was slowly reviving the group's career. Dave Robinson was delighted with this modicum of success, even if it was only in the back room of a pub. On 7 May 1972, Brinsley Schwarz performed in torrential rain at the Bickershaw Festival, as one of the opening acts for headliners, the Grateful Dead. In the audience was 17-year-old Declan MacManus, an aspiring songwriter, then living in Liverpool.

Declan MacManus (destined to become Elvis Costello) was a Brinsley Schwarz fan and, as one half of a Liverpool duo called Rusty, performed several of Nick Lowe's songs from *Silver Pistol*. On 27 July, Brinsley Schwarz played Liverpool's Cavern Club and MacManus was there too, befriending Lowe in The Grapes, a nearby pub, prior to the show. 'Nick was at the bar and I went up to him,' recalls MacManus. 'There was a barrier at first. I was just an amateur musician. I offered to buy Nick a drink and hesitantly got talking to him. That night Brinsley broke a string and the gig just stopped. I think I liked that, together with the self-deprecating way they talked.'

Meanwhile, Dave Robinson was beginning to think in terms of a London Pub Rock circuit. 'I'd had the experience in America of seeing people like Muddy Waters playing in bars to about four people – mostly drunk or asleep,' recalls Robinson. 'And here's the great Muddy Waters – look at where he's playing! It was a question of finding more venues, so I thought, "We'll take over the jazz pubs." I heard that The Kensington in Russell Gardens was wanting to get rid of the jazz, so I went there and met the manager, Matt Farley. He and I hit it off very quickly. I put the Brinsleys in straightaway and told the crowd where we were playing and Matt said, "This is fuckin' it!"'

In the excitement of the moment, new groups began to form with the pub circuit in mind. Martin Belmont, having worked as a roadie for Brinsley Schwarz, had his ear closest to the ground and began plotting a new group with Sean Tyla, an all-round street hustler and Tin Pan Alley songwriter who, like Belmont, had also been a roadie. Tyla's employers were former Famepushers act Help Yourself, whose guitarist, Richard Treece, recalls, 'Sean wanted to be in Help Yourself.

He told us he had been a member of Geno Washington's Ram Jam Band and showed us a photograph to try to prove it. But even though the picture was badly blurred, we could see it was Pete Gage on guitar and not Sean. We got used to Sean's stories and he became a sort of court jester.'

Martin Belmont recalls:

Dai Davies, who I met through the Brinsleys, had been wanting to manage a band. I introduced him to Sean Tyla. Dai liked Sean's bullet-proof ego and attitude and offered to manage us. Having spent a year immersed in the Brinsleys' music, I'd formed my own ideas. It was a really good lesson, being close enough to a band to see how they actually did it. It was the idea of playing songs that made sense. Prior to that, the song was incidental to the clever arrangement.

We were gonna be a song group. As soon as I heard Sean's songs, I knew it was going to be rockier songs, as Sean was influenced by Lou Reed and the Stones. Ken Whaley, who had been in Help Yourself, was our first bass player. We did our first gig in our back yard at Kentish Town. Me and Sean and Ken and Magic Michael hitting oil cans. We didn't have a name at that time, but when Tim Roper joined on drums we became Ducks Deluxe.

Richard Treece says, 'The origin of the name Ducks Deluxe was an amusement machine called The Duck Deluxe, which Sean Tyla had come across at the Severn Bridge Service Station while working for Help Yourself.'

Originally, Belmont thought he was going to join Clancy, a group fronted by former Robinson protégé and Eire Apparent vocalist, Ernie Graham. Belmont recalls, 'I got a call from Ernie Graham saying he was forming a band and he understood I knew a really good bass player. I could be in the band if the bass player came along as well. I said, "Yeah, great." I did two or three rehearsals. Twink was on drums. Me and Twink got fired after the third rehearsal. I should have read the signs!'

Ducks Deluxe were soon ready to go public, hitting the Tally Ho on 30 September with some hard-driving punk rock. Drawing on the uptempo drive of the MC5, the street drawl of Lou Reed, and the precocious teen angst of Eddie Cochran, the group's performances were liberally peppered with Sean Tyla's often offensive stage patter. 'Encore?' Tyla would shout. 'You don't fucking deserve one.' This offended the more sensitive members of the audience, but only Tyla's facial hair, premature baldness and excess kilos stood between the Ducks and rock 'n' roll immortality.

Ducks Deluxe wowed the Tally Ho and soon joined Brinsley Schwarz and Bees Make Honey at other pubs, such as The Kensington and The Cock Tavern in Kilburn High Road (not to be confused with The Cock Inn in Holloway Road, where Brinsley Schwarz would make just one appearance on 2 April the following year). 'The Ducks did a few weeks at The Cock Inn,' recalls Martin Belmont. 'The Irish landlord said to us, "You guys are good but you're a bit scruffy. What you should do is all wear matching shirts." '

'The Cock Tavern was a brilliant place,' says Nick Lowe. 'But the landlord had never heard of Pub Rock. We persuaded him to give us a gig by offering to do it really cheap. We had a big following and it was so packed, he got freaked out. The landlord was mainly interested in selling beer and would often shout, "Keep filling up those glasses!" from behind the bar.' Belmont adds, 'When the Ducks played The Cock Tavern, the place was heaving, yet, in the break, the landlord got up on stage and berated the audience for drinking only half-pints! He was furious. Talk about killing the vibe. He said, "If you lot don't buy more drinks, I'm stopping this!" The pub was packed.'

Minor problems at The Cock Inn and The Cock Tavern notwithstanding, a viable circuit was developing, largely due to the legwork of Dave Robinson, often with Dai Davies and several hungry musicians in tow. 'I was essentially looking for gigs for the Brinsleys,' says Robinson. 'The other bands came with the package, so I could say to the landlords, "You've got six or seven groups here, one for each night of the week – you'll do well." I felt we were inventing an entirely new musical shape and I needed a real format.'

11. CRIPPLED WITH NERVES

One of the most important unifying influences during the growth of Pub Rock was Charlie Gillett's *Honky Tonk* radio show, broadcast every Sunday morning on BBC Radio London. Gillett was author of *Sound of the City*, the definitive history of rock 'n' roll. Published in 1971, Gillett's highly regarded thesis bestowed on its author great credibility as a music historian and an authority on the roots of pop.

Gillett's radio show started in March 1972, originally playing rock 'n' roll and soul music. Occasionally, Gillett would throw in an unexpected track by the Velvet Underground, the Beach Boys, or ? And The Mysterians. This musical catholicism was another direct influence on the musicians who were tuned in, further encouraging the 'anything goes' attitude that the Brinsleys had acquired from Eggs Over Easy.

In addition, Gillett's radio show became a bulletin board for London music fans and musicians alike. 'If a band was looking for a new member, they would get in touch,' recalls Gillett, 'because there was the assumption that if a musician was listening to *Honky Tonk*, he could be trusted and was therefore worth contacting. It also acted as a sort of community service for musicians. I distinctly remember publicising the Brinsleys' housing problems!'

Due to 'needletime restrictions' and Radio London's 'talk' policy, Gillett was limited to playing only 10 minutes of recorded music in each 45-minute show and therefore had to find ingenious ways to present more music. Sometimes he would 'review' a new release and then play the record to 'illustrate the review'. This was allowed. Gillett would also conduct interviews with various musicians and, of course, there was a Gig Guide, usually announced by *Time Out*'s music editor John Collis, credited by some as the man who first coined the expression 'Pub Rock'.

'I know the term Pub Rock is not liked by musicians,' says Collis. 'It might seem to imply a lack of ambition, but it does describe a certain expectation that the music would be unpretentious, well played, based on the roots of rock 'n' roll and there wouldn't be too many shapes thrown.'

Bees Make Honey typified the genre as described by Collis and, because of their connections with jazz, had been one of the pioneers of shifting rock 'n' roll into pubs, at the expense of jazz, to a certain extent.

'I think the tradition of jazz in pubs was already established,' continues Collis, 'and rock 'n' roll had been there since the 60s, but something began to happen in the early 70s. They put a penny on a pint and had free admission. I believe Matt Farley wanted to charge admission at The Kensington, but Dave Robinson said it wouldn't work. Of course, the Brinsleys were worth fifty pence, but had they have charged it, in the early days, it might have killed it.'

Collis's position at *Time Out* allowed him to promote the Pub Rock scene and the magazine's music pages reflected the fervent activity in the capital's hostelries. 'I discovered that there was a certain amount of power in *Time Out*'s caption reviews and the general tone of the editorial attitude at the time. Although the magazine had to concern itself with previewing acts like Uriah Heep at Wembley Arena or Hammersmith Odeon, of more potential excitement to our readership was what I could see was beginning to happen in the pubs. I think *Time Out* was instrumental in defining the genre.'

Although BBC Radio London's signal was not particularly strong, Charlie Gillett's broadcasts could certainly be heard within a 40-mile radius of the capital, where a number of frustrated musicians were lurking, unconsciously waiting for Pub Rock to happen. 'I think it's quite significant that a large number of people in this scene we're talking about didn't themselves grow up in London,' says Gillett. 'We all came to London as outsiders and I'm sure we all had different ideas about what we thought London would be like – the metropolis, the source of the media, the embodiment of our dream city.'

At Canterbury School of Art a group of musically minded students, together with their tutor and a few of his jazz musician friends, were struggling for bookings under the illustrious name of Kilburn And The High Roads. The group was musically erratic yet engaging, with a raucous repertoire that swung wildly between calypso and reggae, rockabilly and 50s novelty pop. As art students, the group paid a great deal of attention to the visual aspect of their act, the importance of which was continually emphasised by their lecturer and group leader, Ian Dury.

Ian Robins Dury was born in May 1942, in Harrow, Middlesex. At the age of seven, Dury fell victim to the polio epidemic that swept through postwar Britain. A visit to the open-air swimming baths at Southend-on-Sea in August 1949 was thought to have been where he contracted the disease, which first manifested itself while Dury was on holiday in Cornwall.

Dury recalls, 'I spent six weeks in an isolation hospital, in Truro, because I was infectious. My dad sent me a postcard every day and my mum gave me a toy farm animal every day. I had a farm on my bedside locker with a mirror for the duck pond. My mum came down on the milk train, and they said I was going to die, but I rallied round after six months in the Royal Cornish Infirmary. I was encased in plaster, both arms and both legs, and they took me back to Essex on a stretcher.'

Dury was soon sent to Chailey Heritage School in Sussex, where children with special needs were educated and catered for. Dury says, 'My education at Chailey wasn't very good. There were twelve of us in what they called the tutorial group, who could read and write. Eighty per cent were affected mentally. Those of us that could write would have a queue of boys behind us asking us to write their letters home. "Did you get a parcel this week? A letter?" We were all tough little fuckers. It was a bit like Wandsworth D-wing. Once I got strong, I became quite a little tyke.'

Dury's parents, Bill and Margaret, had separated. 'Mum and Dad came from two different worlds,' says Dury. 'My dad was a chauffeur. My mum and her sisters were middle-class university types. They all went to university and their father was a doctor. Dad told me he would come home from driving a bus and the three of them would be talking medicine. I think he got quite frustrated by it, their genteel doctorly ways. He was bright but he wasn't educated. He came from a long line of bus drivers, as they say.'

Dury's mother encouraged him to sit the Eleven Plus, an examination he passed. This allowed Dury to attend grammar school and in 1954, with the help of his aunt, who was a doctor, Dury received a grant to attend the Royal Grammar School in High Wycombe as a boarder.

'Ian took a great interest in rock 'n' roll,' says Warwick 'Rocky' Prior, a contemporary of Dury's. 'He particularly liked the music of Gene Vincent. Although he displayed no great musical ability, we allowed him to play washboard in the school skiffle group. During the holidays, Dury developed his rock 'n' roll persona and returned at the start of each term with tales of teddy boys and jukeboxes, demanding to be called "Seven", his self-appointed nickname. He could also draw great pornography.'

'I was 14 when I first heard Gene Vincent,' says Dury. 'I was also interested in New Orleans jazz – Louis Armstrong, Jelly Roll Morton – and rock 'n' roll. In that closed society of boarding school you get people, complete nutters, who are interested in one narrow little area of music. I played drums in the Black Cat Combo and sung the deep bits. I really rated Gene Vincent, the visual aspects of him as much as the sound of it, though I loved that as well. I had no idea that he had a bad leg until after he was dead. That was a sort of coincidence.'

At the age of 16, Dury passed three O Level examinations, allowing him to gain entry to Walthamstow School of Art. Dury had artistic talent and, in 1964, won a place at the Royal College of Art, where he was taught by the eminent artist, Peter Blake. Dury recalls:

I was into jazz then and I'd go and see Roland Kirk at Ronnie Scott's Old Place. My tastes were towards modern, free-form jazz – Albert Ayler, Don Cherry, Pharoah Saunders – and we were all insane about Ornette Coleman. In the art-school days I'd gone through a Bohemian phase, long hair, but now, at the

Royal College of Art, we all dressed like bricklayers. Tuf boots, rolled-up jeans and nice macs. Rugged Working Man Today. We also got heavily involved with rhyming slang. There was a nice club effort going on.

It was partly the Bohemian lifestyle that attracted me. Van Gogh, Lautrec, Renoir. I'd been playing the washboard in a skiffle group round Soho when I was 14. Someone told me I should go in the café bar in Old Compton Street and see a bloke in there called Iron Foot Jack. I went and met him, a real Soho Bohemian, long white hair, a cape, iron foot, he was a well-known Soho character. I fell in love with Soho and the whole idea of being a Bohemian, before they said beatnik. I used to draw all the time and I knew I wanted to go to art school. It was very easy to get into art school with three O levels. All the people who taught us at Walthamstow, including Peter Blake, were practising painters who had to teach to make enough money to stay alive.

I was four years at Walthamstow. The first two years I think my mum kept me. I might have had a travelling grant and she just kept me fed and clothed. You had to do a four-week teaching practice in a school, in Essex; then they'd give you a grant for another two years 'cos they thought you'd become a teacher. I worked at Culver House Secondary Modern School for Boys in South Ockendon. Then I concentrated on painting and we found out about the Royal College of Art.

There were only ten painters in this country who were making money. I wanted to teach art. As a fine-art lecturer the bread was good, twenty pounds a day, a shit load of money if you're doing two days a week. That was enough to live on, plus it involved me in running it on with the younger ones. If you're a full-time teacher you end up sharpening pencils and doing the register, but part-time teachers are expected to be working painters. That's what they wanted. It was a lovely life, but it was hard in the holidays. I had to sign on.

In 1971, Gene Vincent died. He was the same age as Van Gogh and I remember thinking I ought to get a band together. I had the name Kilburn And The High Roads, which I thought was very funny. It existed in my imagination for about three years, since 1969 probably, when I was teaching at Luton. I knew a lot of jazz musicians, so I gathered all my mates together. We had Charlie Hart on bass, Ted Speight on guitar, Terry Day on drums and Russell Hardy on piano. Davey Payne wandered in, but I'm not sure if he played that day. I think George Khan was on tenor.

I was teaching at Canterbury and two of my students, Keith Lucas and Humphrey Ocean, joined the group. I said to the social secretary, Allan Upwood, who also happened to be one of my students, 'Do you want a good result in your assessment at the end of the year? You do a college dance, don't you? Put us on the bill.' He said, 'All right. Forty quid.' I said, 'You're on!' I gave him excellent marks as well. At the first gig we did in Canterbury, we appeared with The Magic Rock Band, whose drummer was David Rohoman.

When I met Rohoman after the gig, he was sitting on his drum case putting his gear away. I had no idea he was disabled. I asked him for his number, 'cos I thought he'd be a great guy to have in the band. Then he stood up and he was on fucking crutches. I thought, 'Oh God, I won't phone him.' Two raspberry ripples in the same band would have been stretching it a bit.

Then Croydon Art School wanted us, then Rochester Art School . . . by early 1972, we started taking it a bit more seriously, digging in deep. We got an agent, a bloke in Bedford, who got us one gig – at Luton Airport Social Club, so we decided to get our own.

On 11 November 1972, Kilburn And The High Roads played London's Speakeasy Club. 'We got a gig at the Speakeasy, simply by going down there,' says Dury. 'I went there one afternoon with Keith and Russell. Leo Sayer was practising there, doing "Summer In The City" and all his gear was Fender, every scrap of it – Fender splendour! They gave us a gig and we thought we would die a death down there, because it's all roadies, but after the first set they all clapped. We thought, "Fucking hell!" '

In the audience that night were Dave Robinson and Nick Lowe. 'I couldn't take my eyes off the Kilburns,' says Robinson, recalling the sighting. 'I thought, "Geronimo!" During the interval, Robinson and Lowe introduced themselves to Dury. Robinson made a note of the group's number and soon visited a vicarage in Aylesbury that was home to Dury and his wife, Elizabeth and two children, Jemima and Baxter. The vicarage also acted as a crash pad for various members of the Kilburns.

Dury recalls, 'The rent was five pounds a week. It had two acres of grounds and eight bloody big rooms. The condition was I had to decorate it, which took six months, but we lived there for five years. That's how I started the band. They could all stay there and we had a big room to rehearse in. I was very broke 'cos I wasn't teaching that much then. All the Kilburns came with me to sign on in Aylesbury.'

Ian Dury recalls Robinson's visit to the vicarage. 'Dave sat on the floor, had a bowl of rice and said he thought that music would grow by word of mouth if you had an environment where it could develop in one locality. You'd have local radio supporting it, which had just started up then, plus this vibe you'd create and the most important thing, playing three hours a night is an excellent way of learning your trade. That appealed. He said we'd get a reputation in a locality that would sustain us. Dave made it sound very logical.'

Robinson soon arranged for Kilburn And The High Roads to play the Tally Ho, where they made their debut on 10 January 1973.

Up to a point, what Dave Robinson said was true [says Dury]. Although the dressing-room facilities were somewhat disgusting: fourteen-year-old junkies shooting up and you're three inches deep in piss and water . . . but we pretended we were at the Albert Hall, even though it was the Tally Ho.

We were playing all our own gear plus Bill Haley and obscure B-sides. I wanted each song to be unlike the one that went before it. It was a deliberate policy . . . reggae, calypso, it was hard to pin down, mostly so I wouldn't get bored. The other bands I saw in the pubs were a bit samey. We wanted to be a little more brittle, plus most of us had been to art school and we considered ourselves a bit snappy. It was always important to us that it was funny, not that we pushed it.

At the Tally Ho, there used to be these two girls in rolled-up trousers and seamen's jerseys, mean-looking women. When I sang 'You're More Than Fair', they'd shout, 'Sexist!' I said, 'Ten out of ten, love.' Then we did 'I'll Have You . . . Girl of 15'. I used to say, 'This is for all you 15-year-old girls hanging round the toilets!' There was also this Caribbean geezer called Jerry. He said to me, 'Ian, Gary Sobers was born with a cricket ball in his hand; you were born singing!' Jerry! He was lovely. Then I was changing behind the p.a. one night and this bird grabbed my bollocks and said, 'Are you gonna play "Crippled With Nerves" tonight?' I said, 'Yes dear.' It gave me the feeling that we were on our way to the Albert Hall!

Every night, you'd always meet somebody who knew what you were trying to achieve. That encouraged me; it was like sharing a secret. The other really good thing is you could change back into your civvies and go back into the audience. You'd meet a lot of nice people and get a lot of feedback. All those aspects were good, although there was a conscious desire not to do it for too long.

Although Dave Robinson had acted as unofficial manager to Kilburn And The High Roads in the early months of 1973, he was reluctant to become fully involved. As well as looking after Brinsley Schwarz, he'd also taken on management of Bees Make Honey, for whom he was handling production chores at Rockfield Studios. 'Dave had got a bit romantic about the way we were operating,' says Barry Richardson. 'We had no roadies. We'd carry and set up our own gear, because Dave had decided that this was good for the soul. Carrying the gear was part of that general back-to-basics concept. He also fired the Brinsleys' roadies and had the group do all the humping, which caused nothing but sore backs.'

Wishing to see the Kilburns in safe managerial hands, Robinson called Charlie Gillett.

> Dave said he wanted to come and see me [says Gillett]. He said he had some things he wanted to talk to me about. Firstly, he said that what I was playing on the radio was great, but there was an implication that I wasn't quite aware of who my audience was. He told me there were a lot of musicians listening. Then he said I should go and see the Kilburns, so I went to the Tally Ho. They did the Alma Cogan song, 'Twenty Tiny Fingers', followed by some wild Albert Ayler type jazz, then 'Tallahassee Lassie'.
>
> Most of the Pub Rock groups, to me, were generic. They were either slightly country bands, or slightly rock 'n' roll bands, or slightly R&B bands, though Ducks Deluxe were something different again. With most of these groups after you'd heard the first two songs, you kind of knew which way it was gonna go. The Kilburns were more eclectic, more English.

Ian Dury recalls meeting Charlie Gillett at the Tally Ho. 'I remember I saw this geezer wearing a sort of handmade, orange, Crown wallpaper jacket. He was bopping about. Turned out to be Charlie Gillett. Dave Robinson introduced us and I said, "In for a penny" straight away. Charlie was looking for a group to go on his label, I think, so that it wasn't all Groovy Joe Poovey from Louisiana. I liked what Charlie did. I knew his name from his record reviews in *Rolling Stone* and I thought he was a pretty cool geezer. There was a good vibe coming from him and his partner, Gordon Nelkie.'

Charlie Gillett plugged the Kilburns on his radio show over the next few weeks until eventually Ian Dury said to Gillett, 'You keep going on about how good we are on your radio show, why don't you come and manage us?' Gillett says:

> It had never crossed my mind to get involved in management, but I was sufficiently flattered and

bemused and asked Gordon what he thought. Gordon was much more of a jazz fan than I ever was but we both recognised in Davey Payne a musician of the highest level. The piano player, Russell Hardy, had an amazing range of references, from Charlie Kunz to Fats Waller and everything in between. For better or worse, we got involved in managing Kilburn And The High Roads.

Then the classic thing happened. Within days of taking the band on, Ian sacked the bass player, Charlie Hart. To us, that was unimaginable. You think you're taking on something that is fixed. Coming from the outside, one didn't realise how fluid and arbitrary these things that look like bands actually were. Bands normally keep that fairly private. We were disappointed when Charlie was fired because he seemed to be the senior musical person in the band. On the one hand, Charlie and Russell and Davey were very good musicians. On the other, Keith Lucas, the guitarist, was relatively new to the game. The drumming was the weakest area because David Rohoman was crippled and therefore his bass drum control wasn't very good.

Ian Dury says, 'Me and Charlie Hart had a parting of the ways. It was a kind of leadership struggle. I just knew that I wanted to do it a certain way. It wasn't musical differences or anything because it was really early days. We didn't have any musical differences.' Charlie Hart's replacement on bass was Humphrey Ocean who, like Keith Lucas, had been an art student at Canterbury, where Dury was a teacher. 'Humphrey really wanted to join the band,' continues Dury. 'He had been in an early line-up with a green Gretsch guitar, a boiler suit with nothing on underneath and his hair in pigtails. His guitar wasn't plugged in, but he looked so great on stage.'

Charlie Gillett has this to say about Ian Dury:

I never knew Ian's logic in choosing musicians. He definitely went for the look as well as for the competence. A black crippled drummer was a very memorable thing. If musicians were too single-minded and not prepared to kow-tow to Ian, he found it hard to handle and he would rather not have them around. He was the boss and he needed to be the boss and he needed to take arbitrary decisions and not have people argue with him. He had some of the things of a London music-hall guy, but there was nothing remotely showbiz about him. It was a slouch and a glare and a stare and it did look as if he might be angry about something. He would scowl at the musicians and the whole place would be under a certain amount of tension – the musicians really didn't know if he was suddenly going to throw a wobbler at them, either later or at that moment.

With Humphrey Ocean back in the group, Kilburn And The High Roads reconstituted themselves but they were experiencing difficulty in attracting a record label, despite generating a buzz on the London scene. The Kilburns' physical characteristics and disabilities had helped to stir up interest, although some record company executives saw these as a minus point. 'I didn't go and see the Kilburns for ages,' says United Artists A&R head Andrew Lauder. 'Mainly because people would say, "You must see this group. They've got a couple of cripples." So I stayed away for a while.'

'I didn't even know what a record deal was,' claims Ian Dury. 'When we came off the road and out of the pubs in late March 1973, we went to Jacksons in Rickmansworth and did a day's banging. We also used to record our rehearsals. Charlie Gillett arranged a day at Island in Basing Street with Muff Winwood and then he took us to CBS to meet with Maurice Oberstein. Charlie wanted Russell and me to write some stuff, a lot more than we had been doing, but I had no thought of recording. Charlie did, but I didn't think we were ready.'

'Ian was very worried about his age,' says Gillett. 'He was approaching 31. This was the time of T Rex, Gary Glitter, Roy Wood's Wizzard and all those guys were around thirty. I kept pointing this out to Ian. They'd all been through the 60s, doing their apprenticeship, whereas Ian had been living a life which had resulted in him becoming a brilliant lyricist. As far as I was concerned, he wasn't lagging behind Marc Bolan or Roy Wood in any way. But with Ian, it was literally, "God, I'm 31. This pop music is for kids." That's what he was worried about.'

On 3 May, Brinsley Schwarz, Bees Make Honey and Ducks Deluxe performed together at Camden Town Hall, with organiser Dai Davies stressing in the press that this was 'a dance, not a concert'. The event had been organised as a benefit for Kilburn And The High Roads, whose van had packed up. 'We'd had big-end problems,' says Dury. 'Dave Robinson said, "Right, we'll have the Kilburns Van Benefit night." We got £250 out of it and bought a new van. I'll never forget that. Matt Farley said, "Look! I own that wheel!" '

12. SEVEN NIGHTS TO ROCK

Pub rock was an attempt to revive what had been going on before. With Dave Robinson and Nick Lowe being around, there were many attempts to philosophise about it. It wasn't enough just to turn up in pubs and play. You had to have accompanying theories! The theory was that we were recreating what had made the Stones and The Who great. This culture had been killed by progressive rock and the college circuit and we were bringing it back. Dave Robinson and I then started looking for other venues. Dave was in the lead as usual. He said, 'This could be a scene, like it is in America.' We'd get in the car and drive along streets looking in every promising-looking pub that might have had a big room. (Dai Davies)

On 4 January 1973, on his quest for more venues, Dave Robinson discovered the Hope & Anchor, a Victorian pub in Islington. The Hope did not have a 'big room', only a tiny basement where jazz, folk and blues artists were presented by the pub's landlord, Fred Grainger.

I always loved music [says Grainger] and I had the idea of a big house full of musicians. It wasn't going to be a pub, just a fantasy place where musicians could come and create. It was complete bullshit really, but I used to have big parties at my house when I was earning a lot of money in the building trade. A friend told me that I was a frustrated club owner, so I started thinking club . . . pub. My mother had a pub in Hornsey and she put in a good word with the local area manager of Watneys brewery. We applied for a tenancy, which meant you paid your money and sank or swam on your own merits.
The Hope was like a bad outpost that they sent you to as part of your education as a pub manager. I was the first tenant at the Hope for forty years. Previously they just had temporary managers coming in for a few weeks

and consequently the place was never cleaned. It was absolutely filthy. One day I was behind the bar and a customer told me there was a horrible smell coming up through the floor. At first I thought he was being funny, but when I went and sat where he was sitting, there was a really bad smell. I went downstairs to the cellar and eventually located this cracked manhole cover, which was where the smell was coming from. I discovered eleven rooms in the cellar that were full of rotting sacks and old bedding.

I'd spent six months getting a jukebox that worked properly and sounded right. I wanted to control it. I had the key and I put the records in. Once I'd got that I started to think about my next love, live music. One night after closing time, I was sitting in the bar talking to my friend, Paddy Mounter. I told him about all the room there was downstairs, but the only access was either through the beer flaps outside or down a very narrow staircase. I suddenly got the idea that if I knocked down a partition wall I could get into an area where I could make a new entrance and a staircase. It was three in the morning and I was stoned. I immediately went and found a tree-felling axe and proceeded to knock the wall down. My wife and three kids were upstairs and there was school in the morning. She woke up and heard the banging. The bar was covered in dust and I'm knocking down the wall of a pub which belongs to Watneys. She was in tears. She thought I'd flipped.

Despite the domestic conflict, Grainger soon created a small space in the cellar of the Hope where he was able to present live music, commencing in October 1971 with The British Jazz Company, featuring former members of the Temperance Seven. The Stan Greig Trio and Don Weller's Major Surgery followed, along with skiffle-cum-jazz group Tight Like That.

In April 1972, the legendary drummer Phil Seaman and his trio commenced a residency at the Hope & Anchor. 'The cellar was absolutely packed,' says Grainger. 'You could not physically get any more in. It was only a third the size of what it eventually became, but it didn't work because nobody could get to the bar and we weren't taking any money. Overnight I knocked another wall down. I'd chipped away at this huge brick pier. I had a steel prop and I had to get it in place. If the whole lot lurched down now, we were dead. I've never concentrated more on anything as much as I did on getting that steel prop in place.'

In autumn 1972, with a much-enlarged cellar, Grainger was able to attract more customers for live jazz. However on 13 October, Phil Seaman died – he was due to play the Hope that night. Seaman had been the Hope's main live attraction and his sudden death left a void, causing Grainger to rethink his musical policy. 'Jo Ann Kelly was up the road at the Kings Head,' says Grainger, 'and I went up there and asked her to play at the Hope. She agreed to do Thursday nights and I said I was going to charge fifty pence. "Pay to go in a pub?" said her brother Dave, who was a bit of a communist. He didn't want her to do the gig if I was going to charge! I told him that if anybody complained I would give them their money back.'

In December 1972, the Jo Ann Kelly Band commenced their Thursday-night residency at the Hope & Anchor. In the drum chair was the Brinsleys' Billy Rankin, deputising for regular drummer Bruce Rowlands. Rankin was moonlighting during a rare quiet period in the Brinsleys' schedule and it was his involvement with the Jo Ann Kelly Band that fortuitously led to Dave Robinson's visit to the Hope & Anchor. Fred Grainger recalls:

Dave went to walk in and I asked him for fifty pence admission. He said he didn't have to pay because he was 'with the band'. I pointed out that the band were going to be paid, so it wouldn't hurt him. When I offered to pay his fifty pence, it led to a conversation. We liked each other and we ended up drinking together. We talked about building a studio at the Hope. Dave was looking for gigs for Brinsley Schwarz, though it never occurred to him that I'd never heard of them. He thought everybody would know about Brinsley Schwarz. Asking him for fifty pence had really amused him.

One week later, on 11 January, Brinsley Schwarz made their Hope & Anchor debut. 'Fred wanted rock 'n' roll, but he needed a bit of help,' says Robinson. 'The Brinsleys went straight in and flooded it; then Fred got the other bands. Again, where the Brinsleys went, others followed.'

Following further appearances at the Hope & Anchor by Jo Ann Kelly and isolated gigs by the John Dummer Band and Carol Grimes And Uncle Dog, Kilburn And The High Roads made their debut at the Hope on 6 February, followed swiftly by Bees Make Honey and Ducks Deluxe. With the Hope transformed into a rock venue of note, Grainger concentrated on enhancing the atmosphere of his tiny cellar.

'My whole thing was that the vast majority of pub gigs were presented in such an awful way,' says Grainger. 'Upturned beer crates and bare light bulbs. It didn't work. What I wanted at the Hope was that when a band had travelled down from Glasgow and they'd seen write-ups about the Hope in the press, I wanted that magic to continue. So when the band arrived I was usually there with a plate of sandwiches and a beer and made them feel at home. I wanted to magic the band up a bit so they felt good. My theory was that if the band felt good, then they would play well and the crowd would get off. If it doesn't happen on stage, it doesn't happen.'

With the Tally Ho, The Kensington and the Hope & Anchor all presenting rock 'n' roll most nights of the week, the Pub Rock circuit was now firmly established, with Dave Robinson generally regarded as its chief architect, although at the Hope & Anchor it was Grainger's groundwork, literally, that made the venue special. Another entrepreneur who helped to expand the circuit in 1973 was Paul Kennerley, an advertising agent whose clients included Trumans brewery.

'Paul was in a band called Holy Roller with Guy Humphries and Mike Desmaris,' recalls Phil Rambow, who would later front the Winkies under Kennerley's management. 'Paul was the original singer and songwriter but he quit because he couldn't sing to save his life. Representing Trumans, he had a lot of venues available to him and that was the rationale behind the Winkies. If we could get a band together we'd have a lot of places to play.'

The most prominent venue to be opened by Kennerley was The Lord Nelson in Holloway Road, which would regularly present Ducks Deluxe and Kilburn And The High Roads. 'The majority of these pubs were tenancies as opposed to managed houses,' says John Eichler, who would later become landlord of the Hope & Anchor. 'Tenants had more freedom than managers and they were able to follow their instincts, usually to put a few more bob in the till. I always distinguished the key Pub Rock venues as those where people other than music fans might have gone. If non-music people drank there too, it was Pub Rock.'

The goings-on at the Tally Ho and the Hope & Anchor merited little attention from the mainstream rock audience. As far as the masses were concerned, this was the era of the Marshall stack, the multi-speaker p.a. system and larger-than-life onstage posturing; the dawning, in fact, of Pub Rock's diametrically opposed second cousin, Stadium Rock. 'What you have to keep sight of,' says Martin Belmont, 'is the fact that Pub Rock had nothing to do with what was popular at the time. It was under the underground, two storeys down.' While not exactly a secret nocturnal world, Pub Rock was, to its followers, a preferable alternative to the bombast of Deep Purple and their ilk.

In the *Guardian* on 17 March 1973, Robin Denselow reported on 'A new phenomenon: pub rock' and interviewed the Bees' Barry Richardson who explained: 'We are reasserting the old values in the music business. The business is in a terrible state because of the belief that the action is in the big halls ... to play that circuit you need a large amount of transport, you need to fill the stage with movement, and you are unfamiliar with your audience. It means you are financially lumbered from the start ...'

The Pub Rock scene soon attracted more press coverage with Bees Make Honey enjoying the lion's share of the publicity. *Time Out*'s new music editor, John Collis, had already championed the group and *Melody Maker* was now on the scent. On 5 May, Richard Williams wrote: 'Something new

is happening in rock – a movement away from giant venues
. . . back towards a more intimate atmosphere . . . and right
in the forefront are Bees Make Honey . . . Bees Make Honey
are an "honest" band – they seem to be playing for all the
right reasons.'

By the summer of 1973 the pubs were busting at the seams.
All of the original groups were still working regularly and
some new names were starting to emerge. Starry Eyed And
Laughing were Byrds soundalikes, led by guitarists Tony
Poole and Ross McGeeney. The Winkies, led by Phil Rambow,
were a four-piece rock 'n' roll outfit with just a hint of glam
quotient. Charlie And the Wide Boys, from Cornwall, were
particularly entertaining.

The Wide Boys were a six piece guitar-based outfit, playing
in a Rolling Stones/Faces style, led by overgrown schoolboy
Charlie Ainley. In interviews, Ainley emphasised his group's
'beat group' qualities and his predilection for skinny ties and
drainpipe trousers. Ainley's striking image and outstanding
original material, such as 'I Don't Mind If I Do' and '(Man) You
Better Find My Boys A Venue' helped the group win a contract
with Anchor Records. True to style, the Wide Boys' first release
was an EP. The Wide Boys' harmony singer, Greg Phillips, was
a hotel wrecker in the rough (not that the Wide Boys ever
stayed in hotels, preferring the comforts of their eight-berth
coach). Based in Cornwall, where they could poach salmon
and terrorise the countryside in untaxed jalopies, the Wide
Boys found it hard to gain a foothold in London.

In the sweaty atmosphere of a packed cellar, fuelled by jugs
of Carlsberg, the Pub Rock audience was able to witness some
truly exciting performances almost any night of the week. It
was still essentially a London scene, although provincial
venues such as Sheffield's Black Swan and JBs in Dudley
helped to expand the circuit.

The major record companies were also dipping their toes
in the water. Ducks Deluxe, managed by the energetic Dai
Davies, were touted around the London record companies
and, in a rare outbreak of suss, were signed by RCA. The
Ducks went on to make some great rock 'n' roll records for
RCA. Sean Tyla proved that he could rock for real, as on his

composition 'Fireball', released as a 45 and favourably reviewed by John Peel. Tyla's songs were complemented by those of Ducks bassist Nick Garvey, a former roadie for the Flamin' Groovies. 'Nick Garvey was a songwriter and he could sing,' says Martin Belmont. 'The song of Garvey's that I thought sounded like a hit was "Please Please Please". You know, the slightly Beatlish one!'

Dai Davies says, 'RCA didn't understand Ducks Deluxe at all. It was doomed. Their plugger was Dave Most, Mickie's brother. Imagine Dave Most talking to Ted Beston at the BBC about Ducks Deluxe! It didn't happen. RCA in the States put the album out and wanted the Ducks to go on tour with Mountain. We wanted to go on tour with The Band! We were so snobbish. We thought Mountain were crap!'

Musically, the early Pub Rock groups were diverse, but all were united by the common desire to get back to the excitement of playing real songs in small venues with minimal equipment. To paraphrase the Kenny O'Dell song, as covered by Bees Make Honey, many of these musicians had thought they'd 'Said goodbye to their Rockin' Days', but now they were coming out of the woodwork in droves. There was, however, a Pub Rock hierarchy, as Dai Davies recalls: 'Everyone was comparing notes, to see whether a band qualified to be on our select list or not. The Kilburns, for example. Were they too "Art School"? No, because Ian Dury is influenced by Gene Vincent, so they're cool!'

Today, Nick Lowe succinctly describes the Pub Rock phenomenon as, 'The regrouping of a bunch of middle-class ex-Mods who had been through the hippie underground scene and realised it wasn't their cup of tea.' If Lowe's observation is accurate, no one fits this description better than guitarist Alan 'Bam' King, former member of definitive 60s Mod group, The Action (1963–68) and definitive English hippie ensemble, Mighty Baby (1968–71). King was now in the process of forming Ace, a group that would become one of Pub Rock's rare commercial successes.

Though devoid of hit records, The Action were one of the most exciting of the Mod R&B groups of the mid-60s. The group's sound was built on the superb vocal harmonies of Bam King and Reg King (no relation), enabling the group effortlessly to cover second division Motown and pack the Marquee and other Mod haunts. The Action later went through a number of line-up changes and, with a change of musical direction, briefly became known as Azoth and later, Mighty Baby. Mighty Baby made two LPs, played at numerous outdoor events and gained a reputation as 'the British Grateful Dead', due to similar-sounding vocal harmonies and their boundless instrumental work-outs.

Four-fifths of Mighty Baby became practising Muslims (Bam King declined to join the faith). When the group played a low-budget tour of Holland during Ramadam, the Muslims were fasting, and tetchiness set in. Mighty Baby disbanded in December 1971. Bam King and his former Action colleague Reg King, who had, in the interim, made one solo LP for United Artists, reunited to form a new group called Clat Thyger.

Clat Thyger's Tuesday-night residency at the Tally Ho during the summer of 1972 failed to stir up any interest and Bam King soon left. With a guitarist named Phil Harris, King formed Ace Flash And The Dynamos. This suitably tongue-in-cheek name typified a trend, both in London and the USA, where groups started to adopt colourful and extravagant names, parodying styles from the 40s and the 50s, perhaps in the hope that a little light-hearted self-deprecation might counteract the intensity of their psychedelic years.

In March 1973, Bam King and Phil Harris enlisted Hammond organist Paul Carrack. Carrack had previously played in the Sheffield-based C G Morris and The Reaction Soul Band, which, in 1969 had evolved into the mildly psychedelic Warm Dust. Detailing this change of musical direction, Carrack recalls:

In 1967, we came down to London and went to the Golden Star Club in Caledonian Road where they held all-day auditions, with hundreds of groups. We played three numbers for the guy who would give you the gig at the Storyville in Frankfurt. We got the gig, took on two girl singers and became Red Beans And Rice.

Basically, we discovered pot and we decided we were going to go progressive. In Hamburg we met these other two guys, multi-instrumentalists – John Surguy and Alan Solomon. They played saxes, flutes, oboes, the lot. We ditched the two girl singers and turned into Warm Dust. We were listening to the Mothers Of Invention, *Hot Rats*, *Freak Out*, the Beatles' *White Album* and Jimmy Smith at half speed to analyse it. Man was the only other British group we liked. We played with them at The Paradiso in Amsterdam and they did all this avant garde, free-form stuff. Bing bong! The Germans thought it was fantastic.

Returning to London, Warm Dust lived in squalor in a series of squats, interspersed with tours of Germany and Scandinavia in their van, which they christened the Mothership. 'We signed to a peculiar label,' continues Carrack, 'and our first album was made in one session. It was a double album! At the time, our music was our whole life, but it must have been the most horrendous load of old tosh. We were relatively unambitious. We only wanted to be as big as Family or The Nice because they had the big p.a.s and the Marshall rigs, and a few roadies. That was the ambition. It was very uncool to be ambitious back then, but you had to have the accoutrements. We would have liked the house in the country. It would have been like *The Young Ones*, except we were all Neil.'

After much of the group's equipment was stolen, Warm Dust disbanded in 1972 and Carrack took his first job since leaving school, cleaning cars at Henleys, the Jaguar dealers in Camden Town. Meanwhile, former Warm Dust members bassist Tex Comer and drummer Steve Witherington had met up with Bam King and Phil Harris and joined Ace Flash And The Dynamos. Comer soon contacted Carrack, who went to see the group at Highbury Polytechnic and subsequently joined. Carrack recalls:

Phil Harris used to run the group. He was the leader and I looked up to him. I was used to being in groups and just going with the flow, but here was a guy who seemed to control his own destiny. He had a bit of a plot – not ambitious, but one level up from me, that's for sure.

I sang a couple of the songs. Then we started introducing songs I was writing. Then I gradually became the lead singer. We'd just acquired a Revox and I would sit in our little place in Camden Town, and mess about bouncing the tracks, writing songs. Then I moved again up to Muswell Hill, which was where the others lived. I was having a ball, playing the pubs with the group. We were getting the newspaper delivered and I think we might have even had a phone. That was when I wrote 'How Long'.

At the suggestion of Straight Music's John Curd, Carrack's group soon abbreviated their name to Ace. 'How Long', something of a Pub Rock anthem, would become the group's sole hit the following year. John Curd had also run the independent label, Head Records. Head's roster included Bam King's Mighty Baby, in which Martin Stone, also formerly of The Action, played guitar.

Stone was now hovering on the fringes of the pub scene and, with songwriter Phil Lithman, a former colleague from Junior's Blues Band, formed a country blues duo named Chilli Willi And The Red Hot Peppers. Chilli Willi would soon sign to a new label, Revelation Records. The fact that Revelation was a hippie stronghold would suit the laid-back lifestyles of Lithman and Stone. Revelation's founder, John Coleman, would gently guide Chilli Willi's 'career' and for a few months they would remain blissfully happy, unaware that their lives were about to be shaken up and turned inside out by one Andrew Jakeman, the manager from another planet.

13. FROM GLASTONBURY TO REVELATION

Barney Bubbles was still smarting from his involvement with Edward Molton. Although he had spent the intervening years successfully designing LP sleeves and posters for Space Rock pioneers Hawkwind, he was still in dire financial straits due to huge tax demands that had snowballed since his days at Portobello Road. Also, Barney Bubbles and his girlfriend Giana Cioffi were now parents. Their son, Aten Ra, was born in August 1972. 'We named Aten after an Egyptian Sun God,' says Cioffi. 'Barney and I wanted a name that was different.'

Through his friendship with Martin Stone, Barney Bubbles had become the resident artist at Revelation Enterprises, a multifaceted organisation that had been formed as an offshoot of Solstice Capers, organisers of the early Glastonbury fairs, headed by Andrew Kerr and Arabella Churchill. The original aim of Revelation was to raise money to pay off the debts of the 'Glastonbury Fayre' of the previous year. The Grateful Dead, although billed, failed to appear: the legendary West Coast combo were holed up in the Chateau d'Herouville in France at the behest of their label, Warner Brothers.

Andrew Kerr says, 'I'd had a disagreement with Warners over the spelling of the word "Fair". They wanted it to be spelt "Fayre". Then they also wouldn't allow the Dead to play. The group themselves wanted to appear. I knew Alan Trist, who was their business manager and he and Phil Lesh had visited the farm several times during the build-up. They told us, "We really want to play Glastonbury." The Dead were very welcome and their album, *Workingman's Dead*, was played constantly throughout the build-up, but Warners simply prevented them from appearing.'

Revelation had set up a record label and, in September 1972, Revelation Records released a triple LP set commemorating the 1971 Glastonbury event. *Revelations – A Musical Anthology For Glastonbury Fayre* was a compilation of tracks from various sources by artists who were directly or indirectly involved, including the Grateful Dead, Brinsley Schwarz, Mighty Baby, Marc Bolan, Pete Townshend, David Bowie, Hawkwind, Gong, the Pink Fairies and Edgar Broughton. The three long-playing records were housed in a complicated tri-fold sleeve designed by Barney Bubbles. The elaborate package included numerous inserts and a 'Build Your Own Pyramid' cut-out model.

Revelation Enterprises Ltd, whose office was above Compendium Books in Camden Town, was run by John Coleman, who says, 'Apart from the estimable Topic Records, we were probably the first totally independent record company in London. After distributing 20,000 Glastonbury albums and, full of ourselves, we decided to tackle what was at that point, the Chilli Willi project. Barry Everitt and I produced Chilli Willi And The Red Hot Peppers' debut album, *Kings Of The Robot Rhythm*.'

Nick Lowe, Bob Andrews and Billy Rankin of Brinsley Schwarz, performed session duties on the LP and it was released in November 1972. Chilli Willi played a number of low-key pub dates, including a support slot to Help Yourself at The Railway in Putney.

The 'Robot Rhythm' packaging was designed by Barney Bubbles and is an early example of the graphic style for which he would later become celebrated, including an insert depicting: 'The Very Amazing Cut Out 'n' Colour Me In Chilli Willi Bow Tie'. On the record label, the standard copyright message is modified, warning those contemplating contravention: 'We'll Be After You With A Very Big Stick'. The label also bears the humorous legend: 'Electrically Recorded'.

During the winter of 1972/73, Chilli Willi gradually expanded to a quintet. First to join Stone and Lithman was multi-instrumentalist Paul 'Diceman' Bailey, swiftly followed by Paul 'Bassman' Riley who recalls:

Martin and Phil were looking to expand their line-up into something that could promote the record. I was living in Richmond in the same house as Robin Scott, a songwriter who was trying to get himself a deal. He had quite a good network and he took me to 48 Queens Gate

Terrace where John and Evie Coleman lived. There I was introduced to Phil Lithman, Martin Stone and Paul Bailey. We had a bit of a strum and a twang and I thought this was much more akin to where I wanted to be, rather than everything else that was going on at the time. I joined and we rehearsed as a four-piece. On Christmas Eve, we did a gig at the Roundhouse supporting Hawkwind. We performed with Dorothy, our tap-dancer, who was known as 'Astrella From The Astral Plane'. Then I suggested we needed drums.

Lurking in the wings was Pete Thomas, also a friend of Robin Scott's.

I'd met Robin in Seaford [says Thomas], where I lived with my parents. Robin used to live in our back garden in a tent with his girlfriend. My parents were subsidising him because they thought he was arty and we did some demos in our dining room. Robin wrote a song called 'Shit House Johnny' and I took the tape to London to get him a record deal. I walked into Charisma Records dressed like Gilbert O'Sullivan. I figured that was how it was done. I met Glen Colson, who was really friendly, and Tony Stratton-Smith. They wanted to sign Robin, but when they eventually met him, he made a lot of demands, so they blew him out.

Pete Thomas soon moved to London and met Paul Riley. 'It was in Noel Brown's kitchen,' recalls Riley, 'where we made another demo for Robin Scott. When it came to drummers, I thought Pete was absolutely fantastic. He was in the frame before 1972 came to a close.' When Thomas was invited to join Chilli Willi, he initially found it difficult to accept. 'I went through this awful soul-searching,' says Thomas. 'I was offered the job, but I was still playing for Robin as well as a group called Ocean.'

Pete Thomas joined Chilli Willi in January 1973. The group's repertoire was varied, consisting of country rock, Western swing, blues and psychedelic pop and, with Riley and Thomas on board, their work rate grew, mainly through their association with Revelation. Shelagh Walsh, who was the girlfriend of the group's roadie, Mouse, booked the dates. Walsh says, 'Mouse and I had gone to work for Revelation for a combined wage and I volunteered for the job. I started booking gigs for Chilli Willi and, because I was naïve, I phoned absolutely everybody and I did quite well.'

By April, Chilli Willi had secured residencies at the Tally Ho and the Kensington as well as playing numerous outdoor events around London.. 'Anything that was big on the old hippie bush telegraph, Chilli Willi would be at,' says Paul Riley. 'Street parties, benefits, dodgy festivals . . . it was the only way we could get work. Any sniff of a microphone, we were there.' One such event was the 'Ding Dong Festival', held at a children's playground in North London's Agar Grove, where Chilli Willi had been booked to appear with Ace. The event was organised by Pink Floyd drummer Nick Mason, whose wife distributed commemorative Toby jugs to all.

'Mouse' (Mike Laslett), an experienced road manager, was now dividing his time between Chilli Willi and Ace. Mouse's mother, Rhaunie Laslett, was a well-known community-spirited Notting Hill resident, who supported the West Indian locals and had helped to found the Notting Hill Carnival and the Housing Trust. Through her involvement with the London Free School, Rhaunie Laslett also co-promoted the first Pink Floyd concert at The All Saints Hall, billed as 'A Pop Dance With Special Lights'.

When Revelation needed to vacate Camden Town, Rhaunie Laslett found the ailing record label a flat at 115a Holland Road, courtesy of the Notting Hill Housing Trust. In the early 70s, the basements of the grand houses in Holland Road were full of squatting musicians, including Gary Moore, Carol Grimes and members of Quiver and Vinegar Joe. Paul Riley recalls, 'We all became acquainted with the Holland Road scene via Mouse and his mother. In Revelation's new office there was a wonky table that was supported at one corner by about thirty Glastonbury triple albums. There were so many of the records lying around that we used them to block drafts and solve plumbing problems.'

Around this time, Chilli Willi acquired a new road manager. Paul Riley recalls, 'We were summoned to John Coleman's flat at 48 Queens Gate Terrace. In walked this chap in an Afghan coat, a tank top and enormous steelworker's clogs. Most notably, he had a back-beard haircut – that style where you have long hair at the back but it is cut very short at the front, so it looks, at first glance, as if you've got short hair. His name was Andrew Jakeman and he seemed rather keen.'

Andrew 'Jake' Jakeman (who would later reinvent himself as Jake Riviera) was born in Edgware, Middlesex, in February 1948. As a teenager, Jakeman was a keen follower of the Middlesex beat group scene. At school he was in a rehearsal group called Wham!, which included future *Oz* director Felix Dennis and later was in The Method. On leaving school, Jakeman desperately wanted to become an advertising copy-writer and was briefly a messenger for the Mather & Crowther agency. But his time in the advertising industry was brief and, in 1967, he set off for France, as tour manager for a group called Fun Shop.

Over the next two years, Jakeman spent a great deal of time in Paris, where he mastered the French language and became a road manager and translator of lyrics for a French group called Les Variations. On returning to England, Jakeman had several jobs including a stint at the Record & Tape Exchange in Notting Hill Gate, where he discovered a lot of American music on second-hand imported records, but his employment was terminated the day he accidentally walked into his boss's office and caught him enjoying sexual activity with his secretary.

By 1972, Jakeman was living in a communal house in West London's Moscow Road and running a stall in Kensington Market, from which he sold his own home-made candles. He also drove a van for *Time Out*, where his girlfriend, Sue Barber, worked. He would often spend his evenings at The Kensington, watching Ducks Deluxe or Kilburn And The High Roads and pursued his love of music as a roadie for the progressive rock group, Daryl Way's Wolf.

After five years of bouncing from one scene to another, Jakeman was hungry for his big break. On accepting the job as part-time roadie to Chilli Willi And The Red Hot Peppers, he was on his way.

Still employed by Daryl Way, Jakeman offered to supplement Chilli Willi's meagre stage set-up with various items from Way's inventory and, over the next few weeks, Chilli Willi's back line expanded. Jakeman's generosity was cut short one night when a friend of Daryl Way's walked into The Kensington, midway through a Chilli Willi set and noticed that most of the amplifiers onstage were stencilled 'WOLF'.

Jakeman was summoned to Daryl Way's manager's office above the Spaghetti House in Knightsbridge, where he was accused of renting out Way's equipment. Jakeman's defence was that he was only 'loaning the gear', but this made Way's manager even more furious. It might have been better for Jakeman if some money had changed hands. He was immediately sacked and now free to concentrate on Chilli Willi full time.

'When Jakeman became Chilli Willi's roadie,' says Paul Riley, 'the burden of responsibility for maintaining the infrastructure of the group suddenly became his and, believe me, it was a burden. But he started to try and make something of it and we said, "Hang on, this geezer is all right." Also, Jakeman didn't mind turning round to people and going, "Fuck you!" That was a phrase I could understand. I'd had it up to here with hippies by this time, and all that "OK man, that's cool, never mind," kind of bollocks. Jakeman started to get things done.'

In between gigs, Jakeman would often find himself at the Revelation office, working alongside Chilli Willi's manager, John Coleman. Jakeman recalls, 'I was just the roadie and he was the manager, but gradually it was like the cuckoo in the nest. The less he did, the more I would take up the slack. So if he didn't show up, I did it and when he did turn up, everything was done.'

At Revelation, Jakeman befriended Barney Bubbles, who had designed the sleeve artwork for Chilli Willi's *Kings Of The Robot Rhythm* the previous year. Jakeman was clearly impressed by Bubbles's work and together they forged a creative partnership that they would later develop with the release of Chilli Willi's next LP.

Chilli Willi sticker, artwork by Barney Bubbles, 1974
(courtesy Jake Riviera)

In many ways, Revelation Enterprises personified the dying days of the London hippie scene, in which everyone was superficially 'nice' to each other and nobody wanted to rock the boat. To be 'together' was to be admired, but to be seen to be ambitious was decidedly 'uncool'. This fake bonhomie was anathema to the driven Andrew Jakeman, who loathed the empty gestures and endless procrastination.

Paul Riley says, 'Chilli Willi was still very much Phil's and Martin's group and Pete and Paul Bailey and I were the junior members. Martin Stone was like an "Old Man of Rock" to us and we were treated as hirelings. We always had to defer to Martin and Phil who would in turn defer to Revelation, but what we were having to work with was stupid. We had two microphones, one lead, a token speaker or two. It was totally unrealistic and unfocused.'

With John Coleman's help, Chilli Willi had at least acquired a new p.a. system with an enormous 24-channel mixer. 'We took it into the Kensington,' recalls Pete Thomas. 'When Matt Farley saw it, he placed his hands on the controls and said, "Take me to Mars!"' But although Coleman had chosen to burden himself, on Chilli Willi's behalf, by purchasing the massive p.a. system, costing in excess of £2,500, he would soon be ousted.

Pete Thomas recalls, 'There was a long conversation in the van one day. Jake talked a good game. He was very keen on practical things like saving the gig money to buy equipment or a van. He was going on about how he could do it all better, but Phil and Martin were standing up for John Coleman and there was a big row.' Paul Riley adds, 'The organisation was becoming threadbare, so we said amongst ourselves, "Why don't we get Jakeman to take over; he'd be much better at it."'

Andrew Jakeman personally viewed Chilli Willi as a potential pop act along the lines of Lindisfarne, who had recently scored hits with some folk-based pop. As he gradually took on more responsibilities it eventually became obvious to Chilli Willi that Jakeman should become their manager. With the demise of Revelation Enterprises looming, there was only one way forward. Lithman and Stone were becoming more dissatisfied and eventually agreed to let Jakeman take over. Soon he would impose on the group a strict work regime to help bring about his vision of a bright new future.

Although the group's date sheet was growing, it was still 'Amateur Hour'. Jakeman announced that the group needed a shake-up. Pete Thomas recalls, 'First, Jake got us into the outfits. That was one of his things, giving everybody an image.'

As Paul Riley recalls:

Jake's girlfriend, Sue Barber, had a property in Camelford in Cornwall, and Jake suggested we all went down there to rehearse. It was the first time we'd all been away with Jake. No one else was around. There was some sort of discussion or argument with Martin and Phil going on about something. Jake was shifting his weight from one foot to the other, when suddenly he turned around and let Martin and Phil have it. Both barrels. He told them all the home truths and in my mind I was saying to myself, 'Tick, yes, you are right, Jake, 100 per cent, tick, yes, quite right there too . . .' What he said was absolutely true and he didn't mind saying, 'I'll tell you what . . .' Jake didn't fuck about.

Pete Thomas adds, 'It wasn't only directed at Martin and Phil; we got it as well. '"It's no good staring at the posters on the wall," Jake ranted at Paul. "You've got to project."'

Chilli Willi album advertisment, Barney Bubbles, 1974
(courtesy Jake Riviera)

By now, Jakeman's own image had changed. Gone were the beard and the Afghan coat and in their place, some snappier clothing. 'That was the beginning of everybody taking Jake seriously,' says Paul Riley. 'He was well worth listening to. I think it dawned on Martin and Phil that if they were going to survive and get Chilli Willi off the ground at all, Jake was the person most likely to make that happen, rather than John Coleman, who was ailing.'

Chilli Willi were instructed by Jakeman to rehearse solidly and restructure their set so that it flowed smoothly. 'When they started, they used to change over instruments a lot,' says Jakeman. 'Well, one of the first things you do, if you're doing a set list and you have tons of instrument changes, is you actually work out where the changes should occur, irrespective of songs or keys. You start to realise, "Hey, these four songs all use the same instruments. Let's do them all together, so we don't spend most of the set waiting for people to tune up and change instruments!" '

'Jake also had the great record collection,' says Riley. 'It was great going round there. Phil and Martin were the big Geoff and Maria Muldaur fans. Jake had those records. Also, we all liked the same kind of stuff. Poco, the Burrito Brothers, Manassas.' Thomas adds, 'Formerly Fat Harry and Quiver were the two bands over here I really dug. Martin Stone played a bit like Tim Renwick.'

After Jakeman's drilling, Chilli Willi became a somewhat tighter live act and their work rate increased. Obeying the adage, 'One gig is worth a dozen rehearsals', the group played anywhere they could. This included a regular trek to Cambridgeshire, to play 'for a rich guy who had a windmill', to quote Jakeman. Dick Lawson recalls, 'Chilli Willi used to come and play for us at our acid weekend house parties. Robert Hunter, the lyricist for the Grateful Dead came once or twice.'

Eventually, Revelation Records went bust and John Coleman left London, handing the task of managing Chilli Willi entirely to Jakeman. Not only did Jakeman acquire Coleman's group, but also his flat, when he took over the lease of 48 Queens Gate Terrace. The address would soon become the

Chilli Willi headquarters, from which Jakeman would run Downhill Management and distribute a Chilli Willi fanzine called *Up Periscope*. Paul Riley says, 'Out moved one manager and in moved the next. It was the same address, business as usual. We still had to climb those stairs though.'

In spring 1973, the lease on 10 Carew Road was about to expire and the Brinsley Schwarz operation was forced to seek alternative accommodation, with some of the group finding temporary refuge at the Hope & Anchor. For the second time in three years, roadie Malcolm Addison scoured the estate agents' lists. Addison eventually discovered Wilton Park Farm in Park Lane, Beaconsfield, which became the Brinsleys' new home.

Musically, the Brinsleys were in a rut and Nick Lowe, now partially recovered from his psychedelic nightmare of recent years, was feeling a certain amount of frustration. 'I'd started to think that what we were doing was real old-fashioned,' says Lowe. 'We were still doing our residencies and we tried to have at least one rehearsal a week to learn up some new tunes, but the morale was fading. I remember wanting to do Gilbert O' Sullivan's "Get Down". It had a good tune, it had been number one in the nation, we'd only do it once, and it would have been a good move. But I ran into some serious flack from the others over it and that made a real impression on me. From this minor thing a huge row blew up and I said to the others, "You don't get it." '

Despite Nick Lowe's desire for Brinsley Schwarz to stay one jump ahead by unleashing unexpected cover versions on its audience, Dave Robinson remembers events somewhat differently. 'The band was playing well, but Nick had decided he didn't really groove on it, although he never said anything. I had a big argument with Nick, saying, "Without your leadership musically it won't go anywhere and we're now at the point where we need to pick up a gear. I need you because the musicians listen to you." He didn't want to lead and left it all to me. Nick grooved on the power but he didn't want the responsibility.'

At the time in the process of recording their fifth LP, *Please Don't Ever Change*, Brinsley Schwarz were guaranteed to pack any pub venue with their hugely entertaining repertoire, but the group was trapped. What had started out as an inspired, back-to-the-roots, stance had now become a straightjacket, worn, it must be said, with some pride. 'I enjoyed being the big fish in a small pool,' says Lowe. 'I can't deny that. Being the darlings of the Pub Rock scene had a certain cachet, but it was going nowhere.'

Dave Robinson was also feeling frustrated:

We'd done the pub thing, the band were coming on a great deal, but we were not really getting anywhere. We could get a grand a night in the colleges and we were on television. We owned two vans and our equipment and Brinsley had his 35th guitar, but . . . all the money was going into running the group. There was no profit.

Henry McCullough had joined Wings and they were going on the road. I said to the Brinsleys, 'Let's go out and see what a real tour is like.' Henry got my name on the door at *Top of The Pops* and pointed out where Paul and Linda McCartney's dressing room was and then said, 'Right, you're on your own.' I'd already tried to get on the tour through McCartney's guy, Vince Romeo, but he wasn't having it without a buy-on and we didn't have the money. So I had my speech prepared, tapped on the door, and it's Paul McCartney. He looked more like Paul McCartney than I'd imagined.

Paul was very polite and said he'd talk to his people and I should call Vince again in a couple of days. Vince was having none of it. 'I know you've spoken to Paul, but there's no way you're gonna get this bloody tour and that's that.' I got on to Henry and said, 'Maybe Paul's giving me the elbow without saying so himself, getting Vince to say no.' Henry said, 'That's not like Paul at all. If he says he's gonna do something, he does it.' I got Paul's home number and he invited me over to his house and we had a half-hour chat. Then Vince Romeo called me up and said, 'OK, but you'll have to travel on Paul's coach!'

Suddenly, Pub Rock's greatest outfit had been booked to open for the world's most famous pop star. With the Wings tour in the bag, Robinson and the group set about restructuring their company. Dot Burn-Forti had been out of the picture for several years and the company she had set up with Robinson in 1970 now officially changed its name to Down Home Ltd. Directorships were given to the five members of the group and to Dave Robinson and road manager Malcolm Addison. Each of these seven directors was allocated a 14 per cent share in the company with the remaining 2 per cent going to the group's solicitor, David Gentle.

> We still didn't believe we had the Wings tour [continues Robinson], yet I was really having to chase the band to rehearse and get the right 45-minute set together. They'd got a bit lazy. I said, 'We've got to be good, he'll watch us, and there are these big concert audiences. We've got to make an effort.' It was hard work; they were difficult to motivate. Nick just didn't seem to want to do it. There was a point where I'd elevated Nick to be the musical leader of the band. Shortly before the Wings tour he'd started to not want to lead. Maybe in his mind he was leaving. He didn't exactly down tools but he stopped wanting to be the leading light.

The Wings tour commenced on 11 May 1973 at Bristol Hippodrome and wound up two weeks later with a series of shows at London's Hammersmith Odeon. 'McCartney wasn't doing any Beatle numbers,' recalls Robinson 'This got to Ian Gomm in particular. One night Paul came to a late-night do. Ian picked up a guitar and started singing, "It's been a hard . . ." We were there until five the next morning singing Beatle songs. Paul couldn't remember the words to most of them, but after this, he'd put the odd Beatle number in his set.'

Robinson watched McCartney like a hawk. 'I was amazed by Paul McCartney's professionalism,' he says. 'Each sound check was an effort to improve on the previous day. He would use it to fix anything that was wrong. As a result, Wings' set kept improving. I remember thinking, "Of course, that's how you do it." I was trying to get this over to Nick and the band but they were in the pub when they should have been sound checking. Getting a sound check for a support band was a minor miracle in itself, but McCartney made a point every night of taking his band off stage to give the Brinsleys their sound check. The Brinsleys didn't appreciate it. I was totally embarrassed.'

'At the end of the tour, we had a showdown,' says Robinson. 'It seemed they were not serious enough. I was prepared to listen to their complaints and go and do things for them like I'd done for four years, but I needed them to want it. I was beginning to sound like an old nag. Brinsley, I think, said, "We don't really see it that way Dave." That was that. I left.'

Brinsley Schwarz says:

I don't know how Dave can say he was disappointed with our performances on the Wings tour because our opinions and attitudes towards the music industry were moulded by him. We'd turned down a tour with Elton John on Dave's advice. We did what Dave said. Towards the end, Dave and I crossed a lot. We had a conversation at Beaconsfield where Dave said he thought he'd come to the end of the line with us and he thought he should make sure we're OK and move on. I said, 'If you're going to move on, why don't you go now?' He was quite shocked by that and he went.

Dave Robinson was suddenly homeless and turned to Fred Grainger at the Hope & Anchor. Before long, Robinson had moved into the Hope, where he and Grainger continued their earlier discussions about building a studio on the first floor. 'There was a function room up there,' recalls Grainger. 'The problem was it had glass all the way round and so it would be difficult. I researched some lightweight brick. Dave said, "If you're serious and do the construction work, I'll equip it with recording gear." Three weeks later, I'd finished building the wall. Dave was knocked out. We went to Dublin and bought a Studer machine from Eamonn Andrews' studio.'

'Fred Grainger and I had wanted a studio at the Hope for a while,' says Robinson. 'We could foresee the time when the Hope would become an important venue, so I moved in and built the studio, booked the bands and lived there. The studio took about a year to finish. I got a valve desk from Decca and I wrote to Willie Mitchell, asking him about his drum sound. He sent me his microphone set up. The Shure SM57 was used for the snare drum sound, at a certain angle on the rim. Any drummer could have free drinks for as long as he liked if he'd just sit and bang while I twiddled.'

Soon, Robinson and Grainger set up the Upper Street Music Company, primarily to exploit the recordings of any promising new groups that came through the Hope, as well as Bees Make Honey, whom Robinson was now managing. 'We went to see Joop Visser at EMI,' says Grainger. 'My name was on the contract as being responsible for any advances and I asked for it to be taken off. I'd had nothing to do with the Bees and there was no way that I was going to be responsible for moneys from EMI. That was the first time Robinson and I crossed swords. He was pretty pissed off and that probably made a difference to what happened from that point. Up until then I think he was pretty happy with the idea of us being a partnership.'

'I never understood why Fred was involved in the deal,' says Barry Richardson. 'Dave negotiated a very good deal for the Bees with EMI. It was a lease tape deal. We owned the copyright and EMI pressed and distributed it. Then there came a moment when Dave Robinson said, "I want you all to be pro." I told Dave that I couldn't give up my job. I had commitments and needed "x" pounds a week. Dave said, "I'll guarantee you that!" To put it mildly, he was an optimist.'

Following their bust-up with Dave Robinson, Brinsley Schwarz were not without management for long. Waiting in the wings was Ducks Deluxe manager Dai Davies. 'Dave Robinson and the Brinsleys had been living in each others' pockets for three years,' says Dai Davies. 'They were getting on each others' nerves. The group was getting a little less purist and they now wanted to become successful. Success was all right for Ronnie Hawkins or Lee Dorsey. It was a laudable thing! Nick Lowe, who did all the thinking for everybody, reached a point where he wanted to make classic pop records and be in a successful pop group, although he had to invent an ideology to justify it.'

When Brinsley Schwarz played live on BBC2's *Old Grey Whistle Test*, performing 'Surrender To The Rhythm' and 'One More Day', Nick Lowe chose the high-profile TV appearance to unveil a new image. On the day of the show, Lowe had his hair dramatically cut into a spikey Mod style, but failed to tell the group he was doing so. 'I was really pissed off,' says Ian Gomm. 'Most of us still had long hair and Nick made us look like a bunch of old hippies.'

Nick Lowe says, 'I'd met a German woman named Ula Heathcote. She was quite a scene-setter who used to design knitwear for a chain of shops called Crocodile. She took me up and showed me the good life a bit. She used to get on my case and say, "Wear this; do that." There was a bit of resentment amongst the group because she would turn up in her sports car and whisk me off to nightclubs and parties. She said, "What are you doing this old man's stuff for? You're not a bunch of old men, you're only 24 or 25." Up until then, we'd wanted to be old blokes, like The Band.'

14. LAND OF MILK AND ALCOHOL

If London is made up of a series of villages, it was true to say that each village had its own Pub Rock venue, with its own set of fans who had no need to venture very far to see their favourite group. Only Brinsley Schwarz could lay claim to drawing fans from all over London, whereas familiar groups like Ducks Deluxe or Kilburn And The High Roads would be coming round again in a week or so and people would wait. But a new group was about to emerge that would quickly develop unprecedented pulling power.

By summer 1973, Dai Davies had become a major player on the Pub Rock scene, having taken over the booking arrangements of several venues, including the Tally Ho. But the Tally Ho had tired of Pub Rock and was in the process of switching to Country & Western evenings. For what was intended to be one of the last rock bookings at the venue, Ducks Deluxe were due to appear on 13 July. A week before the engagement, Dai Davies accepted an alternative offer for the Ducks to appear at the Nightingale Hotel in Wood Green, supporting progressive rock group String Driven Thing. Davies was now desperate for a replacement act at the Tally Ho.

For several months, Dai Davies had been hearing about an R&B outfit from Canvey Island called Dr Feelgood, who were keen to try their hand on the Pub Rock circuit. This information reached Davies via a colleague at the Savage Aries agency, Kevin Percy, who was a friend of Feelgoods associate and early stand-in drummer – and this book's author – Will Birch. By the summer of 1973, Davies had been pestered enough by the Percy/Birch lobby and was now in a position to give Dr Feelgood their first break, as a replacement act for Ducks Deluxe at the Tally Ho.

The roots of Dr Feelgood can be traced back to the rash of teenage jug bands that operated on Canvey Island in the 1960s. Canvey Island lies some 38 miles to the east of London, in the Thames Estuary, close to the seaside town of Southend-on-Sea. In the early seventeenth century, Canvey was occupied by the Dutch, who came, hung about for a bit and left, after a nasty set-to over a few churches in the early eighteenth century.

The agricultural depression of the 1870s resulted in the acquisition of acres of farmland by land speculators, including one Frederick Hester. Hester, a local entrepreneur of note, carved up the land into small plots, which he then marketed to East Londoners, offering them the opportunity to start life anew on 'The Old Dutch Island', or, when business was not so brisk, 'Canvey-on-Sea'.

The Cockneys came to Canvey, via Benfleet, by the trainload, seduced by the prospect of securing plots for a 10 per cent deposit followed by 'easy payments' to Hester. Any notion of town planning went out the window as the newcomers spontaneously built holiday homes and village shops, which were often little more than ramshackle dwellings, on crude lanes and unmade roads that criss-crossed and abutted each other at peculiar angles.

In 1931, a bridge was built to connect Canvey to the mainland. This was a turning point for the prosperity of the island. Prior to the bridge, access was only possible by ferry boat, or stepping stones at low tide, but now Canvey was opened up to new commercial possibilities. Canvey developed as a holiday destination for Londoners, with the building of hotels, holiday camps and a casino.

In 1953, disaster struck. Throughout late January, violent storms had been gathering in the Thames Estuary and, on 1 February, a surge of water began to breach Canvey's sea wall. At around 1 a.m., a devastating flood hit Canvey Island, resulting in the loss of 58 lives and irreparable damage to hundreds of homes. As the waters rose, people climbed onto their rooftops and awaited help.

At a semi-detached bungalow in Woodhurst Road, six-year-old John Wilkinson spent eight hours perched on top of a wardrobe to escape the rising water level. At dawn, rescue workers came and, later that day, the children of Canvey were evacuated to various schools on the mainland.

As a teenager, John Wilkinson (later Wilko Johnson) was captivated by rock 'n' roll, especially American rhythm and blues and was particularly keen on early British R&B act, Johnny Kidd And The Pirates and their outstanding guitarist, Mick Green. Wilkinson says, 'I saw Johnny Kidd on TV. Mick Green had a Telecaster, a Fender amp and a clean sound. He's a rhythm player first and foremost, which is what I've always tried to be. Johnny Kidd And The Pirates were a three-piece with singer for the reason that Kidd thought it looked better to have just one guitarist on either side of him. Mick Green had to devise that guitar style because Johnny Kidd wanted to look good!'

Wilkinson soon adopted the 'Mick Green' style of playing, which he brought to his early mid-60s groups: The Roamers (with childhood friend and flood evacuee John Martin on drums); The Heap; and The Flowerpots. In 1967, Wilkinson won a place at Newcastle University to study English, but continued to play music around Canvey during the holidays, often in jug bands with his brother, Malcolm.

On 29 July 1967, John Wilkinson's North Avenue Jug Band played the Canvey Carnival talent contest. Three teenage boys in the audience watched Wilkinson's group intently and were so impressed that they were inspired to form their own group. Lee Collinson, John Sparks and Chris White formed The Southside Jug Band in August 1967. Over the next three years, they progressed towards rhythm and blues, went electric and eventually became The Fix, then The Pigboy Charlie Band.

John Wilkinson had, in the meantime, gone off to India to pursue the hippie trail, reading Shakespeare and listening to Bob Dylan along the way. On his return to Canvey in 1971, Wilkinson hooked up with Collinson and Sparks of the The Pigboy Charlie Band. With the addition of drummer John Martin in 1972, the quartet began trading as Dr Feelgood.

On 13 July 1973, around 40 people – mostly Ducks Deluxe fans – were present to witness Dr Feelgood's Tally Ho debut. This wasn't the Feelgoods' first London appearance – in August 1972 they had appeared in a rock 'n' roll revival show at Wembley Stadium, as the backing group for ex-Tornado and 'Just Like Eddie' star, Heinz. Jerry Lee Lewis and Chuck Berry topped the bill.

Now, playing London for the first time in their own right, they received only a lukewarm response. Their music was, unfortunately, nothing new, closely resembling the sound of the Rolling Stones, circa 1963, complete with songs such as 'Route 66' and 'Bye Bye Johnny'. The group's appearance, however, was a little more interesting.

The bass player and the drummer were both stocky chaps and looked as if they might be bricklayers or car mechanics. Indeed, these were their respective trades. The guitarist, who sported shoulder-length hair and jerked erratically around the small stage, was a little harder to pin down. Although he didn't exactly resemble the average secondary school teacher, this was, in fact, his profession. And the singer, a spindly fellow in a denim jacket, was, by day, a solicitor's clerk. The group also had a 19-year-old manager, who had been a child TV actor, with appearances in *Z Cars* and *Please Sir*.

Davies watched Dr Feelgood's performance from the middle of the room and was sufficiently amused to offer them a second booking, this time at The Lord Nelson in Holloway Road. The group's confidence was now boosted and in the short time between these two London dates, Dr Feelgood carried out some minor surgery. John Wilkinson became 'Wilko Johnson' and cut his hair. Johnson remarks, 'Ever since I was 16, I'd let my hair grow long and then cut it short, so I was cutting my hair every 18 months or so. It was time to cut it anyway, but we were starting to get these feelings about the way we ought to look.'

Lee Collinson became 'Lee Brilleaux' and John Martin adopted the name 'The Big Figure', in keeping with his slightly sinister appearance. By the time of their second or third Lord Nelson date, Dr Feelgood looked like no other rock 'n' roll group on earth. Within a few years, the Feelgoods' image would be a major factor in a universal shake-up of the rock 'n' roll look.

The essence of the Dr Feelgood look was: shorter-than-average hair; the street clothes of an out-of-work bank clerk; and, most importantly, a menacing on-stage presence. This was achieved by a disinclination to smile and a refusal to acknowledge what the other members of the group were up to at any given moment. For example, bug-eyed guitarist Wilko Johnson would skitter, mid-solo, from one side of the stage to the other, 'accidentally' colliding with singer Lee Brilleaux. None of the group would react to this. It was not a big deal. It was all in a night's work and, at first, it completely fazed the London audience. But soon, everyone would be waiting for Dr Feelgood's next display of nonchalance.

By the autumn of 1973, Dr Feelgood were packing out The Lord Nelson every Thursday night and The Kensington every Saturday, although their fee at both venues remained a fixed £20. Says manager Chris Fenwick (formerly Chris White):

> It was very badly paid. For five people and a van, even in the early 70s, it wasn't much, but it meant more than that of course. We started picking up other dates, £150 for a college, £75 for Dingwalls, which was a bit more like it. But some of the publicans took advantage of the vibe, saying, 'If you play at my pub you will be written about in the *NME*. We get all the A&R men here . . .' At The Lord Nelson we had hundreds in and they took fortunes at the bar. The publicans couldn't believe their luck. Bands queuing up to get bookings; music six nights a week; it was a wonderful boom time for them.
>
> Matt Farley at The Kensington got himself laid loads of times by ladies trying to get their acts on there. Matt would say, 'Send the tape down. I'll see what I can do for you.' There was one girl who managed a band. Matt told her if she'd sleep with him, he would get her band on, so she did. For some reason, the diary got screwed up and he couldn't give the band the gig. She came into the pub screaming, 'You bastard, you promised . . .' She was causing a right scene and she said, 'And I'm going to tell your wife.' Matt said, 'Hold on a minute . . .' Then he went and got hold of the nearest barmaid and told her to say she was his wife. The girl said, 'Your husband fucked me!' and the barmaid said, 'Matt you bastard, I'm going to leave you.' The girl thought she'd wrecked his marriage!

Fenwick recalls that some landlords tried to take advantage of his rapidly rising act, as on 9 November, when Dr Feelgood played The Greyhound in Fulham Palace Road:

> I had an awful row with the manager, Duncan Ferguson. An agency had booked us in for an agreed fee of £60. It was stuffed. I went to get paid and Ferguson weighed me out thirty quid. He said it was only thirty quid because his was a prestige venue. According to Ferguson, it had nothing to do with the group at all; it was the venue that brought the people in. A screaming match started and Ferguson said, "You're never gonna play London again." The agent, who was there, slipped a piece of paper into Lee's pocket, saying "Your manager has just blown it. This man is very powerful. Here's my phone number; get in touch." We eventually got paid and we all had a giggle about it in the van driving along the Embankment. We tore up the piece of paper and threw it out the window.

Fenwick's managerial abilities and the group's confidence in him were often underestimated by the wheelers and dealers that Dr Feelgood encountered during this period. 'Chris was incredibly self-confident from a very young age,' says Wilko Johnson. 'He was really good at it and all business decisions were left to him. Usually when a band starts making it, the local manager gets the elbow pretty quickly, but Chris would take on all comers. People were sniffing around but we always closed ranks and kept faith. No outsider could have penetrated it. I think Chris used to tell people he had an exclusive contract, but we never signed anything between each other and we've never disputed anything.'

'We were consolidated,' confirms Fenwick. 'If any outsider tried to chisel their way in and fuck our game up or tried to take advantage of what they considered was a weakness, they picked the wrong mob. Also, the geography was brilliant. We could drive up to London four times a week and come home and go to bed. We didn't have to get all messed up with that staying-in-London bit. That wasn't part of the gig. We were in a very exciting position and we had a very intelligent core on the firm. Wilko and Lee were clever blokes. They could see that it was cooking and it wasn't going to be a problem.'

At this point, Dr Feelgood were still operating on a semi-professional basis. Fenwick says, 'When we first started hacking into London, all of the group had their day jobs. I was still acting, doing *Dixon Of Dock Green* or a film for a cash and carry firm. But we quickly came to the conclusion that if we were going to embark on long runs and European jaunts, we had to be serious and attack it on a pro basis.'

It wasn't long before the music press caught on to Dr Feelgood. One of the first journalists to latch on was Tony Tyler of the *New Musical Express*, who reviewed an early show. Wilko Johnson recalls, 'He burst into The Lord Nelson one evening and told us who he was and that he wanted to write about us. But unfortunately, the *NME* was not being published at the time due to a printers' strike. He started telling the other guys, people like Mick Farren and Charles Shaar Murray, who were very positive.'

In autumn 1973, Dr Feelgood recorded their first Radio One session for the *Bob Harris Show*. Wilko Johnson had stayed up the previous night, putting the finishing touches to his first original composition for the group, 'She Does It Right'. This song became the blueprint for the Feelgoods' style: a minimal guitar riff, super-tight drums and bass and a manic growl from Lee Brilleaux as he related the virtues of the girl in question. The formula was successfully repeated by Johnson with 'Twenty Yards Behind' and 'Roxette'.

The radio and press buzz on Dr Feelgood brought a number of record companies to Chris Fenwick's door, but initially he had to cope with the offers of 'production deals', whereby independent companies sought to sign acts and then lease the tapes to a major label. 'We were very wary of production deals,' says Fenwick. 'Bob Harris and Tony Woolcott had a production company and came down to Canvey very early on, offering us this kind of deal and there were a few others, but my situation was very clear — we didn't want any involvement with third parties. When I saw a contract for a direct signing to a record company, then I would talk.'

Unfortunately for Fenwick, the record companies were not interested at this stage. 'I remember going to see Dave Dee at Atlantic Records in London,' continues Fenwick. 'Atlantic were looking for British groups to crack the US market, but Dave Dee passed on the Feelgoods. He said it would be "Taking coals to Newcastle". He couldn't see it at all. We got a fair few rejections and it seemed to be taking a long time to get a deal.'

'It was a time of real frustration,' says Wilko Johnson, 'because we didn't seem to get a record deal fast enough. We were getting companies sniffing around, but other bands were getting deals quickly and I remember thinking it was taking forever, but it was probably only a few months. We were getting a lot of press off our own bat, so naturally we thought we were going to get signed.'

Despite the lack of an immediate recording deal, venues across the country welcomed the Feelgoods with open arms and attendance records were broken almost everywhere. Wilko Johnson says, 'At The Kensington, I felt something was happening. After we'd played there two or three times, I was standing outside before the gig and a taxi pulled up and I thought, "Wow! We're really happening. People who can afford to ride in taxis are coming to see us." At The Torrington, we'd done a good show and we were doing an encore, with Lee, Sparko and me standing in a line. Lee was pointing his microphone at the audience and the three of us were moving from side to side in sync and it was rocking so hard. I could have burst out laughing but we didn't laugh on stage. I had to laugh inside.'

In March 1974, Dave Edmunds was hired as musical director for the film *Stardust*, starring David Essex and Adam Faith. The script called for a backing group, named the Stray Cats, and Edmunds suggested Brinsley Schwarz for the part. Nick Lowe recalls:

Dave Edmunds had phoned me up and told me he was producing Del Shannon and he wanted me to play bass. Then he got us in *Stardust*. David Puttnam was the director and we stayed at the Post House in Manchester for three glorious days whilst they filmed the concert sequence at Belle Vue. Our job was to play live to these kids before David Essex came on, but they booed and howled at us. The night before the filming we got drunk with Keith Moon, who sent out for copious quantities of curry, which he dumped over actor Karl Howman's head.

The next day we had to be on call at six in the morning, but we failed to get up. I had this irate phone call from David Puttnam, who was beside himself with rage. 'You get up and you get down here now!' he yelled. He put the fear of God into me. I jumped out of bed and I was the first one down there. He was seething and things didn't improve when Dave Edmunds managed to persuade them to open the bar so he could get a Bloody Mary. I said to Puttnam, 'Look, have a heart. We've never done anything like this before. We can't help it if we were up late.' It was the straw that broke the camel's back. Puttnam screamed, 'Look, I know what your name is, and yours, and yours, and believe me, I will see that none of you ever work for me again.' He was absolutely right.

Edmunds became our producer after that and with his help we made *The New Favourites of Brinsley Schwarz*. Whereas we were intimidated by the recording studio, Edmunds treated it with contempt. He was fearless and he got us to do little tricks that had never occurred to us – double-tracking only selected lines, radical pushing up of faders, guitars surging, echoes keeping the mix moving all the time. I'd remembered the time he came in while we were recording *Nervous On The Road*. That was when I thought he might be the guy to produce our next record. I rather set out to get him to do it. I thought he could really sort us out.

The New Favourites of Brinsley Schwarz became the group's first truly ambitious recording and the first time that any attempt had been made to give the material a production sheen. The LP opens with '(What's So Funny 'bout) Peace

Love And Understanding', a great Nick Lowe composition, blatantly based on the power chords of The Who's 'Baba O'Reilly'.

By 1974, 'peace and love' had become a cliché and the butt of a thousand anti-hippie jokes. Nick Lowe says:

> By now, the old hippie thing, which I'd invested a lot of my time and energy into, had become a load of old bollocks and I'd seen that for a while. I was thinking about some old hippie saying, 'It might be all changing now but when it comes down to it – you might laugh – what's so funny about peace and love?' I thought it was a fantastic title. I couldn't believe my luck. As long as that title popped up now and again it didn't really matter what I sang about in-between. I had that ginchy little lick that I think I pinched off of Judee Sill's 'Jesus Was A Cross Maker'. Of course I thought peace and love were basically good, but suddenly the old dream was over and I was in the right place at right time, front and centre, to come up with something like that. It was a sort of waking-up song.

Several more strong Lowe compositions follow: 'Ever Since You're Gone', 'The Ugly Things', and the country ballad 'The Look That's In Your Eye Tonight'. With Dave Edmunds at the helm, *New Favourites* was a great step forward for Brinsley Schwarz, but another spectacular commercial flop.

The Brinsleys had, however, managed to bring Dave Edmunds out of his shell. Such was Edmunds's enjoyment in working with Brinsley Schwarz, he decided he would undertake a UK tour with the group accompanying him. In June 1974, the 'New Favourites Tour', a co-promotion between Brinsleys' manager Dai Davies and Asgard Agency boss Paul Fenn, hit the road, starring Dave Edmunds, Brinsley Schwarz and, as opening act, Dr Feelgood.

Billy Rankin didn't make the tour. He recalls, 'I was out with John Collis playing cricket. I went back to his place for dinner and got pissed and drove home. I hit a roundabout and the van went out of control. I broke my thumb and the van was a write-off. I ended up in hospital and they got Pick Withers in on drums for the whole of the tour.'

'Edmunds got fed up with the tour halfway through,' says Dai Davies. 'Dave didn't quite get it. He bought a sort of leather outfit to wear, but the Brinsleys were in the lumber-jack shirts and Levis.' Nick Lowe remembers, 'Dave Edmunds kept getting his illnesses. At Bristol, he wouldn't go on, saying, "My hands won't work." He had us completely fooled.'

Brinsleys' fan Declan MacManus recalls seeing the tour. 'Dave Edmunds was absolutely howling and so loud. He was the loudest thing I'd ever heard in a club, playing through a Fender Dual Showman flat out. I suspect he was being propped up at the microphone, but he seemed to have amazing powers of recovery. Five minutes before he went on he didn't seem to be with it at all, then he'd get up and do it.'

Nick Lowe recalls the impact of the Feelgoods on the bill. 'They made us look real pedestrian, blowing us off stage every night. They were fantastic – no contest.' Lowe spread the word and badgered United Artists A&R chief Andrew Lauder, who made moves to sign the group after witnessing their performance in Cardiff.

Chris Fenwick recalls the initial meeting at United Artists. 'Andrew Lauder was the A&R man and Martin Davies was the business head. I was thinking to myself, "This is what we want, a direct deal with a label." I went up to UA and Martin Davies took me into his office and said, "I think it would be better for you, Chris, to sign to our production company." I couldn't believe it. I told him, like I told everybody else, that I wanted to deal direct with a record company. Three weeks later the contract was ready. The second contract! The one with United Artists at the top of it!'

It was during this period that Wilko Johnson, in many ways the focal point of Dr Feelgood, was head-hunted by a number of established acts. An early offer had come from Kevin Coyne, seeking a replacement in his group for Gordon Smith. Then news reached Johnson that David Bowie was interested. Next was Sparks.

'We were playing The Roundhouse,' recalls Johnson. 'We were second on the bill and we'd done a good gig and Chris and I were wandering about and these guys came up to us. They asked if I'd like to do some sessions for some American band that was coming over. I said yes. They kept talking for awhile until Chris wandered off. Then they steamed in and said, "Listen, we're the managers of Sparks and we want you in the band." I told them I wasn't interested, but they said, "Look, do you want to be a professional musician or do you want to waste your time with these people?" I said, "I want to waste my time with these people." '

With a major record deal in the bag, there was now the necessity for Dr Feelgood to find a regular agent. 'I viewed a lot of the agents very cautiously,' says Fenwick. 'I was a bit stubborn at first. We'd handled most of the bookings ourselves until we signed to UA, who called me in for a discussion. Martyn Smith, who ran the Iron Horse Agency, which was a division of UA, took me up the pub and pointed out that because things were going to get bigger, we needed an agent. We went straight to Paul Conroy and Nigel Kerr at Charisma Artists.'

'I first saw Dr Feelgood at The Lord Nelson,' recalls Paul Conroy. 'I started to book gigs for them, but it took a bit of time before Chris and the group really trusted us. No one realised how young Chris was and we had to prove ourselves before he would give us "the full agency". Lee used to like the old cash in hand. No cheques to the agency, thank you very much. Unlike some groups, the Feelgoods came with a bit of street suss.'

As plans were being made for Dr Feelgood to record their debut LP, the group went out as support act to United Artists stablemates Hawkwind. 'In Manchester, they threw pennies at us!' recalls Wilko Johnson. 'I remember Lee calmly picked up one of the pennies. Then he bit it, and with a mean look, tossed it aside, as if it were a dud. The place erupted. It was a turning point. It made us feel so strong.'

In November 1973, Kilburn And The High Roads had been invited to support The Who on a UK tour. 'Pete Townshend had apparently been down the Speakeasy the same night as Nick and Dave in 1972, and he knew we were about,' says

Dury. 'We did eight gigs with The Who. Then there was talk of us going to America with them. I've never really tried to find out what was behind us not going, but I think they wanted us to be on their record label. It was a hectic fortnight with The Who. I saw what could be done with extreme volume. At The Lyceum, the flunky came down with the plates of gear and Keith Moon smashed the lot. Same the next night. The third night they came down with paper plates and he tore them all up. He lived by his convictions that man.'

The road antics of The Who had a serious effect on Kilburns bassist Humphrey Ocean. Dury recalls, 'Humphrey witnessed a load of dodgy reporters telling Roger Daltrey and Moon to throw things and kick the walls down. Winding them up so they could get some shots. Plus Humphrey had done the best part of a bottle of Pernod. He had to be laid on his left side, in this hotel in Manchester, so he didn't choke on his vomit.'

'I left the Kilburns having had enough,' says Humphrey Ocean, who went on to become a highly regarded fine artist. 'I realised that it was not for me. I wanted to be a painter and all of the hardships that one had to endure, I would endure for painting, but not for music. My heart wasn't in it. I knew very well that I didn't want to be a bass player, having tried it and been quite good at it. It wasn't really what I wanted to make of my life.'

Humphrey Ocean's replacement in Kilburn And The High Roads was Charlie Sinclair, who, at a little under five feet tall, further enhanced the Kilburns' unconventional appearance. Dury recalls Sinclair's audition. 'The day we auditioned little Charlie, at a church in Brixton, we'd had 'em all in, six foot two, banging their basses. Charlie was easily the best. We were rehearsing in the vicar's office and Charlie was waiting in a pew while we had our group discussion. I was sent out to talk to him. I said, "Well, Charlie, you're the best bass player we've had, but you can't join the band." He said, "Why?" I said, "Because you're too small." He exploded with rage and said, "That's no fucking reason." I said, "I'm pleading with you Charlie, three out of six?" He said, "No, I'm joining." We went, "Oh, all right then."'

In January 1974, Charlie Gillett and Gordon Nelkie secured a recording contract for Kilburn And The High Roads with Raft Records, a subsidiary label of Warner Bros, run by former Soft Machine manager, Sean Murphy. Seasoned session musician Tony Ashton, formerly of Family and Ashton Gardner And Dyke, was hired as producer and recording took place during February and March at Apple Studios in Savile Row. By the time the record was finished, the Raft label had been closed down by Warners.

'We shopped the Kilburns around again,' says Gillett. 'The only company that was interested was Virgin. Ian said, "I'm not going with that hippie company," and went off and hired a new manager.' The Kilburns' new manager was Tommy Roberts, proprietor of the garish Kings Road boutique, Mr Freedom. 'By this time I suppose I had started getting more ambitious,' says Dury. 'We got Tommy to manage us at Paul Conroy's suggestion. I knew him vaguely. He was a mate of Peter Blakes's. He was more like Flash Harry and he knew about clothes.'

'Ian still had a contract with Warners,' recalls Tommy Roberts. 'It wasn't going anywhere and Warners were certainly not interested in doing anything. I told Ian I'd try to get him out of the contract. I said to Warners – the chap was in a wheelchair – "I'm the new manager, when shall we come in and start recording?" In the contract they were obliged to record a second album. "Can you book some nice studio time so we can make a start? We'll need a studio with a nice ramp because, like you, the drummer's in a wheelchair. We'll need a few hours, about three weeks actually, because they're not experienced musicians, plus their meals, because they've got no money." Their faces went grey. I knew they didn't want it. I said, "You'd prefer not to have the group really, would you?"'

With one bound, the Kilburns were free and Tommy Roberts commenced his search for a new label. 'I went to Pye Records,' says Roberts. 'Charlie Gillett had been to all of the others, he'd done the lot, but he hadn't done Pye. It was their Dawn label. They'd had a hit with Mungo Jerry. The A&R guy wore cowboy boots, feet up on the table and his briefcase was covered in stickers.'

'What I tried to put into the Kilburns was the secretive aspect of sartorial elegance,' says Dury. 'If you talk about it, you spoil it. As Oscar Wilde said, "The greatest stylist is the one that remains the most obscure." Meaning that once it's public knowledge, it's not stylish any more. It wasn't that one didn't want to share these things, but . . . my friend, Smart Mart, made me a razor blade earring. I hung that on the end of my safety pin.

'I knew the New York Dolls a little bit,' continues Dury. 'We'd been to their gigs at Bibas. I read somewhere that their audience used to wear safety pins through their nipples. I thought, "Lighten Up!" So I unwound the safety pin and put it through my lughole. Sartorially, I'm not a claimer, but I would say that I must have worn the first razor blade. A year later I was in a pub on Exmoor and there was this lovely plump milkmaid girl with short hair and tiny gold razor blades through her ears and that was just a common thing that went whipping round. It wasn't as exciting once it had become public, once you'd seen somebody on Exmoor wearing it. But it was great that it had gone that far that quick.

'Then I had the Billy Bentley dressing gown, which was made by Malcolm McLaren. He used to work for Tommy Roberts. Indeed, Bernard Rhodes did as well. They were shop assistants. Tommy had that kind of verbal. He had it down; he had the humour. "I got the instant hippie kit here. Go to Pontin's, get the Indian bedspread, cut it in half, get the bell, today's the first day of the rest of your life, instant hippie kit! Forty-two bob!" He'd been bankrupt three times when I met him.'

Kilburn And The High Roads signed to the Dawn label and released their first recorded product. The Chris Thomas-produced single, 'Rough Kids' c/w 'Billy Bentley (Promenades Himself In London)', was full of promise, but failed to make any impact on the charts. Its follow-up, 'Crippled With Nerves', also bombed. An LP, *Handsome*, produced by Hugh Murphy, failed to rectify matters and the Kilburns would remain prisoners of the Pub Rock circuit.

But Kilburn And The High Roads were, without doubt, the most musically adventurous and sartorially inspired group on the scene. Delivering semi-autobiographical songs such as 'Upminster Kid' and 'Billy Bentley', the musicians would bump and jerk while the polio-stricken Dury, all black leather glove and grimace, dispensed sinister vibrations and sudden unexpected gestures. For those seeking a glimpse of how rock 'n' roll might develop in the next half-decade, the Kilburns were, on a good night, a life-altering experience.

Under Andrew Jakeman's management and with the help of Paul Conroy and Nigel Kerr at the Charisma Agency, Chilli Willi And The Red Hot Peppers became extremely busy. In addition to a full date sheet, the group also secured a recording contract with Mooncrest, an offshoot of the Charisma label. Now it was time to get down to some serious recording.

When it came to hiring a producer, a number of ideas were mooted, including Ted Templeman (The Doobie Brothers, Little Feat); Lenny Waronker (Ry Cooder, Randy Newman) and Geoff Muldaur. None of these was available. Out of left field came the idea of approaching Mike Nesmith, formerly of The Monkees.

In his 1996 sleeve notes for the Chilli Willi reissue, *I'll Be Home*, Paul Riley recalled:

Unbeknown to us, some time between Monkeydom and taking on our album, Mike had become a Christian Scientist. Professionally, perhaps, this should have made no difference to us at all, but it did – specifically to Martin, Phil and Jake. After we'd cut five tracks, Jake came out of the control room (where something had apparently 'gone down' between Martin, Phil and Mike), and announced to the rest of us that we were bailing out!

Chilli Willi adopted Plan B. The group hired Ronnie Lane's mobile studio and, with American engineer Ron Nevison, recorded all of their stage favourites at Sue Barber's house in Camelford in Cornwall. The resulting LP, *Bongos Over Balham*, which included two of the Nesmith-era tracks, was released in November 1974.

The packaging was designed by Barney Bubbles and contained several humorous slogans, including 'Bohemian Revivalist Series Volume 2' and 'Should you hear the word culture on this waxing return as faulty product'. A press advert, copy-written by Jakeman, read:

> Vinyl Mogul says: Chilli Willi And The Red Hot Peppers is not a frozen food. It's a band. And their first real album *Bongos Over Balham* is available now on Mooncrest Records. Buy it. It'll look good in your fridge.

Life on the road with Chilli Willi was a scream, with Martin Stone in the back of the van, engrossed in drawing cartoons, Phil Lithman rolling enormous joints and Andrew Jakeman in the front seat, leading the attack. The group's agent, Paul Conroy, recalls, 'There was nothing quite like a day out with the Willies. Once, we were driving through Lewes with tons of drink in the van. We got in a car chase because Jake had shouted "Fuck off" to some bloke. Then we stopped at the lights and there was a pedestrian with a white suit on, so Jake, being the angry young man, sprayed the poor chap with beer. Jake was extremely hyperactive.'

One afternoon in September 1974, the telephone rang at Wilton Park Farm and Brinsley Schwarz answered the call. 'It was Martyn Smith, phoning from Warner Brothers,' recalls Schwarz. 'He said, "Do you mind if The Band come up and rehearse?" I took it that he'd said, "a band". He said, "No, man, THE Band! Now!" I said, "Fine!" Then I put the phone down and told the others The Band were coming to rehearse, now. They said, "Sure . . ."'

The Band were in the UK to appear in a concert at Wembley Stadium on 14 September, with Crosby, Stills, Nash and Young and Joni Mitchell. 'We were crazy for The Band,' says Nick Lowe. 'We didn't believe they were coming to our place. We thought it was a wind-up, of course. Someone was having a joke.' It transpired that, some days earlier, Bob Andrews had called Martyn Smith at Warners because he had wanted to meet his idol, Band organist Garth Hudson and

Smith had arranged the best possible introduction. Once convinced that The Band's imminent arrival was not a hoax, the members of Brinsley Schwarz hurriedly began making preparations.

'Billy Rankin made sandwiches,' recalls Martin Belmont, 'and Nick Lowe started hoovering the rehearsal room in readiness for their arrival. And Nick is a man who loathes the sound of Hoovers.' Soon The Band's equipment arrived, followed by a stretch limousine. 'Five cardboard cut-out figures got out,' recalls Bob Andrews, recounting the mass outbreak of hero worship.

'They brought their own guitars and Garth's Lowry organ,' adds Lowe 'and they used our amps and drums. It was a lovely warm evening. We stayed away from them because we didn't want to crowd them, so we just sat on flight cases outside.' After a while, the members of Brinsley Schwarz drifted into the barn and nervously attempted to strike up conversation with their heroes. 'We were babbling about their music,' recalls Schwarz, 'and Rick Danko changed the subject. He just wanted to talk to my wife about the kids. I said, "Never mind about them. Now, when you recorded the brown album . . ."'

They stayed for an hour or two [recalls Lowe]. I remember Levon Helm and Rick Danko looking around the old implements in the yard and the stables. Right at the end, Garth was playing his Lowry, making incredible music that sounded like it came from the spheres and we were all leaning on the organ listening to him. Suddenly Bob couldn't contain himself any longer and said something to the effect of, 'This is a dream come true. You don't know how incredible you are.' It was a sweet speech. Sadly it freaked Garth out. The spell was broken and he just said, 'I guess it's time to leave.' He was confused and embarrassed by this kid telling him how great he was. It was a shame. Bob got the piss taken out of him for it, but if he hadn't said it, I would have done.

After The Band's departure, several souvenirs were retained in the hope that some of The Band's magic might rub off on

Brinsley Schwarz. Ian Gomm kept the empty orange liqueur bottle from which Richard Manuel had been drinking and Schwarz held on to Robbie Robertson's straight guitar lead. Schwarz was besotted with Robbie Robertson and had been desperate to learn a few of his tricks. 'I'd spent years trying to perfect the Robertson sound,' says Schwarz. 'As soon as Robbie plugged into my amp, which he'd decided to use, he sounded just like Robbie Robertson! It really pissed me off.'

By the autumn of 1974, Brinsley Schwarz were living on borrowed time. Their recent *New Favourites* LP, had failed to find favour with the record-buying masses, despite the fact that it contained some of Nick Lowe's best songs, one of which – '(What's So Funny 'bout) Peace Love And Understanding' – would one day bring riches to its composer, but the Brinsleys' records had enjoyed only mediocre sales. 'The old ship had lost its steering somewhat,' says Bob Andrews. 'It all splintered up and we'd become frustrated.'

It was in this state that Brinsley Schwarz entered Rockfield Studios, with American producer Steve Verroca, to record their seventh album. 'Steve told a few porkies,' says Lowe. 'He'd worked in Turin where they used to demo stuff and he reckoned he came over to New York from Italy in the 50s, bringing with him the popular song, "Volare". "Anything to declare, Mr Verroca?" "Yes, 'Volare'!" '

With Verroca at the controls, Brinsley Schwarz recorded a dozen new tracks, including the original compositions 'Cruel To Be Kind', 'As Lovers Do' and 'God Bless Whoever Made You', plus cover versions of William Bell and Judy Clay's 'Private Number' and Tommy Roe's 'Everybody'. But as the sessions progressed the group was slowly disintegrating.

In an attempt to recoup some of its investment by way of a last-minute stab at the charts, United Artists Records asked the Brinsleys to record cover versions of Beatles songs, including 'Tell Me Why' and 'I Should Have Known Better'. 'They gave us a list of songs they wanted covers of,' says Nick Lowe. To avoid the stigma associated with the name Brinsley Schwarz at Radio One, the recordings would be released under the name of Limelight, one of a number of pseudonyms used by the Brinsleys during this period.

On the London pub circuit, where the group could still be found defending their status as the unchallenged kings of cool, spoof names such as Reg Lowe And The Electricians, or Bert Rankin And The Electricians, were used in an attempt to control attendance at the tiny venues. But despite being a strong live draw, the Brinsleys were lacking a consolidated direction, performing in a range of styles that was now more diverse than ever.

One minute it was out-and-out pop, typified by Lowe's 'There's A Cloud In My Heart' and the next minute, a blue-eyed Philadelphia soul pastiche, resulting in the Nick Lowe/Ian Gomm collaboration 'Cruel To Be Kind'. 'That song was our take on "The Love I Lost" by Harold Melvin And The Blue Notes,' confesses Lowe.

It was as if Brinsley Schwarz had reverted to their identity crisis of 1969 and, as before, the seeds of musical change were in the air.

The Kursaal Flyers first appeared on the London pub scene in the summer of 1974, with more than a little help from the Feelgoods, who had arranged our first dates at the Kensington.

We first assembled in Southend in October 1973. Paul Shuttleworth, Graeme Douglas and myself had previously played together in various groups, the most stable of which was Surly Bird who, in 1970, were spotted by Peter Meaden, the legendary early manager of The Who. Meaden vainly attempted to get us a record deal through his association with the pioneering independent record producer, Tony Hall.

During this period, we would lamely imitate the hot musical trend of the moment, whether that was 'Blues', 'West Coast', 'Progressive' and so on. We were more about youthful enthusiasm than musical ability, although we did 'compose' our own material, with titles like 'What Was Wrong With Wednesday' or 'Rocking Horse On The Roof', all mercifully lost. Peter Meaden arranged a recording session at Thames Television Studios in Teddington, where our musical ineptitude stunned Tony Hall. I remember naively asking him, 'Will there be a photo session now we've finished recording?' Hall retorted, 'Before thinking about photos you should learn to play in time with the bass player.'

Prior to us meeting Meaden, Paul had broken away to sing country music in a group called Cow Pie, having been inspired by the Byrds' *Sweetheart Of The Rodeo* and the first Dillard and Clark LP. Moving in country circles, Paul ran into Vic Collins, then learning the pedal steel guitar, banjo wizard Richie Bull, and Dave Hatfield, who had previously played with Graeme in Saints'n'Sinners (their motto: 'Heavenly music with a devilish beat').

It was Hatfield who got us all together: me, Paul, Graeme, Vic, Richie and Dave himself. Dave was the early driving force, offering his tiny terraced house as the venue for our first practice sessions. During the winter of 1973–74, we learnt about 25 songs, mainly country and western standards, with a bit of Monkees and Eddie Cochran thrown in. By February 1974 we were ready to expose ourselves to the danger of public scrutiny and persuaded the landlord of the local Blue Boar pub to let us play twice a week in his saloon bar. At first we were nameless, but Dave came up with 'Kursaal Flyers', taken from a mocked up wild west train that appeared at the Southend carnival. Paul designed a witty poster and we mounted a local publicity campaign.

The Blue Boar soon became busy as we struggled to perform newly learned songs from the latest US imports I was acquiring by the skip load – Jackson Browne, The Band, that sort of thing. Graeme and I also started to write songs, such as 'Hit Records' and 'Kung Fu', the latter being a spoof on the then-popular TV series. Paul rose to the challenge of conveying this novelty number by stripping to the waist and donning a comedy rubber bald head.

Despite our local success, I was getting itchy feet, and was desperate to quit my day job. Through Dai Davies, I heard that Charlie And The Wide Boys were looking for a drummer. They were hot on the London Pub Rock circuit, yet were based in Cornwall. I booked some time off work, put my drums on a train and headed west, with the intention of never returning. It lasted seven days. As Wide-Boy-for-a-week, I played Sutton-in-Ashfield Golden Diamond and London's Lord Nelson, then returned home to the Kursaals.

Having seen the Wide Boys operation at close quarters, I was convinced that the Kursaals could make it in London. Fortunately, Dr Feelgood offered to get us some gigs when the time was right. Although the Feelgoods had been making a noise in London for a year, they were still without a recording contract, but the minute they secured their record deal, they fixed us up with the two Sunday lunchtime gigs at the Kensington, each worth £15.

We thought that this was the most exciting thing that could possibly happen, never dreaming that within six months we would have our own recording contract. The first Kensington date was a nervous affair and we didn't have quite enough material for the two 45-minute sets demanded by landlord Matt Farley. So we repeated a couple of the songs and inserted a torturous slow blues. Despite our inability to evoke the atmosphere of post-war Chicago, we went down a storm.

Unbeknown to us, our Kensington debut was witnessed by Chilli Willi drummer, Pete Thomas, who brought along his manager, Andrew 'Jake' Jakeman, the following week. A crucial chain of events was then set in motion: Jake liked us and told Paul Conroy of the Charisma agency, who offered to get us gigs, Conroy told Zig Zag's Pete Frame who told CBS press officer John Tobler who told Clive Selwood of UK Records. Selwood told his boss, hit-maker Jonathan King.

During the autumn of that year, Paul Conroy became our manager and we appeared regularly at most of the prominent Pub Rock venues, picking up much positive press, spear-headed by *Melody Maker*'s Geoff Brown and Mick Flood-Page at *Sounds*. When Chilli Willi And The Red Hot Peppers headlined a 'Big Xmas Beat Extravaganza' at London's Round-house on 15 December 1974, we were given a support spot. Also on the bill at the Roundhouse were Ace and, billing themselves as The Electricians, Brinsley Schwarz.

The Xmas Beat Extravaganza was conceived by the exuber-ant Andrew Jakeman, who was also in the process of organising a national tour to bring Chilli Willi to the masses. In addition to Chilli Willi, the tour would also feature

Kokomo and Dr Feelgood. None of these three groups alone was famous enough to fill large provincial venues and so the 60s-style 'Naughty Rhythms Tour' was conceived.

Chilli Willi enjoyed a modest following after two years' solid slog and Jakeman's enviable marketing style came with the territory. Kokomo, a highly accomplished nine-piece soul review, were signed to CBS and enjoyed the heavyweight management of Steve O'Rourke, who also represented Pink Floyd. Therefore, Kokomo were able to provide a businesslike p.a. system, a bus and a team of roadies for the tour. The Feelgoods, with their debut album *Down By The Jetty* ready for release, were the rising stars at the time and were probably capable of selling at least 200 tickets in any UK town, having slowly built a grassroots following. It would be a revolving bill.

The Naughty Rhythms Tour kicked off with two warm-up dates, Bristol University on 11 January 1975 and Guildford Civic Hall on the 12th. After a two-week gap, the tour proper opened at Watford on 28 January. By the time the Naughty Rhythms Tour reached London's Rainbow Theatre on 15 February, Dr Feelgood were causing riotous scenes.

Paul Conroy, booking agent for Dr Feelgood and Chilli Willi, recalls the outcome of the tour, using a sporting analogy. 'If it was a breakdown on Sky Sports, Dr Feelgood would have had 75 per cent of the play. But Chilli Willi and Kokomo could produce some surprises. The Feelgoods had the most obvious act. It was a press-led buzz and they'd be hanging out with people like Nick Kent.'

Dr Feelgood had emerged as the stars of the Naughty Rhythms Tour and were poised to become a headlining attraction in their own right, but for Chilli Willi, this last-ditch attempt at national acceptance had failed and the group never recovered from the ignominy of being upstaged nightly by the Feelgoods. Jakeman says, 'Phil Lithman became very disillusioned because he couldn't conceive of the fact that people could be oblivious to his amazing talent! When he saw the audiences lapping up Lee Brilleaux, who was nothing more than a bank clerk who could hardly get two chords together, the old bitter and twisted came in a bit.'

The Feelgoods' debut LP, *Down By The Jetty*, with its stark monochrome packaging and radical monaural sound, had become an instant classic, but it was not the group's original intention to make a mono record. Wilko Johnson says, 'Vic Maile, our producer, said he wanted to record bass and drums first and then build it with overdubs. We told him we wanted to play together and we said, "If it can't be done live, fuck it!" We tried mixing it like our stage line-up but it sounded lopsided. So we started panning everything in towards the middle until we virtually had mono. I said to Andrew Lauder at UA, "Look, don't write mono on the label. No one will ever know." Andrew started blabbering on about the Trades Descriptions Act, so I said, "We've got a stereo record here. It's just a monaural mix!"'

With their explosive stage show, Dr Feelgood started to exert a real influence over the younger musicians in their audience who were contemplating a rock 'n' roll career. It was on the Naughty Rhythms Tour, at Guildford Civic on 12 January, that 17-year-old Paul Weller got his first taste of the Feelgoods, inspiring the musical direction of his own group, The Jam. For the next few months, Weller strove to master Wilko Johnson's guitar style and The Jam covered Feelgoods songs such as 'Going Back Home' and 'Cheque Book'. Within a few years, The Jam would become the most popular group in Britain.

Also in the audience at Guildford was a South London singer/songwriter named Graham Parker. 'I probably went with a few mates,' says Parker. 'Basically I was always the one to turn them on to new stuff, I was always first. The Feelgoods were really something – short hair, straight trousers. Wham, in the face!' Parker was so inspired by Dr Feelgood that he immediately placed an advertisement in the *Melody Maker*, in search of a backing group.

Of Dr Feelgood's transfer to the bigger venues, Lee Brilleaux says, 'When we began playing the big halls we were able to make our stage act much more demonstrative. For example, in a small pub like The Kensington, there wasn't much room for Wilko's famous skittering and I think that one of the things we realised was that our strength was visual as well as musical. Both Wilko and myself adapted ourselves to filling up a bigger area of stage.'

The Feelgoods' transition to the larger stage signalled the beginning of the end for many of the Pub Rock groups and the musical diversity they embraced. Brinsley Schwarz, in particular, were feeling a little left out. 'We liked that soul stuff . . . the Philadelphia sound,' says Nick Lowe. 'I thought it was great music but what were we doing trying to play it? There was no point.'

In recent months, Chilli Willi manager Andrew Jakeman could often be found in and around the Brinsleys' camp, due to a growing friendship with Lowe. Jakeman had accompanied the group on a tour of Holland in November 1974 and there had even been a suggestion that he might manage Brinsley Schwarz.

'I met Nick at the Marquee,' says Jakeman. 'He was there with Billy Rankin to see some band and they were speed-ing out of their lids. I went back to Beaconsfield with them in Billy's Ford Anglia that had a three-litre Zodiac engine in it. It was the most scarey drive! Billy kept saying, "It's all right man. The pills cut through the booze, no problem!" I went out and stayed at their house and talked to them, because we all knew each other, and I suggested to Nick that I would look after them.'

But the Brinsleys were beyond rescuing and, with the lease on Wilton Park Farm about to expire, the end was nigh. Nick Lowe and Ian Gomm, as the main creative forces within the group, toyed with the idea of forming a production company as a vehicle for their songwriting. Ian Gomm says, 'Nick and I were the only ones coming up with songs. We'd just written "Cruel To Be Kind". The plan was to go to America and get a new record deal. Island Records were interested, but UA wouldn't release us from our contract.' Lowe and Gomm discussed the idea with Jakeman, but the concept was short-lived. Suddenly, it was clear that Lowe was on his own.

'I was spending more and more time with Jake,' says Lowe. 'He and I felt the same way. We used to listen to records all day and all of the night. I was very influenced by Jake. He kept saying, "There's something coming and we've got to do it, whatever it is." There was something else out there but I didn't know what it was. I felt that the music was about to change. Things were certainly getting faster.'

PART IV
A CASE OF THE SHAKES

15. TIME GENTLEMEN PLEASE

The early months of 1975 represented a black period in the annals of Pub Rock. With the exception of Ace, who had recently scored with 'How Long', none of the groups had achieved hit status.

Nick Lowe says, 'My theory is that when they let the groups make their own records it all went horribly wrong. They let them write their own songs and more or less produce their own records when they knew bugger-all about it. This new multi-track recording thing had just come in. Those three factors are the reason why those records sound so awful and why there's no great legacy from Pub Rock.'

> I was quite often disappointed by the music [says Charlie Gillett]. Most of the pub bands felt stiff and unexciting, unlike American musicians, and because they were playing music that invited comparison, I felt I wasn't being unfair. The scene was endlessly fascinating, with some great characters, but if you go back and dig out the records, you start to wonder what all the fuss was about. I don't know how great Gene Vincent And The Bluecaps would have been if you saw them live, but there was something magical about their recordings. How did they get that spontaneity, that sheer vivacity? The British records sound inhibited and small: it's like the difference between British and American movies. There's some diminished ambition in the UK.

Gillett has a valid point, although Pub Rock was not about ambition, it was more about a bunch of enthusiastic amateurs getting the opportunity to break out and play in front of an audience. And those records that were a let-down were never allowed to get in the way of a great night out. Pub Rock was essentially a live scene and no amount of studio wizardry could have captured the excitement of seeing the Kilburns or the Ducks on a sweaty night in the Hope & Anchor. You literally had to be there.

Although the Brinsleys, the Feelgoods and Chilli Willi all managed some sterling performances in the studio, recording was often secondary and if one wished to pinpoint a single reason for any of the disappointing Pub Rock records, it was probably because many of the participants, including musicians, producers, engineers, managers and A&R men, were still learning their craft. The blind were, in most cases, leading the blind drunk.

Bees Make Honey's leader, Barry Richardson, says, 'We recorded too much material of a rabble-rousing nature and it was not a good first album. All I can say is that we were a bloody good live band, but I wish we'd have met George Martin at that time.'

The Bees had already called it a day the previous autumn. 'We'd been touring like idiots,' says Richardson. 'Our records sold poorly. In order to make enough money we had to play anywhere and everywhere. I think we were getting very tired and very frustrated. The fundamental mistake was the band turning pro. We had the music; we just got the business wrong. It was absolute misery.'

Now, Pub Rock groups were about to disband at an alarming rate. Disillusionment was infectious and some of the scene's biggest names disintegrated within weeks of each other. Next to go, at the end of February 1975, were Chilli Willi And The Red Hot Peppers, following the disappointment of the Naughty Rhythms Tour.

Paul 'Diceman' Bailey says, 'We'd been eclipsed by Dr Feelgood. They were working the audiences and we weren't. I think Jake had definitely seen an opportunity and faced with the choice of reshaping Chilli Willi or going with the Feelgoods, he might have found the latter more attractive.'

There were a number of things that happened [says Paul Riley]. We're moving into a contentious area, because I have a strong opinion about this that I don't think is generally shared, but Jake was very keen to get off and become Dr Feelgood's tour manager. Jake actually pulled the plug on Chilli Willi. One day we were in a group, the next day we weren't. One day we had a van, the next day we didn't. And, evidently, something had gone horribly wrong between Martin Stone and Phil Lithman, but nobody witnessed it. We kept hearing, 'All that time you were on twelve quid a week, Phil Lithman had a private income.' Did he? Do I give a fuck!

My guess is that Jake had got fed up with Phil and I think he'd chosen to light a bit of a fire underneath it and use it as an excuse to go off and do something he'd rather be doing. The only thing is, in doing that, he made sure there was no way we could continue. When we were hit, we were hit and we couldn't get up. The carpet was firmly pulled from under our feet. Not only did we not have a manager, we had nothing. No infrastructure, it was all gone – the van, the manager, and the two main guys, whose band it was, were at each other's throats. Also, Jake was very keen to see Pete on the plane as soon as possible. Now we had no drummer. What could we do?

Willies' drummer Pete Thomas had been invited to work with American country artist John Stewart. 'I'd made sure I was alright,' says Thomas. 'The Willies had done a *Zigzag* benefit with John Stewart and I sat in on drums. It was a triumph apparently. In the dressing room afterwards John Stewart said, "Pete, if you ever want a gig, just give me a ring . . ." It was storybook. When Chilli Willi broke up, I remember calling John from the phone box by the Holland Road squat. I got very excited and legged it to the States.'

On 18 March 1975, Brinsley Schwarz played their farewell performance, at the Marquee. It was an emotional show, with the Brinsleys delivering two sets for their hard-core fans and Nick Lowe referring to some of the songs as the group's 'hit singles'. They closed their first set and opened their second with the classic 'Country Girl' and encored with 'Brown Sugar'. 'It was the best gig we'd done for years,' says Brinsley Schwarz. 'Afterwards we said, "If it could be like this every time, we'd keep doing it," but Nick said he thought it was time we all did something else. I was horrified. I was married with two children and we had no house. Not only was I not in a group any more, I had no idea of how to earn money or where to live.'

'The last gig was quite poignant,' says Ian Gomm. 'I was crying. But we had to break up. There wasn't a future in it. The thought of continually playing in Britain wasn't appealing. We'd return from somewhere like the Penthouse Club, Scarborough, and realise we'd done this country umpteen times. Also, living in a commune didn't help. We were getting on each other's nerves.'

The break-up started with us all having our own little section in the fridge [says Nick Lowe]. We'd always been quite happy to split everything, but dissent had crept in. Billy Rankin and I often wanted to go to the Speakeasy to get laid, but we didn't even have enough money to put some gas in the van. Billy pointed out that the single members of the group were subsidising those with families. Also, towards the end of the Pub Rock thing, I had an inkling that something else was about to happen, but I felt that some of the other guys in the group didn't. That made me think, but I didn't want to rock the boat. I realised that if the group broke up, I'd have to find somewhere to live. But the boat was rocked. Brinsley Schwarz broke up and I was terrified.

I didn't know anyone outside our little scene except for Jake. At first I went to share a flat in Fulham with my sister, but it didn't last long. She had a high-powered job and went to bed at ten o'clock. We'd come in from the pub and get the guitars out. She'd come bursting out of her room, covered in face cream and scream at us. It was a disaster, so I went and slept on Jake's couch for a week and ended up staying 18 months. Jake went out and drove the *Time Out* van while I stayed home and wrote songs. Being with Jake, I felt released after the Brinsleys. I didn't have a plan but I was ready for anything. Jake made me think that absolutely anything could be done, if you say it positively enough.

Meanwhile, the Kursaal Flyers had 'gone pro'. Whilst still at work in Barking, I'd spent most of my lunchtimes either in Guy Norris's record shop or the Brewery Tap where I would slave over cash flow projections for the group. Could we afford to chuck in our day jobs? The married members of the group needed £40 a week, whilst the rest of us could exist on £25. After adding in van hire and petrol, I came up with the magic figure and told Paul Conroy that if he could get us £235 a week, we would turn professional. Paul soon responded with a solid date sheet.

Then there was a sort of Davy Crockett at the Alamo scenario, where I announced we would be turning pro in six weeks time. I took out my imaginary sword and made a line on the carpet. Those who 'wanted in' should cross the line now. Richie had no hesitation – he was already a professional musician with a lucrative session career. There was a bit of hesitation from the others, but I must have talked a fairly good talk, because only Dave, who ironically had been Mr Energy a year earlier, didn't fancy it. He left the group and the rest of us 'went pro' on 1 January 1975.

One of our first jobs was a stint at Boddy's Music Inn in Amsterdam. It was the first time I had ever been abroad and our roadies, Dave Murdock (co-writer of 'Speedway') and Stuart Cook (both former members of Surly Bird), refurbished our hired long wheelbase Transit with aircraft seats for the trip. We were now a real group. Amsterdam was a hoot and our imitation Flying Burrito Brothers music was received warmly. The Burritos themselves – legends in Holland – were due to tour Europe that spring. I'm not quite sure how, but we were asked to become the Burritos' support act for the tour on the understanding that they could use our p.a. system and occupy some of the seats in our van. Wisely, they opted to travel by rail.

Meanwhile, Jonathan King was waving a UK Records contract about. His top act at the time, 10cc, were leaving the label and we were earmarked to replace them, but the music press's comparisons between the two groups were ludicrous, especially since the Mancunian quartet were experienced studio geniuses and we were a bunch of enthusiastic amateurs.

Our musical shortcomings became painfully obvious when we recorded our debut LP, *Chocs Away*, produced by the late Hugh Murphy. Hugh was a wonderful chap but he just couldn't get us to play in time (or, I'm reliably informed, in tune). Also, he made our songs sound as if they had been recorded inside a small cardboard box, with virtually no deployment of proven studio effects, like 'echo'. Jonathan was disappointed and wrote to Paul Conroy to say so. 'Only a really great album should be released', said Jonathan, who attempted a remix of 'Pocket Money'. It turned out rather well but got no further than the acetate stage.

After the break-up of Brinsley Schwarz, United Artists exercised its contractual option on Lowe's solo services and was now envisaging the 26-year-old Lowe as a potential pop star. 'Maybe I wanted to be a bit more pop,' says Lowe, 'but I think UA had a view to make me into some kind of Rock Lite artiste, like James Taylor or John Sebastian – quirky and be-denimed.'

'Be-denimed' was anything but the image that Lowe adopted in the spring of 1975. With hair trimmed short and a trilby on the back of his head, Lowe would hit the hot spots as a songwriter-about-town. With demo cassettes bulging from the pockets of his natty three-piece suit, Lowe boldly exploited his 'Have I got a song for you' routine, like an old-time Tin Pan Alley hustler.

I think Jake perceived me as a pop artist, but we got such a kick out doing things a little bit skew-whiff. We liked being perverse, and then we got more and more emboldened when we saw it ruffle a few feathers. That was a terrific thrill after being seen as a bit of a loser. I got much more arch under Jake's influence and I thought, 'Look, we don't need to be just underlings in this pop business. We can be taste-makers here. This is our time.' Pop journalism was changing. No one swallowed that line: 'And Nick's dislikes are – "phoney people and girls who wear too much make-up!" Favourite meal? "Chinese!" ' By now, pop music had been round the circuit and we were the first generation to benefit from that.

One of Jakeman's pranks was to spread the rumour that Lowe had been selected to replace Peter Gabriel in the progressive group, Genesis. 'It was at Dingwalls,' recalls Lowe. 'Jake told a few faces, "Don't tell anyone, but it looks like Nick's got the job singing in Genesis." Pure mischief. We were hip then, in our own little world. We were looking to make a mark. Feather-ruffling could still be done. The *NME* and the *Melody Maker* were still big sellers. I'd open them up each week and it would be like my personal diary. I'd say to myself, "Now, let's see what I got up to this week." '

Jakeman's first managerial priority was to extricate Lowe from his United Artists recording contract. He conceived the idea of Lowe cashing in on the popularity of the Bay City Rollers, by making a tribute record, under a pseudonym naturally. It would be a no-lose situation. If the record was successful, much-needed money would be generated. If it was a flop, Lowe might be released from his contract and a new, more lucrative deal could be sought. Whatever the outcome, Lowe's name would not be directly attached to the Rollers project. At the very worst, Lowe might gain kudos as the shadowy mastermind behind the tacky tribute.

Fired up by Jakeman's masterplan, Lowe wrote and recorded 'Bay City Rollers We Love You' under the tongue-in-cheek pseudonym, Terry Modern. Recording took place at Vic Keary's Chalk Farm Studios and children from a nearby school provided the sing-along backing vocals under the tutelage of their music teacher, Penelope Tobin. Credited to the Tartan Horde, 'Bay City Rollers We Love You' was released in Japan and, much to everyone's surprise, became a hit. Far from losing Lowe his recording contract, United Artists demanded a follow-up. Lowe quickly composed 'Rollers Show'. 'Nick had these gimmick hits,' says Jakeman, 'but it was pushing him away from credibility really. But I thought it was really cool doing these cash-in things, speeding up the tapes, and making him sound young.'

Lowe's next recording project was with American guitarist and singer Danny Adler, leader of Roogalator, a highly accomplished combo that would soon make a big noise on the pub circuit. With producer Dave Edmunds, Lowe and Adler entered Rockfield Studios and recorded 'Let's Go To The Disco' and a cover version of Dr Feelgoods' 'Keep It Out Of Sight'. An earlier Lowe/Adler session, recorded by Dave Robinson at the Hope & Anchor, had yielded 'Everybody Dance' and these recordings were released by United Artists, credited to The Disco Brothers.

Nick Lowe says, 'Danny Adler and Roogalator, on their night, were really sensational. They were like Captain Beefheart, with a funky weird groove. Danny called it "Roogalation" and nobody else has come up with a better word for that groove. Danny was a much better musician than all of us, but his one foible was that he took it too seriously. No one could get his arrangements. By the same token, if I'd sat and listened to him, my thing would have been better too.'

In spring 1975, Nick Lowe performed some club dates in Amsterdam alongside members of Dr Feelgood, the Kursaal Flyers and the recently disbanded Chilli Willi. 'I feel the hand of Jake on that,' says Lowe. 'I think it was essentially the Feelgoods and a few floating people who were in town. It was a jolly up. We were having a laugh.' Jakeman christened the makeshift combo 'Spick Ace & The Blue Sharx' and even suggested recording an EP, with the working title *All Meat Diet*, but the Spick Ace project was short-lived.

Eventually, United Artists grew tired of Lowe's dilettante approach to making records and released him from his contract. Lowe was at a loose end, but Jakeman had suddenly found gainful employment. Dr Feelgood were about to embark on their 'Speeding Through Europe' tour and manager Chris Fenwick was in need of a full-time tour manager. Jakeman, who conveniently spoke fluent French, following his days busking on the streets of Paris, was the ideal candidate. Chris Fenwick says:

After Chilli Willi broke up, Jake was in a vacuum. I was feeling more confident, having got the record deal but, quite honestly, I needed some help. Jake had a great deal of vision and he had a few years on me in the business as well. It had gone off a bit fast and furious for us. Out of the sticks – band . . . management . . . Transit van. Jake was a total pro and he had good ideas for marketing, with logos and slogans. He was very 'on board' and a complete asset. Jake was in United Artists a lot, on our business and on Nick's behalf. They took a bit of a shine to him. It was never mooted that it would become a joint management deal, but it was pointed out by Martin Davies of UA that I should hold on to Jake. Jake was free to do his own thing as well. It got us both through a difficult period.

On the Pub Rock circuit, the established groups continued to disband. Ducks Deluxe were next to throw in the sweaty towel, although they did manage to limp on until the early summer of 1975 with an eleventh hour line-up that included drummer Billy Rankin and, after a little cajoling, guitarist Brinsley Schwarz. Ducks main man Sean Tyla recalls:

We'd gone off on a French tour, which was to end up in Holland. Billy Rankin was on drums. The French tour had been sensational and we came into Amsterdam on a real high. When we walked into the Hotel Weichmann, Mrs Boddy, the promoter, said, 'Where's Brinsley?' We replied, 'What are you talking about? He's not even in the band!' She said, 'Dai told me he was in the band.' It was news to us!

What had happened was that no promoter in Holland was interested in booking Ducks Deluxe, but one promoter had asked, 'What's Brinsley up to?' So Dai had promised him faithfully that the band now included Brinsley and on the strength of that, the promoter put the tour in. All the posters for the tour carried the caption: 'Ducks Deluxe – featuring Brinsley Schwarz.' I rang Dai up, in an absolute foul mood and said, 'What the hell is all this about Brinsley?' Dai said, 'He'll be at the airport in about ten minutes!' And poor old Brinsley wasn't party to any of this; he'd just been told by Dai, 'You're in the Ducks!' And good old Brinsley 'Have Guitar – Will Travel' Schwarz was there.

I was absolutely furious. It was my first-ever encounter with any form of manipulation in the rock 'n' roll business, apart from Dai booking us into the London Gay Ball without telling us and waiting until the sound check to inform us that our name for the night had been changed from Ducks Deluxe to the Iron Boys, but everything would be all right because we were getting thirty quid. But Brinsley brought quite an interesting thing to the band. He played tenor sax and he was a musician, which I wasn't, but it didn't make any difference to the tour. Everywhere was empty.

Prior to the Ducks' final fling there had been some personnel changes and political wrangling within the group. Sean Tyla says, 'There was a great deal of skill in the band in so much as Nick Garvey was a great singer. He has one of the classic, all-time great singing voices, but when we got a piano player in, that was the end of the Ducks. We split into two camps – the Nick Garvey/Andy McMasters camp and the Sean Tyla/Martin Belmont camp. We didn't need keyboards. Martin was against it, vehemently; Nick was wholeheartedly for it. He just wanted to get more musical, which was fair enough, but at that point we should have changed our name to Kansas or Boston, because it lost what it was all about.'

Garvey and McMasters later re-grouped as The Motors, scoring hits in 1978 with 'Airport' and 'Forget About You', showcasing Garvey's vocal talent and the duo's songwriting skills to great effect.

The Winkies had also disbanded. Leader Phil Rambow remarks, 'Pub Rock was fabulous. We started later than everybody else, but we were the second band to get a major record deal. We backed Brian Eno on his one-and-only tour and for one week we were the hottest band in London!'

In June 1975, Kilburn And The High Roads joined the growing list of casualties. Ian Dury recalls, 'After about the third time our bubble had gone up and burst again we were still doing Cleopatra's Club in Derby. It was a step up from the pubs, but one you'd rather not take. We knew we were on a sticky wicket. Also, I'd seen the Feelgoods go screaming past us like a rocket ship and I started worrying that we were doing it wrong.'

Dury was soon to continue as Ian Dury And The Kilburns with a new set of backing musicians, but it would be a short-lived venture. 'We got a really good buzz going,' says Dury, 'doing new stuff and old Kilburns gear. I had brilliant musicians but they weren't stylish like the original Kilburns and I felt a bit sad because I knew we weren't going to be stars.' It was during this period that Dury met his future co-writer, Chaz Jankel.

'I was in the dressing room at the Nashville, a bit disgruntled,' recalls Dury. 'Jankel walked in with his big white teeth. I said, "Do I know you?" He said, "No," so I said, "Well do us a favour and fuck off!" Then I sent Ted Speight out to apologise to him.' Dury and Jankel soon teamed up and began co-writing a body of work that would become the basis for the next stage in Dury's career.

As the Pub Rock casualties lay around licking their consider-able wounds, a number of new developments took place. Graham Parker, who had been jolted into action after seeing Dr Feelgood at Guildford Civic, had received a response to his classified ad in the *Melody Maker*, in search of a backing group. 'I got all the usual replies,' says Parker. 'From the trombone player, the A1 accordion player . . . but I did meet Noel Brown. Noel got me a gig in a hamburger joint in Finsbury Park and introduced me to Paul Riley, who had just broken up with Chilli Willi. I thought, "Wow! I've met somebody in a band I've seen!"'

Graham Parker was born in London in November 1950 and first picked up a guitar at the age of 13. As he recalls:

I had a group called the Deep Cut Three. We did Beatles songs, but we couldn't play. I wrote one or two songs and we became the Black Rockers and wore polo necks and had Beatle haircuts and winkle pickers. Then I took a break when I was 14. At 15, I started a group at school with various names. The Way Out was one of them – R&B, Stonesy, 'I Can't Explain'. I was a serious Mod between 14 and 17 and I had a scooter. At 16, I started going to the discos and got into the whole Stax music scene. The fashion then was more moddy boy, crew-cut, proto-skinhead. We wore the white shirts and red braces and pinstripe suits.

I started growing my hair around 1968, but more because I was into the white blues revival. Peter Green's Fleetwood Mac was a big influence on me. From that, I got into the LSD scene, dope, Pink Floyd, Captain Beefheart. I went full pelt. A typical youth thing where you'd be into one thing and six months later you were into something else. I had a caftan and hair down to my ass!

Then I started travelling. France, Spain, Morocco. I took an acoustic guitar with me because I'd got into James Taylor. I was well immersed in the hippie thing. I joined a band of spaced-out rich brothers who were playing Wishbone Ash. We were probably called Pegasus, which I promptly changed to Terry Burbot's Magic Mud. I couldn't stomach Pegasus, I said to them, 'This stuff is over guys – you can be stoned but you've got to have a bit of wit.' I came back to England, did various jobs and ended up back at my parents like all good boys. I worked in a gas station around the corner and started to seriously write songs. The soul influence started coming back to me. I found myself buying Gladys Knight And The Pips, The Staples Singers and for some reason, Bob Marley's *Catch A Fire*. Then it became apparent that my songs were getting stronger and they were of a different stamp. They were three-and-a-half minutes long with a beginning, a middle and an end. I started to appreciate pop music again and dropped the pretensions of the long guitar solos; that was gone.

I was also listening to Dylan, the Stones and Van Morrison – *Astral Weeks* and then those middle-period records like *St Dominic's Preview* and *Tupelo Honey*, which profoundly affected me. I started to pick up on that idea of acoustic guitar and horn section. I was also listening to Busby Berkeley soundtracks and Bob Marley. It was this big stew of music.

The Feelgoods were a stylised R&B band, I thought, but there was something new going on there. In the suburbs it was still people with long hair, listening to *Dark Side Of The Moon*. I knew something was gonna happen and I thought I was It. I'm The Man. I'm the only one who knows! Then I saw these other bands and I thought, 'Oh, OK . . . maybe they know as well!' But now I knew it was time to move. It was like, 'Let's Go!'

Paul Riley liked Parker's songs but was reluctant to form a band and introduced him instead to Dave Robinson, now ensconced in his studio at the Hope & Anchor. Within days, Parker was recording demos with Robinson who, realising that the unknown singer was hot property, proceeded to handle him with special care. Robinson also began to find musicians for Parker's sessions. 'Dave took me round the circuit and introduced me to people,' recalls Parker. 'He knew all these musicians. I didn't know about paying for anything. I just assumed they played on my demos for nothing because I was going to be a star.'

Having amassed dozens of demos by various acts that had passed through his studio, Robinson's next move was to contact Charlie Gillett for some input. 'Dave rang me up and said he wanted to come and play me some of the stuff he'd been recording,' recalls Gillett. 'I told him that my tape recorder only played seven-and-a-half-inch reels, so he had to make sure he brought that size of reel. He replied, "No problem," but of course he came with ten-inch reels, so the first hour was spent with the two of us using pencils to spool the tape onto smaller reels. The tapes mostly contained variations of Ducks Deluxe. I'd heard of everybody except one and I didn't like any of them except one, which was "Between You And Me" by Graham Parker. I said, "I'll play that one this weekend." '

Parker remembers the broadcast. 'It was postponed the first week. There I was out in the suburbs tuned in to BBC Radio London and it didn't come on. Then the following week Charlie Gillett did play it and Phonogram's A&R man, Nigel Grainge, called up and asked, "Who is that Graham Parker guy? He sounds like Van Morrison." Suddenly we'd got a record deal. Piece of cake! That was absolutely what was gonna happen.'

As Parker's manager, Dave Robinson began negotiations with Vertigo, the Phonogram imprint usually reserved for progressive rock acts. At the same time, Parker became one of the principal beneficiaries of the Pub Rock scene when he finally located his dream backing group. While Robinson had been recording Parker's demos upstairs at the Hope & Anchor, he'd also been quietly assembling a virtual Pub Rock supergroup in the basement.

'I moved into the Hope & Anchor and worked behind the bar,' recalls Martin Belmont, now plotting the next move with Brinsley Schwarz, following the musical partnership they had forged during the dying days of Ducks Deluxe. 'I lived on the top floor. It was handy. I had a job, somewhere to live and in the afternoons we had somewhere to rehearse. Bob Andrews came in and then Dave Robinson told us about Andrew Bodnar and Steve Goulding from Bontemps Roulez. They were young and really good, a crack rhythm section.'

But it was a great bunch of musicians without a focus. Custom-made, in fact, for Parker. 'We'd started rehearsing as a five piece,' continues Belmont, 'and we had some original songs plus covers like Paul Simon's "One Man's Ceiling Is Another Man's Floor". None of us knew exactly what we wanted to do but we all knew what we didn't want to do and that was to end up just another pub group.' At Robinson's suggestion, Parker hooked up with the band in the basement and, after a few tentative rehearsals at The Newlands Tavern in Peckham in October 1975, emerged as Graham Parker And The Rumour.

News of Parker's progress and record deal was not music to the ears of Fred Grainger. 'Dave Robinson and I fell out over Graham Parker. I'd heard about Graham but Dave told me he was just a petrol pump attendant from Camberley. He was "recording a few things acoustically in the studio, with Nick Lowe and Bob Andrews," but they were only "checking things out". No major recording was being done. There was always a red light on, telling me, "Don't Interrupt," so I carried on running the Hope. If anything came out of the studio, I'd be first to know. Then one day Nick came down from upstairs and casually mentioned something about a deal being in the air. Then Nick said, "Shit, forget I said anything." '

Grainger confronted Robinson and a blazing row ensued. Grainger says, 'I told Dave I was picking up the tab for the electricity and the telephone. I'd been supporting Dave for two years. I used to bung him a few quid before we went to Dingwalls so he wouldn't be embarrassed. Dave contributed a lot to the Hope because of the bands he brought in, but he never ever bought me a drink because he never had the money.'

Dave Robinson left the Hope & Anchor and the studio was closed down. The equipment was sold off, some of it to former Equal, Eddie Grant. Grainger spoke to Jonathan King of UK Records about the tapes that had been made at the Hope, including recordings by Graham Parker, the Kilburns and Declan MacManus, but although King expressed interest, Dave Robinson was not in agreement to such a deal going through.

Meanwhile, Charlie Gillett was inundated with demos from artists seeking exposure on *Honky Tonk*. 'One of the things I used to do was send out an information sheet of record shops where you could buy good stuff,' recalls Gillett. 'In fact there was a Honky Tonk Records in Kentish Town where John Illsey from Dire Straits worked. He phoned me up and said, "I'm in this band, can I bring a tape over?" '

After the success of Graham Parker, another aspiring singer/songwriter who forwarded his demo tapes to Charlie Gillett was D.P. Costello, otherwise known as Declan Mac-Manus, the Brinsley Schwarz fan who had befriended Nick Lowe in a Liverpool pub in 1972. Like Parker, Costello had recorded with Dave Robinson at the Hope & Anchor, first in an acoustic session and later with his new group, Flip City, a Pub Rock combo that pretty much imitated the Brinsley Schwarz operation.

'The Brinsleys used to switch instruments, a bit like The Band,' recalls Costello. 'I thought that was very hip. Also they played pretty quietly, a club dynamic, and did unexpected covers. One of the artists they covered and made it hip to like again was Lee Dorsey. They did a lot of his tunes. He was somebody they were gonna put back on the map in some way. Flip City ended up sharing a house, just like the Brinsleys. We thought if it had worked for them, maybe it could work for us. We stayed there for a couple of years, mainly copying the Brinsleys' blueprint.'

Flip City's manager, Ken Smith, was keen to get his combo seen at as many Pub Rock events as possible and had spent a great deal of time hustling Chilli Willi and now, the Kursaal Flyers, for support slots. As the Kursaal's drummer, I remember bumping into Ken a lot during 1975. He was always going on about this group called Flip City and he kept pestering us for gigs, but they never happened.

The Kursaal Flyers' debut LP, *Chocs Away*, enjoyed some great reviews and our singles 'Speedway' and 'Hit Records' were played a little on Radio One. Exuding optimism, UK Records exercised their option for another LP, to be produced this time by the group, with some input from Jonathan King. This was a fundamental error; installed for two weeks in a residential studio to which Jonathan would make flying visits in his Rolls Royce Corniche, we struggled to get a 'drum sound'. During breaks at the local pub, Jonathan, then riding high with his cover of 'Una Paloma Blanca', would loudly announce, 'I've made ten thousand pounds from the record industry today, dear.' Unfortunately, none of this was with the Kursaal Flyers. When I said, 'But Jonathan, we're in the *Time Out* alternative chart,' he replied, 'Alternative to what, dear? Alternative to money if you ask me.'

Our manager, Paul Conroy, had been in talks with Dan Loggins at CBS, who was keen to acquire the Kursaals' services, and a transfer deal was arranged. In the hot summer of 1976, sessions for the *Golden Mile* LP commenced with Wombles hit maker Mike Batt firmly in charge. One of our songs, 'Little Does She Know', had started out as a waltz-time country song, but we suspected it might be made more grandiose. Mike asked us how we saw it and Paul, who envisaged an over-the-top Phil Spector-type production, gave him a drawing of a kitchen sink. Mike definitely got the joke and proceeded to add all kinds of orchestrations and effects to create an over-the-top production. The most memorable session was when he decided he wanted cannon blasts a la '1812 Overture' and hired an army marksman with a big rifle. The studio filled with smoke as the poor chap attempted to pull the trigger in time with the music. His excellent work can be heard towards the end of the track.

'Little Does She Know' was released as a single and entered the charts 'with a bow and arrow' the day we played Bristol Colston Hall on our 'Works Outing' tour. It was certainly a thrill to hear ourselves on Radio One three times a day and we were soon on *Top Of The Pops*. A long-held dream had been realised, largely thanks to the existence of the pub rock circuit. Even Jonathan King phoned to congratulate us.

Dr Feelgood had now become one of the UK's top concert attractions, but not before giving a helping hand to other musicians from the Southend/Canvey area. The Feelgoods had already assisted the Kursaal Flyers and also championed the great Mickey Jupp, a Southend legend whose songs were covered by the Kursaals ('Cross Country') and the Feelgoods themselves ('Cheque Book'). Jupp, who had previously fronted The Orioles and Legend, put together a new group to play the pub circuit and went on to record for a number of major labels. His songs would be covered by The Judds, Rick Nelson and Nick Lowe, amongst others. It was now the turn of another Southend group, Eddie And The Hot Rods, to receive a leg-up on to the rock 'n' roll ladder.

Eddie And The Hot Rods were formed in Rochford, Essex, in 1973 by schoolboy boxing champion Barrie Masters, drummer Steve Nichols and guitarist Dave Higgs. Masters and Nichols had previously played together in a glam rock group called Buckshee and Higgs had been in The Fix, with Lee Brilleaux. As Higgs recalls:

The Fix got together at Canvey Youth Centre. Wilko had been in an earlier line-up and later Lee and Sparko were in the group. They kept asking me if I thought Wilko would join this new group they were forming, called Dr Feelgood. I told them to ask him. When Wilko joined they became very good. The Feelgoods were electric at a time when everyone was still sitting on the floor swathed in denim.

When the Feelgoods asked me to jam with them I couldn't sleep for two nights beforehand, but they got me playing again after a long lay-off. Seeing the Feelgoods doing so well gave me the confidence and inspiration to have a go myself. I put an advertisement in Chris Stevens Music Centre and met Steve Nichols and Barrie Masters. We got Paul Gray in on bass and Lew Lewis on harp and started playing around Southend. We got accused of sounding like the Feelgoods, but we were all listening to the J Geils Band.

Now heavily influenced by Dr Feelgood in terms of speed and musical economy, the Hot Rods played their first London pub gig at The Kensington on 17 May 1975. A week later they returned and after a gap of a month, commenced a six-week residency at the venue. After branching out to other venues, including the Nashville Rooms and the Newlands Tavern, they quickly established a following. The timing was perfect. The Hot Rods had picked up the mantle from the Feelgoods, whose own success had signalled a sea change in rock 'n' roll.

Whereas, prior to this moment, younger musicians may have sought to emulate the progressive bombast of, say, Emerson, Lake & Palmer, they would now be more excited by the prospect of performing hard-driving rhythm and blues. This was a sound that hadn't been heard much in Britain since the mid-60s and was therefore new and exciting to younger ears, especially when enhanced by the Feelgoods' – and, now, the Hot Rods' – on-stage menace.

The best indicator of this gradual shift in musical tastes was the UK music press and, more specifically, its readers' letters pages. In the years 1972–74, when the scene was dominated by progressive rock, they were littered with missives raving about Emerson, Lake & Palmer, typified by this letter to *Sounds* in October 1972:

I have just returned from seeing ELP at The Oval. Surely no one can touch them for ability and showmanship . . .

these three men must be the world's best trio ever; they are supermen.

A little later, one Mark Perry from Deptford wrote to *Record Mirror* describing Emerson, Lake & Palmer as 'The Eighth Wonder Of The World!' But by December 1975, Perry's musical tastes had changed, as evidenced by this letter to *Sounds*:

> After seeing Dr Feelgood at two big gigs this year (Reading and Hammersmith), I can't help feeling sorry that they became 'big'. They were much more 'alive' at the Marquee or Dingwalls. Raw R&B at Hammersmith Odeon just doesn't sound right to me. I just hope the Kursaal Flyers don't become too well known, otherwise the pub/club/college circuit is gonna lose another good act . . .

OK, Mark Perry knew an exciting act when he saw one, but his musical appetite was changing fast. It would not be long before he'd form his own group, Alternative TV, and found the UK's first 'Punk Rock' fanzine, *Sniffin' Glue*. In this home-made broadsheet, Perry would sing the praises of Dr Feelgood and Eddie And The Hot Rods, but before long the Feelgoods and the Hot Rods would be ousted in favour of some of the newer punk groups. *Sniffin' Glue* would then humorously dismiss all rock music that had gone before. Rock 'n' roll would never be quite the same again.

It is probable that Perry's evolving musical tastes had been shaped by the more influential writers in the UK rock press in the period 1974–75. Perry would almost certainly have read articles by Mick Farren, Nick Kent and Charles Shaar Murray in the *NME* and Giovanni Dadomo and Chas de Whalley in *Sounds*, reporting the first rumblings of punk.

At this point, punk was usually being written about in the context of acts such as the Flamin' Groovies and the MC5 or mid-60s American garage groups such as The Standells, The Seeds, and ? And The Mysterians. These latter groups had enjoyed reappraisal following the 1972 release of the Elektra double LP, *Nuggets*. Compiled by writer and future Patti Smith guitarist Lenny Kaye, *Nuggets* was a treasure trove of trashy pop, mostly seeking to emulate the Stones, The Animals, or Them, but with a psychedelic slant.

Although there was the odd studio masterpiece on *Nuggets* that suggested intervention by session musicians, such as the Electric Prunes' 'I Had Too Much To Dream Last Night', musical accomplishment was not top of the agenda for the 60s punk groups. Instead they preferred the high energy rush of garage-band R&B, complete with fuzz guitar and snarled vocal. *Nuggets* and the musical trails to which it pointed represented a bonanza for Eddie And The Hot Rods, under the direction of their manager and mentor, Eddie Hollis.

Edwyn 'Eddie' Hollis had been at Rayleigh Sweyne grammar school with Lee Brilleaux of Dr Feelgood and was part of the Canvey clique that surrounded the Feelgoods in the early days. Hollis was an avid record collector and acquired the nickname '1000 Eddie', because of his then staggering collection of over 1,000 LPs. Anyone visiting the Hollis pad would be subjected to his shouting, 'It's brilliant! It's brilliant!' as he played brief snatches from his mighty collection. To say Hollis had catholic tastes would be an understatement; his turntable favourites ranged from Kraftwerk to Sun Ra and from The Osmonds to the MC5. He loved it all and he became a great influence on the local scene. In one of his inspired moments, in a Southend bar in 1973, he exclaimed to everyone within earshot, 'Let's form a 60s group!'

By 1975, Eddie And The Hot Rods had become a living embodiment of mid-60s musical values. Hollis's record collection had fuelled much of the Hot Rods' early repertoire, but guitarist Dave Higgs was now starting to compose strong original songs, often with lyrics supplied by Hollis. With anthems like 'Teenage Depression', the Hot Rods attracted a rabid young audience and soon found themselves described in the music press as a punk rock group. In this role, the Hot Rods would have the London scene almost entirely to themselves for nine glorious months, but there were moves afoot to queer their pitch substantially.

* * *

In the wake of the Feelgoods and the Hot Rods, a number of younger groups came on to the pub circuit, creating a press-led buzz and generally refreshing the scene after the demise of the early Pub Rock groups. For example, at the Nashville Rooms during the latter half of 1975 it was not uncommon to see the Hot Rods sharing the bill with The 101ers, led by the manic Joe Strummer. Strummer was a high-energy front man who could win over a pub audience with sheer gusto. At a 101ers gig, any deficiencies of a vocal or musical nature were more than compensated for by Strummer's alarming presence.

Also creating a stir were the Count Bishops (formerly Chrome), a high-powered R&B act in a similar vein to the Feelgoods, whose *Speedball* EP launched the Chiswick label in November 1975.

Chiswick Records, an important label in this transition period, had been started by Ted Carroll, proprietor of the Rock On record stall in Soho, and his partner, Roger Armstrong. Carroll and Armstrong had both come to London from Ireland, where they had gained much experience as agents and promoters, with Carroll managing an early incarnation of Thin Lizzy. From the general ambience on the streets of London, Carroll and Armstrong sensed that a new mood was imminent. 'There was a reinvention of rock 'n' roll going on,' says Armstrong, 'with the Flamin' Groovies, the Feelgoods and others. It was, "Let's be beat groups again," but it wasn't that revivalist.'

'There were a lot of parallel scenes happening,' adds Ted Carroll. 'In late 1974, we used to get a lot of French guys coming in buying records. Larry Dubais and Mark Zermatti arrived and they had the Skydog label with the Flamin' Groovies EP, *Grease*. Also, by this stage, rockabilly started to happen and we were going to see Crazy Cavan And The Rhythm Rockers, who Charlie Gillett was playing on *Honky Tonk*. The Bobby Sox Club at the White Hart in Tottenham was a big scene.'

Armstrong adds, 'It was mixed. You had had your old teddy boys like Sunglasses Ron. Then all these young kids were coming in on the back of *American Graffiti* – 13-year-olds in baseball jackets with flat-top haircuts. They called it "Graffiti Rock"!'

But for Carroll and Armstrong, the most exciting development in this period was the emergence of a handful of groups who, like the Hot Rods and the 101ers, were bridging the Pub/Punk divide. Ted Carroll says, 'We used to ask ourselves, "Can we sell a record by this group?" If we could sell it in our shop, we could sell it anywhere! That was the idea of Chiswick Records.'

The Count Bishops were already under contract to Chiswick and the next group up for consideration were the Hammersmith Gorillas. Led by one Jesse Hector, the Gorillas did not actually have youth on their side. 'Jess Hector told us he'd played at the 2 "I"s in the 50s,' says Armstrong, who initially doubted Hector's claim. 'Then he produced a photograph of himself standing in front of The Shadows, when they were called The Drifters, at the 2 "I"s in about 1958. Turns out he'd been a boy wonder in the late 50s. When he was 12 or 13, he had a band called the Jesse Hector Rock 'n' Roll Trio, playing Johnny Burnette-style rockabilly. Through the mid-60s he was in a band called The Clique, who made records on Pye and in the late 60s he was in Crushed Butler.'

By the end of 1975, Andrew Jakeman had become frustrated by the record industry's lack of interest in Nick Lowe. Although Lowe's recently signed publishing deal with Rock Music Company was keeping the wolf from the door of 48 Queens Gate Terrace and Lowe had been hired to produce Graham Parker's debut LP, *Howlin' Wind*, Jakeman's frustration was beginning to show.

When the fast-rising Kursaal Flyers headlined at London's Roundhouse, within only a year of their bottom-of-the-bill slot at the Chilli Willi 'Big Xmas Beat Extravaganza', Jakeman was present. Five minutes before the group was due on stage, Jakeman entered the dressing room and launched a torrid verbal attack on me. 'Just because you all think Nick Lowe is some kind of poet . . .' he ranted, trailing off into a hail of invective.

Admittedly, the Kursaals were avid fans of Nick Lowe's songwriting, having recently recorded a new Lowe song,

'Television', for their imminent second LP, *The Great Artiste*, but the thrust of Jakeman's outburst was random and incoherent. Perhaps, in Jakeman's opinion, the Kursaals had butchered Lowe's masterpiece. Or, possibly, Jakeman envied the Kursaals' rapid rise, while Lowe's career languished . Reassuringly for me, however, Andrew Jakeman was ranting all over town.

'Jake's explosions were not relevant to any method,' says Chris Fenwick.' There was no built-up angst. It would usually be some daft situation that would set him off, at an airline check-in or an equipment load-in. The game was a lot looser in those days. There was more turbulence. But Jake wasn't pissed off with his lot. It was usually down to the hangover.'

But there was one clear light on Jakeman's horizon. 'In six or seven months I'd made about 12 trips over to New York or LA,' recalls Dr Feelgood manager, Chris Fenwick. 'We could have gone with almost any label for the States, but once we'd signed to CBS, their president, Bruce Lundvall, said he would consider it an honour if the boys would come to play at their sales conference. He would pay to fly us in for the weekend. We told Lundvall that we'd have to take the road crew, of course, including our lighting man and our tour manager.'

Now, nine months into his stint as Chris Fenwick's right-hand-man, Andrew Jakeman contemplated his first visit to the USA and the CBS sales conference in San Diego, California, at which Dr Feelgood would be promoting their second LP, *Malpractice*. It was a crucial trip for the Feelgoods, if they were to reach new audiences beyond the concert halls of Europe. And for Andrew Jakeman, America would provide the inspiration for the next chapter in his unstoppable career.

16. TOTAL UNLIMITED CREDIT

If 1975 had been a transitional year in the development of modern pop, 1976 would be the turning point – an eventful 12 months during which the rock 'n' roll rule book would undergo a complete overhaul. Those embracing the Punk Rock ethos would regard 1976 as Year Zero, while for ailing pub-rockers, the year would present great new opportunities.

In January, Andrew Jakeman, continued to seek a record deal for Nick Lowe. Although Lowe had been dropped by United Artists the previous year, Jakeman could often be found at the UA offices on Dr Feelgood business. 'We all used to love going to UA,' says Paul Conroy. 'We'd visit their plush offices and get our Nitty Gritty Dirt Band albums. It was where Jake used to send all his mail from.' While A&R head Andrew Lauder and his staff turned a blind eye, Jakeman did indeed make full use of UA's facilities, including the telephone and the photocopier. More importantly, Jakeman was able to glean inside information on two labels with United Artists associations, Jet and Beserkley.

Jet Records, a mainstream pop label and home of the Electric Light Orchestra, was owned by Don Arden, a legendary figure in British pop with a fearsome reputation for getting his own way. In the 60s, Arden had managed top acts such as the Small Faces, Amen Corner and The Move. Now Arden was in the process of developing Jet Records and delegating certain A&R tasks to his son David. David Arden was one of the few industry moguls to claim to appreciate Nick Lowe's talent. More importantly, Jet's West Coast A&R man, Greg Lewerke, was a former UA employee who kept himself up to date with developments in London and was familiar with Dr Feelgood and Brinsley Schwarz.

Beserkley, in contrast to Jet, was a San Francisco-based left-field independent label. Founded in 1975 by Matthew 'King' Kaufman, Beserkley nurtured the talents of nouveau-pop artists such as the Rubinoos and Greg Kihn, while the jewel in Beserkley's crown was Modern Lovers mainman, Jonathan Richman.

In terms of style and aspiration, Jet and Beserkley were at opposite ends of the spectrum, but Jakeman was not in a particularly strong position. Beserkley's sense of fun was more appealing, but Jet had stronger commercial clout in the USA, where it had recently signed a distribution deal with United Artists. Jakeman considered the pros and cons of Nick Lowe signing to Jet or Beserkley and found the former less suitable. 'I disliked David Arden on the first meeting,' says Jakeman, 'and after Andrew Lauder played me the *Modern Lovers* album, and all the Jonathan Richman stuff, I thought, "This is the business! Berserkley Records! Crazy as you like! Small guys! Fabulous!" '

But for a deal with either label to progress, it was necessary for Jakeman and Lowe to make the 12,000 mile round trip to California for meetings. With CBS funding Dr Feelgood's imminent visit to San Diego, a plan was hatched to enlist Lowe as a road manager, bringing the touring party up to ten and enabling Lowe and Jakeman to cross the Atlantic together. Chris Fenwick says, 'Bruce Lundvall had said, "Bring what you like," so obviously we loaded it up. If someone wanted to make themselves busy, there was plenty to do.'

The Dr Feelgood entourage travelled to San Diego, via Los Angeles, in January. First to fly out were Dr Feelgood's roadies, Jeff Shaw and Fred Barker. Shaw and Barker knew that they would be staying at the Los Angeles Hyatt, but were unaware that Hyatt was a chain of hotels. On arriving at Los Angeles International Airport, they immediately saw a hotel with a big Hyatt sign and checked in. It was, unfortunately, the wrong Hyatt hotel and two days later they were reported missing by Chris Fenwick, who was awaiting their arrival at the Hyatt on Sunset Boulevard.

After a night in Los Angeles, the Feelgood team drove to San Diego in two hire cars and checked into the Rivermont Hotel, where humorous pseudonyms were used at the registration desk. Nick Lowe, clearly travelling incognito, checked in as 'Dale Liberator, equipment handler'. Perhaps the former Brinsley Schwarz front man was in head-down mode for his first return to America since the humiliation of the Fillmore debacle some six years earlier.

After checking in, the Feelgoods soon discovered the special bar that was reserved for participants in the CBS sales conference. There, they discovered their first source of amusement – a sign that read: TOTAL UNLIMITED CREDIT. Armed with ID cards that would entitle them to said credit, the Feelgoods got stuck in. This was the American recording industry in all its hedonistic glory, rewarding a front-line sales force for another great year. It was also the green light for anybody connected with the event to go hog wild. Jakeman recalls:

The hotel gift shop was denuded within the first day. Swimming costumes, suntan oil . . . all gone. It was my first visit to America and they'd let me into this hotel with total, unlimited credit! People were porking out on steaks, and getting legless. This CBS salesman, with a really dodgy ginger toupee, was tucking into a huge ice-cream. We later found out that the same guy, whose name was Sal, had gone for a swim after his meal, and pegged it at the bottom of the pool.

Apparently, Sal had been with CBS for twenty years. They were saying, 'Well, we've got to stop the convention now, out of respect for Sal!' and I was going, 'Hold on pal, we've come six thousand miles to bang out this R&B stuff! We're trying to sell a record here! What do you mean?' I didn't realise this was the American way of doing things. I genuinely thought they were going to stop the convention. Of course, after an hour, it was, 'Sal would have liked it to go on!' And the show went ahead.

That evening Dr Feelgood took to the convention stage, sandwiched between performances from Michael Murphey and Phoebe Snow. Seconds before the MC announced Dr Feelgood to the packed room, a hapless roadie, possibly Nick Lowe, accidentally knocked Lee Brilleaux's Guild slide guitar from its stand, shattering the neck. Brilleaux turned to see the smashed instrument and, completely unruffled, withdrew a pencil stub from his pocket and calmly amended his set list, striking a line through 'Back In The Night' and 'Rolling And Tumbling', the two songs that were slide guitar-dependent.

After the performance, the Feelgoods hit the bar to enjoy more unlimited credit. In particular, Feelgoods' bassist John 'Sparko' Sparks, rose to the occasion. Sparks recalls, 'It must have cost CBS about ten grand to fly us out there and I soaked it up. I was like a sponge. We could sign for everything, plus a tip! We'd sign for the drinks and say to the barman, "And here's twenty dollars for you, my good man!" Later that night, Martyn Smith and I went on the rampage. The next morning, Bruce Lundvall met Chris in the lift and said, "Sparko was on top form last night!" I think they liked that sort of rock 'n' roll behaviour.'

Feelgoods' drummer, the Big Figure, says, 'I've got this image in my mind of Sparko sitting by the pool drinking cocktails, with the phone on a long lead, phoning his missus.'

'Playing the CBS conference was a wonderful rock 'n' roll hoot,' says Fenwick, 'but we weren't really geared up to playing to an industry crowd, alongside Boz Scaggs and Starcastle. Our appearance caused a ripple – there was a feeling of, "What have we got here?", but it didn't ring quite true. The Americans were all looking for this new huge wall of sound, but our situation seemed very thin, quite honestly. Also, we were used to an audience response, which we didn't get from a room full of salesmen. They would introduce themselves to us. "Hi! I'm Joe. I look after Pacific North West." For us, going to San Diego wasn't a great career move.'

Returning to Los Angeles, everyone in the Feelgood entourage was overjoyed to learn that blues legend John Lee Hooker was playing Hollywood's Starwood Club. This event was attended by most of the party, except for Wilko Johnson, who had decided to stay in his hotel room for the evening and derive amusement from a little of the 'Paki Black' that the Feelgoods had invested in for their LA stay. The other ounce of smoking material was stashed in the glove compartment of the Feelgoods' hire car.

At the Starwood, Fenwick, Brilleaux, Sparks, the Big Figure and Lowe watched John Lee Hooker's disappointing performance. Hooker, who appeared to be inebriated, sacked three drummers during his perfunctory forty-minute set. On the way back to the Hyatt, the Feelgoods' hire car, with Fenwick at the wheel, was stopped by police on Santa Monica Boulevard.

'It was an incredibly well-lit road,' says Fenwick, 'like daylight all night, but I only had my side lights on, not dipped headlights, which was illegal. I didn't see the necessity for headlights. We had the whole routine . . . "Get out of the car, up against the wall, no-one move!" As English blokes, this was very odd. I remember Nick Lowe saying to one of the cops, "Do you mind if I smoke a cigarette, old boy?" He was doing the limey abroad routine, but the cop yelled, "Don't move!" '

'The cop was a young Puerto Rican,' says the Big Figure. 'He was holding a huge gun, which looked like a cannon to me and his hand was shaking nervously. I told Nick to cool it.' Meanwhile, another cop was searching the car and suddenly screamed, 'Driver, step forward!' Fenwick complied but was unable to produce his driving licence. He recalls:

The cop said, 'Turn around!' Then he very skilfully pushed my head over the top of the car and pulled my arms around my back, which hurt, and slapped the cuffs on me. Then he clicked the cuffs up. It was four clicks and it bit into my wrists.'

I was arrested, but I wasn't particularly worried. What could they do me for? Not having a driving licence? I was feeling pretty confident, thinking I'd be back at the hotel bar in an hour. Of course, I was blissfully unaware that there was an ounce of dope in the glove compartment and they'd found it.

They told me I was being charged with possession of hashish. The penny dropped. I was taken to West Hollywood police station. The dope weighed over an ounce and there was a huge debate over whether it was a misdemeanour or a felony. Possession of grass was a misdemeanour, carrying only a $100 fine, but holding an ounce of hard black dope constituted a felony, with a minimum of $10,000 bail, a wee bit of a jump. A lot of phone calls were going down and suddenly I heard this cop scream with delight, 'It's a felony! Fingerprint him! This is just what I need to get my stripes!'

This was the start of my management career in America. Lee called up the police station and went into solicitor mode. He established that we needed a bondsman, but it was the middle of the night. I was put in the cells, which I shared with a sleeping Mexican who had raped a hooker. In the morning, the bondsman came in, signed the papers, took my passport and I was released. I was told that if I voluntarily went on a rehabilitation course, called DANA [Drugs, Alcohol and Narcotics Awareness], and attended college for lectures, I'd just get a slap on the wrist and probation for six months. So I did the course and attended all the lectures and I haven't touched dope since!

Following Fenwick's release, Wilko Johnson and the Big Figure flew home to England while those remaining took the shuttle up to San Francisco, where Andrew Jakeman would meet with Beserkley's Matthew Kaufman. In San Francisco, the Feelgood entourage hung out with Clover, who were playing a club in Fairfax.

Shirley Alford, later to become Mrs Lee Brilleaux, recalls running into the Feelgoods for the first time. 'I had been invited by my old friend, George Daly, to go see Clover. George had a management company at that time, Pyramid Promotions and Clover was one of his bands. They had been playing around the Bay area for years. At the end of their set, they announced that they were happy to welcome "their friends from England, Dr. Feelgood! So, please put your hands together for Lee Brilleaux!" I don't remember what they played, probably "Route 66" or "Great Balls of Fire", but my memory is of Lee getting up there and playing a harp solo that had jaws agape.

With Chris Fenwick's probationary commitments and a six-week wait until the Feelgoods' next US tour, Fenwick, Jakeman and Lowe decided to stay in the USA, renting former

Byrd Skip Battin's house in Laurel Canyon. Andrew Jakeman recalls, 'We just bought some sleeping bags and rented a colour television and went to a garage sale and bought a table and four chairs and some lilos and this huge bag of grass. Nick sat out on the veranda and wrote a load of songs, including "Heart Of The City".'

Nick Lowe soon returned to the UK. Having earned his roadie's credentials with Dr Feelgood, Lowe was hired to tour-manage Graham Parker And The Rumour. Parker had been booked to open for Thin Lizzy on a UK tour. 'I was pretty good at getting them out of bed,' says Lowe, 'but I got all the accounts wrong. I was about £125 out, which was a lot of dough. Robbo fired me.'

In spring 1976, Dr Feelgood reconvened in the USA, where they were due to tour with financial support from CBS. After various shows in the Northeast, supporting acts as diverse as Starcastle and Papa John Creach, the Feelgoods were booked to open seven shows in the Deep South, for glam-metal monsters Kiss. When Dr Feelgood arrived in Mobile, Alabama, for the opening date of the tour, Chris Fenwick made a reconnoitre of the venue. Within minutes he was on the telephone to the group, who were waiting in their hotel.

Wilko Johnson recalls the call. 'Chris said, "It's crap. You're not doing it! I've blown it out." Chris was 22 at the time and he was blowing out stadium gigs with Kiss!' It transpired that the Feelgoods were expected to change in the public toilets at the front of house, so that Kiss could use the entire backstage area for costume changes and the preparation of pyrotechnic effects. Johnson continues, 'Then we got a message through from CBS. They sent along Bob Ringe from the William Morris agency. We told him we'd blown the tour out and he said, "You're shitting me!" It certainly left a gap in the itinerary.'

On 10 May and 11 May, Dr Feelgood played New York's Bottom Line. CBS had papered the room and it was largely a music industry crowd, plus Pop Art legend Andy Warhol. Opening the show on both nights were The Ramones, newly signed to Sire Records and promoting their groundbreaking debut LP, which was to have a monumental influence on the new up-and-coming Punk Rock groups.

Later that month, the Feelgoods played a number of dates opening for Bad Company and began to get used to the American way of serving drinks. This was the start of the Feelgoods' love affair with the cocktail shaker. 'After America, Lee and Sparko were constantly pissed for a good five years,' says the Big Figure. 'I would sit and drink with them, I loved the blokes, but I couldn't do it all day like they could. I fail to understand how they managed to turn in such great shows. We used to hit the Holiday Inns and they would set up their own individual bars in their rooms.'

We used to buy suitcases and cocktail shakers in thrift shops [says Sparks]. I was into Margaritas, so I'd have all the ingredients. Lee was into Banana Daiquiris. You'd go into Lee's room and have a Daiquiri; then in my room you'd have something else. We'd leave our doors open and you'd drink whatever each room was serving at the time. After about twenty cocktails, we'd be sitting at the bar. If anyone offered to buy you a drink and you replied, 'No thanks, I don't want one,' the invisible notepad and pen would come out. 'I . . . do not . . . want one . . . Would you mind signing that?' Hangovers became a way of life.

I don't think we were drunk, not in that way. Occasionally you'd make a mistake, but we always had the antidote. I'd say an average day's drinking in those days was a bottle of spirits, six or seven pints of beer, a couple of bottles of wine, each, and on top of that, the cocktails.

The Big Figure adds, 'I don't know how we came out of it alive. We definitely got the habit in America. Wilko obviously took the opposite stance. He'd ask for a milk and say, "Make it a double." '

For the Feelgoods, America was generally not a rewarding experience, especially after the adulation they had received at home. In the States, there was no weekly music press to spread word of their exciting stage performances. Chris Fenwick says, 'What a lot of people don't seem to realise is that the jurisdiction of the British music press ends at Penzance. In America, these papers sell to the industry, but they don't sell to a kid out in New Jersey. He might get an imported *NME* if he's an out-and-out enthusiast, but there weren't enough enthusiasts for it to really kick in.'

To make matters worse for the Feelgoods, guitarist Wilko Johnson hated his American experience. Johnson recalls, 'CBS really looked after us, flying us everywhere, no Greyhound buses, but I was miserable most of the time. I think any divisions that there were within the band were starting to show then. All the old crap about pressure, but it's true. I had a different way of life. I didn't drink, so I wouldn't be with the others in the bar. I was writing the songs and I had my worries so I'd go really quiet and then people reacted to the quiet. I'd hear them say, "What's the matter with him?" And I was sitting there thinking I wish I could just stand up and say, "Look, I'm all right, don't worry," but you can't. It was building up.'

'We were feeling the pinch,' says Fenwick. 'Another old adage sticks in my mind – "A guaranteed way to break a band up is to send them to America." When you've left a very strong gig base in the UK and Europe, playing to 2,000 people a night and it's electric, and you go straight to a situation where the best gig is one that's been bought by the record company and it's full because they've sent the cars to pick up the key players, Warhol is there and it's an open tab at the bar and when you come on stage they all go, "Wa-hoo!" in that Yankee way, it's forced. The Bottom Line show was OK, but not as exciting as The Lord Nelson. We didn't get too much luck either. When you get a good run of luck you run with it hard, because eventually you're not gonna jump every fence.'

In a commercial sense, Fenwick's observations are indisputable, but as far as achieving critical acclaim and having an influence on other musicians is concerned, the power of the music press in the mid-70s must not be underestimated. Dr Feelgood had enjoyed acres of positive press coverage in the UK and this had not escaped the attention of New York's New Wave elite, including Blondie, the Ramones and Talking

Heads, all of whom were blown away by the little Pub Rock group from Canvey Island.

Back home, Eddie And The Hot Rods had filled the vacuum left by the Feelgoods' absence. Now slimmed down to a quartet, following the departure of harmonica player Lew Lewis, who was fired after a dressing-room tantrum at Brunel University, the Hot Rods had become a big live draw and secured a contract with Island Records. But their punk supremacy was about to be challenged by an improbable new group called the Sex Pistols, who were booked to open for the Hot Rods at the Marquee on 12 February.

Egged on that night by their mentor and manager, Malcolm McLaren, the Sex Pistols caused havoc. During their short set, the Pistols sabotaged the p.a. foldback system, making things difficult for the Hot Rods, and generally stuck two fingers up to the Marquee, an established music business stronghold.

Dave Higgs of the Hot Rods says, 'We were obviously young and naïve at the time. The two managers, Malcolm McLaren and Eddie Hollis, had put their heads together to create a publicity stunt. I watched the Pistols from the side of the stage as they were getting their instructions from Malcolm. "Swear at them Johnny!" he shouted. It was like a puppet show.'

Nevertheless, from McLaren's point of view, all of this had the desired effect. The Sex Pistols made the headlines and the Hot Rods' status as Punk Rock's standard bearers was irreversibly damaged. Interviewed by the *NME*'s Neil Spencer after the event, Sex Pistols guitarist, Steve Jones, had the snappy quote, remarking, 'Actually we're not into music; we're into chaos.'

Despite this setback, the Hot Rods became even more popular and their year would peak in September with the success of their *Live at the Marquee* EP. Guitarist Dave Higgs appeared on the cover of *NME*, under the caption: 'With one B flat chord, Eddie And The Hot Rods Save Rock and Roll.'

Although the outwardly anarchic Sex Pistols may have preferred to disassociate themselves from the Pub Rock scene, they were not above using some of the Pub Rock venues to establish their reputation. There were even those who didn't find anything particularly new in the group's approach. 'I thought the Sex Pistols with Glen Matlock were a pretty good group, a bit like The Stooges,' says Dai Davies, then promoter at the Nashville Rooms, adding, 'but in reality, the Sex Pistols were no less of a Pub Rock group than Ducks Deluxe, only a bit younger.'

On 23 April, the Sex Pistols opened for Joe Strummer's 101ers at the Nashville. This time, photographers Joe Stevens and Kate Simon were on hand to capture the inevitable confrontation between the group and members of the audience, which was sparked off by Malcolm McLaren and his partner Vivien Westwood, both seeking to liven up an otherwise 'dull evening'. Joe Stevens's classic image of the Pistols bundling into the front row would grace the cover of *Melody Maker* some months later. The Sex Pistols were on their way.

On 18 May, Chiswick Records signed the 101ers, whose debut 45 – 'Keys To Your Heart' c/w '5 Star Rock 'n' Roll Petrol' – was scheduled for release at the end of the month. Joe Strummer, however, had already left the group.

'I remember I was standing at the bar of the Red Cow watching The Jam,' recalls Chiswick's Roger Armstrong. 'Joe tapped me on the shoulder. There was a wee thin guy behind him, who I later learnt was Mick Jones. Joe was saying to me, "I've broken the 101ers up. Have I done the right thing?" Joe is terribly moral, but I said, "Thanks a lot Joe. We haven't even put your record out yet!" We weren't pleased.'

Strummer had recently seen the Sex Pistols and was quoted in the music press as having 'seen the light'. Now he was forming a new group, called The Heartdrops, with the aforementioned Mick Jones. Soon The Heartdrops would become The Clash. With their uncompromising image and the radical subject matter of their songs, The Clash were the final nail in Pub Rock's coffin, driven home by Joe Strummer in a dramatic break with his past.

Chiswick Records observed the emerging punk scene. 'Punk got invented by a few people,' says Roger Armstrong. 'You had Rat Scabies, Chrissie Hynde, Mick Jones, Billy Idol.

But, except for Joe Strummer, they had never actually played live.' Ted Carroll adds, 'These people were into the New York Dolls and Bowie and Roxy Music to an extent. But the Pistols used to come in and buy Yardbirds records. They were looking for hard-edged British beat group things like The Thirds. I used to play them stuff like the Paramounts, or the Marauders.'

Chiswick Records, it seemed, was perfectly positioned to sign up the early Punk Rock groups, but ultimately was unable to attract any of them. 'We were in the middle of all this,' says Armstrong. 'But we didn't end up with the Pistols or The Clash, although we nearly got The Jam. The triumvirate of Bernie Rhodes, Malcolm McLaren and Andy Czezowski all had, from day one, ambitions to sign their acts with the major labels.'

'Malcolm and Bernie were just old-fashioned carnival-type wide boys really,' says Geoff Travis of Rough Trade. 'They just wanted the money. They didn't have any kind of principles, yet they were the ones that talked the most about having principles. I think The Clash would have made much better records on an independent label, but I don't think it even crossed their mind that it was a possibility. The Clash were shielded from it by Bernie Rhodes. I think it was a historical opportunity missed.'

Roger Armstrong says, 'The difference between punk and the Pub Rock of five years before, when it was the Brinsleys getting away from The Hype and being down home and playing pubs, was that punk took it back the other way. Malcolm McLaren would have hung on for ages if EMI hadn't signed the Pistols, rather than sign with a label like Chiswick.' Ted Carroll adds, 'McLaren's intention was to sign with a major and have the opportunity to rattle their cage.'

Armstrong says, 'Punk was unsignable one minute, hot the next, but it was a very narrow thing that lasted a year and died. It left a legacy that goes on to this day, but the core of punk started in 1976 and finished a year later. It came and it went.'

Following their American visits, Dr Feelgood continued to build their following in the UK, but not all was well within their ranks. Wilko Johnson was becoming a major pain in the arse and the atmosphere within Dr Feelgood had already become too much for tour manager Andrew Jakeman. 'The Feelgoods could have been enormous on a global scale,' says Jakeman. 'It was slow at first, but when people got it, they got it big time. But Wilko, who was quite amusing early on, was starting to be less fun.'

'Jake had to leave,' says Fenwick. 'We had run our course with Wilko. It could go no further. We couldn't work on that kind of tension.' Despite a regular wage working for the Feelgoods, Jakeman was still intent on securing a recording contract for Nick Lowe, but nothing was happening fast enough and all the people who could have been shouted at had been shouted at.

Beserkley Records were still keen to sign Lowe for the USA and Jakeman considered their offer, but after having been inspired by the dozens of local independent labels he had seen all across America, particularly Beserkley, Jakeman had started to think seriously about starting his own label in the UK, if only as an outlet for Lowe's work.

Jakeman says, 'I'd been to America and I'd seen how some of the labels worked. I thought, "Yes, I can do that. I've had a lesson in American and now I'm ready to take on the world!" '

In June 1976, Jakeman terminated his employment with Dr Feelgood and began setting up his own record company. It would be called Stiff Records. Barney Bubbles was involved in early discussions about the look of Stiff and he and Jakeman plotted and planned together. Both men were overflowing with ideas and a torrent of slogans started to flow, including 'If They're Dead We'll Sign 'Em' and 'Undertakers To The Industry'. While there were no immediate plans to release anything other than a single by Nick Lowe, a number of artists were considered, including the Pink Fairies, Sean Tyla and Motorhead.

Initial finance for Stiff came in the form of a £400 loan from the Feelgoods' Lee Brilleaux, plus a little more cash from photographer Keith Morris and Feelgoods' manager Chris Fenwick. Wilko Johnson also made a contribution. 'Wilko said he'd put in fifty guineas,' recalls Jakeman. 'So he gave me a cheque for fifty-two pounds and fifty pence. I never banked it. I framed it.'

But although Lee Brilleax's investment might have paid for a few 45s to be pressed up, Jakeman also required an infrastructure. For this, he needed to look no further than Graham Parker's manager, Dave Robinson, with whom he had been in contact since Nick Lowe had produced Parker's debut LP. Coincidentally, Robinson had also been dating Jakeman's flatmate, Irene Campbell, who worked in the advertising department of *Time Out*.

Andrew Jakeman says, 'Dave and Irene found this boat in the columns of *Time Out*. When the ads came in, Irene would sift through them, so she could pick out all the good bargains. They saw this boat for three hundred quid and they did it up. The weekend they were going to move onto it, the thing had sunk! So they came back to 48 Queens Gate Terrace, which was such a mortal blow. At that time Dave had Graham Parker and I had Nick Lowe and I had Stiff Records.'

Dave Robinson says, 'Jake was tour managing at the time. I was up and running and Jake came in and used the phones. We had two phones and I said, "You can have the other one." I had been thinking about setting up a label but I was very busy with Graham Parker at the time. I'd already written out a list of seven or eight people that I thought would work on a label including Declan MacManus. I also had an idea to put Dave Edmunds, Nick Lowe and Mickey Jupp together, but their three personalities made it impossible. I told Jake about the tapes I'd made at the Hope & Anchor. When I first played the Declan MacManus tape to Jake, he said, "Next!" '

Declan MacManus recalls recording at the Hope & Anchor studio. 'Dave Robinson had the idea, with his entrepreneurial flair, of recording one particular song from Flip City's repertoire, which was "Third Rate Romance". Some of the hipper stations like Capital were playing Jesse Winchester's version or the Amazing Rhythm Aces' version. Robbo thought we might steal a march on these and got us to come into what was a barely finished studio and record it. It was the first time I'd been in the studio with a band. Another time I recorded acoustically for Dave. I did every song I had at the time. The tape is thankfully lost.'

Nick Lowe says, 'I think that Dave Robinson would probably agree he's not exactly a style-maker, but he can get things moving and get things done. He's also really tenacious.'

Publicist Glen Colson gets to the heart of the matter:

Jake needed Dave because Dave had Graham Parker and he had money. But Dave needed Jake because Jake had all the ideas, which he'd been working on for five years in his head. He'd been travelling and every time he saw a good slogan he saved it and every time he saw people being fucked over he said, 'We don't want that happening to us.' He'd already been burnt by the Chilli Willi situation and he knew all the pitfalls. He was also very clever. He knew how to do publishing and record deals and he knew Geoff Travis at Rough Trade would buy the records off him. He knew where to go and how to do it.'

Jake also knew Barney Bubbles was the best designer in the world and would come up with great graphics. So Jake knew everything. Robbo was a workhorse, who by sheer persistence and soul had come up with Graham Parker, who was their shining beacon then. Graham was the real diamond that the whole Stiff thing was built on. When the Rumour got together with him, it was like The Band and Bob Dylan, or the Lewisham equivalent anyway. When that little man went on stage, it was magic. All those years of Bob Andrews, Brinsley Schwarz and those guys playing around, it was crystallised. And Jake wanted a bit of that and Robbo wanted Jake's marketing ideas. But I'm sure deep down inside Dave and Jake loathed each other.

17. ROCKETHEAD OF A REVOLUTION

Stiff Records was launched on Friday, 13 August 1976, with the release of Nick Lowe's 'So It Goes' c/w 'Heart Of The City'. The production of this double-sided slab of urgent pop was credited to Nick Lowe and Jake Riviera, the latter being the brand new persona of Andrew 'Jake' Jakeman. A plethora of witty slogans graced the label of the record, designed by Chris Morton, informing the listener that the music had been 'Electrically Recorded' in 'Mono Enhanced Stereo' and that Stiff was 'The World's Most Flexible Label'.

As was often the case with Nick Lowe's compositions, both songs contained elements that sounded strangely familiar. Lowe says, 'I used to do it on purpose. In the same way that people nowadays sample their records, I used to steal, very obviously, so that people would say, "Oh yeah, he's with it! What a good sample! He knows a good record when he hears one." '

'So It Goes', with its fast shuffle rhythm and conversational vocal was, Lowe admits, a musical hybrid of Steely Dan's 'Reeling In The Years' and Thin Lizzy's 'The Boys Are Back In Town', rescued, in the interests of modernity, by a Shadows-style instrumental break. Clocking in at two minutes and 28 seconds, its lyrics were sharp, wise and world-weary, as if Lowe was unloading a decade's worth of pop baggage.

> Security's so tight tonight, oh they're ready for a tussle,
> Better keep your backstage passes, cos the promoter hired the
>   muscle . . .
> In the tall building sit the head of all nations, worthy men
>   from Spain and Siam,
> All day discussions with the Russians, but they still went
>   ahead and vetoed the plan . . .

'Heart Of The City' was a much faster item, as if influenced by the Feelgoods, or the recently released debut LP from the Ramones. It also contained echoes of Jonathan Richman's

'Roadrunner' and, in the fade-out, the 101ers' 'Keys To Your Heart'. It was, in other words, a musical summary of the most recent and exciting developments in pop.

Promotion of Lowe's single relied on word of mouth, music press editorial coverage and a lone advertisement in *Zigzag*, copywritten by Riviera:

> Sometimes in life you've got to make a decision . . . this is Nick Lowe. He is a pop musician. Alone is his the privilege of having the first release on Stiff. A 45rpm recording. Titles are 'So It Goes' b/w 'Heart Of The City'. They're really nifty . . . copies available direct from 32 Alexandra Street, London W2 . . . only 65p inc P&P or from hip record shops . . . this offer is not open to medallion purchasers or men who wear make-up . . .
>
> This fabulous limited edition medallion struck in finest re-cycled vinyl and plated in Rio . . . is available to progressive music fans who have the complete works of ELP, Yes & Genesis etc. Just send in all the sleeve artwork (not your precious records) together with a cheque/P.O. for only £99.99 to Stiff Records . . . If you wanna rock . . . we've got Stiffs in stock.

In *Sounds*, 'Heart Of The City' was made *Star Single and B-side to boot*, with the added comment: *It's an A-1 smash . . . the energy is fantastic*. In the same issue of *Sounds*, Chas de Whalley interviewed Riviera under the headline: 'Stiff: a label for hard-up heroes'. 'The policy will be very simple indeed,' said Riviera, capturing the mood of the moment. 'Basically speaking we want to put out singles that are two and a half minutes long and have got two and a half chords in them.'

'Are obsolete bar bands really commercial enough to launch Stiff as a successful record label?' asked de Whalley. 'There's a much larger market there than you might think,' retorted Riviera, who was also hopeful of licensing the *Modern Lovers* album from Beserkeley, for release on Stiff.

Stiff's style found favour with music journalists and musicians alike. Ian Dury says, 'At Stiff you had your Barney Bubbles; you had Jake and Nick; you had such a load of talent there. Speaking as someone who's spent half his life at art colleges, Barney was easily the most incredible designer I'd ever come across. His vision was fantastic. It really did impress me. He scared the shit out of me. He was righteous. He didn't have the faults, or the ego and he made me feel second class. I wanted his approval in a strange kind of way. I wanted the acceptance.'

The first musician to knock on Stiff's door was former Flip City front man, Declan MacManus, aka D.P. Costello. Two songs from his demo tape – 'Lip Service' and 'Wave A White Flag' – had been aired on Charlie Gillett's *Honky Tonk* radio show on 15 August.

Costello, who was now solo and seeking a recording contract, recalls:

I read about the formation of Stiff and the release of 'So It Goes' in *Melody Maker*. I was working in North Acton as a computer programmer and at that time anyone who wore a white coat and worked with computers was regarded as a scientist or a genius or something. They left me alone, so I had plenty of time to read the paper all day, or write songs. I took the next afternoon off and went to Stiff. I expected to find what I knew to be a record company. A Bohemian girl opened the door, who was Suzanne Spiro. She was terribly nice and said, 'Oh, there's nobody in.' She was sort of shocked. They'd only been open for business a couple of days.

Costello purchased a copy of 'So It Goes', left his demo tape with Spiro and made his way home via Westbourne Grove tube station, where he encountered Nick Lowe. 'It sounds like the most romantic coincidence of all,' says Costello, 'but as I was going down the stairs, Nick was coming up and I said to him, "Here's your new record . . ." He asked me whether I was still with Flip City. I had my guitar over my shoulder, because I'd been prepared to do an audition at Stiff there and then.'

Although Costello had left his tape at Stiff, this was not his normal practice. When visiting record companies, he would always insist on a live audition with acoustic guitar, which would often intimidate A&R men, due to the power of his voice. Costello had also tried forming a new group with former Chilli Willi bass player, Paul Riley. 'Paul found some of my songs a bit complex,' says Costello. Riley remembers, 'Costello had been round to my house, but he had the unfortunate disadvantage of wearing horn-rimmed glasses and being extremely intense and I'd just had three or four months with somebody else like that,' referring to Roogalator's Danny Adler.

On 21 August 1976, a number of Stiff acts were booked to play at the Mont de Marsan Festival, organised by Mark Zermatti and Larry Dubais, of the French label Skydog. The event was billed as the 'First European Punk Rock Festival', although this was still in the early days of the punk upsurge and the genre had not yet been clearly defined. In the eyes of Skydog, Punk Rock could encompass Street Rock, in the form of the Hammersmith Gorillas and the Count Bishops; New Wave, represented by Nick Lowe and Roogalator; relatively pure punk in the form of The Damned; and, of course, Eddie And The Hot Rods.

The Damned had formed earlier that year and their guitarist, Brian James, had always kept abreast of the latest developments on the music scene. Rat Scabies, their drummer, recalls:

Brian had heard about Jake and Stiff Records. Brian was very up on all those independent labels. He was a sort of obscurist music fan and into that *Record Collector* thing. He kept an eye on it. Today, anybody can buy an MC5 album in HMV, but you couldn't then. Soon we were all checking out the American labels like Ork with 'Little Johnny Jewel' by Television.

Larry Dubais used to run a record shop called Bizarre in Praed Street. The Damned's geographical connection was that the dole office in Lisson Grove was around the corner. We'd go and pick up our giro and then go round to the record store and rummage through and then go to the pub and have a sausage, which was the start to our weekend. I blagged the Mont de Marsan gig through Larry. We'd only done about two gigs, but the Sex Pistols were gigging by now and we'd done the 100 Club and things were starting to look a bit lively.

When it came to doing the Mont de Marsan thing, we travelled in a St Trinians school bus that Jake had hired from somewhere. We were quite appalled by our fellow travellers. I was expecting it to be punk, but there was nobody under 35 except for us. I was quite interested to see who these people like Roogalator were and we met Sean Tyla and Larry Wallis. Nick Lowe was wearing an Eddie Cochran T-shirt and doing an interview with Caroline Coon. He was waxing lyrical about rock and roll, referring to himself, as in: 'That's the rock and roll life for you.' I remember listening to his interview and I just thought, 'This bloke has lost the plot.' So I ripped up his Eddie Cochran T-shirt.

We all met at Victoria Coach Station. Jake came up to us and said, 'Right, you're The Damned, get on the bus.' He knew who we were and we were quite impressed by that. He had the suss. That was the first meeting. The festival was a complete farce and Jake ended up taking it over. Larry Dubais was just sitting there in tears, a broken man.

Chiswick's Ted Carroll remembers, 'We closed the Soho stall and drove towards Dover. At Streatham, Roger realised he'd forgotten his passport so we drove back to Camden, did some whizz and made for the channel ports. We drove through the night and arrived in Mont de Marsan at 3 p.m. Mark Zermatti was being carried out comatose. Nothing was happening on stage, so Jake was hi-jacking the gig and running around looking for the first complete group he could find to get them on stage. I thought it was a bit too early for the Gorillas to go on, so I told Jesse Hector to get lost. He hid out in a nearby church.'

Rat Scabies recalls, 'We did the first set and Jake came up and asked us if we wanted to make a record for Stiff, with Nick producing. We liked the idea of Stiff because it was an independent. We felt that signing to a major wasn't very punk. Also, Jake knew who the MC5 were. You could talk to him about music. He was a bit older and a hustler and he knew his way around. He also had a good pedigree from working with the Feelgoods, who were a cool band.'

These were the vital factors in The Damned's decision to sign with Stiff, as opposed to, say, Chiswick. 'When it came down to it, Chiswick was a retro 50s kind of outfit,' says Scabies. 'What they were doing was cool, but it wasn't nearly as exciting as what Stiff were doing. Stiff were the darlings of the media and they became the darlings of the industry. There was a much better vibe.'

'The Damned supporting S.A.L.T. at the Nashville was the classic punk gig,' says Chiswick's Roger Armstrong. 'The Damned wouldn't get off, so they closed the curtains. The next thing was, a bass drum came flying through the curtains and landed on a table where these four long-haired guys were sitting, sending their drinks flying. The guys were outraged. Chiswick paid for The Damned's first demos, but Jake dived in and nicked them from under our noses.'

In September, The Damned signed with Stiff and went into Pathway Studios with Nick Lowe to record their debut single, 'New Rose'. 'I had no idea what a producer was supposed to do,' says Rat Scabies. 'I just remember going into the control booth and being totally astounded by the sound. Nick was the producer because he was Jake's mate. If Jake thought he was OK, that was OK. Jake could control us. There was a bit of a dad element to it. We were all quite young and Jake took care of things. But he could also be as badly behaved as us.'

'Nick Lowe was the house producer really,' says Glen Colson. 'Jake loved Nick because he adored Brinsley Schwarz, and he would have done anything for Nick. In those days, Nick was more of a friend of Jake's who was gonna do the producing. His solo career was on the back burner. He made The Damned into magic. Anything that he touched turned to gold, not in sales terms, but in magic terms. He'd walk in and, if there were no lyrics, he'd make it happen in five minutes. He'd go in the toilet and come out with lyrics. Nick was the man who was gonna do it.'

The Damned's 'New Rose' holds the distinction of being the first British Punk Rock single, released three weeks ahead of

'Anarchy In The UK' by the Sex Pistols. 'Stiff put the single out,' says Scabies, 'and there was a bigger response than they could handle, so they gave it to Andrew Lauder at United Artists to distribute. Jake made us ring the office every day to see what was going on. Suzanne Spiro told us we'd gone into the charts at 65 or something. I was amazed.'

Before long, a Damned LP was called for, again to be produced by Lowe. In addition to the slogan 'Made To Be Played Loud At Low Volume', initial pressings featured a photograph of arch rivals, Eddie And The Hot Rods, on the back of the sleeve, with a sticker saying:

Erratum. Due to Record Company error, a picture of Island Recording Artists Eddie & The Hot Rods has been printed instead of the Damned. We apologise for any inconvenience caused and the correct picture will be substituted on future copies.

Rat Scabies says, 'Of course it was a stunt, although it was described at the time as a printer's error. But it's safe to blow it now. Jake had worked out how many LPs we needed to sell to recoup the recording costs. That was the quantity that was pressed with the Hot Rods picture on the back. About two or three thousand only. Jake knew that it would appeal to the collector's market. He was totally hip to all that. The marketing was brilliant.

'I'd go for a walk round the block with Jake and he'd say, "We need some new badges Ratty. What's a good slogan?" We'd have a beer and a chat and it wouldn't take much to trigger his imagination. The next day it would be everywhere. It was all done on the nod. "When You Kill Time You Murder Success" and "In 78 Those Born In 45 Will Be 33" were two of the slogans. Jake had that evil sense of humour, he was great fun and that's why you'd always sign with him over other labels that were around.'

Meanwhile, down at the Hope & Anchor, things were looking rather grim for landlord Fred Grainger. 'I owed Watneys three grand and they'd given me 48 hours to pay it,' says Grainger.

'I needed to put on some benefit shows. I asked Watneys to give me an extension to 72 hours and I phoned up Dave Robinson, hoping he could put a rescue package together. Dave phoned Nicky Horne at Capital Radio and Nicky announced the Save the Hope campaign over the air. Dave Robinson pulled most of it together.'

'Over three nights, we had Graham Parker And The Rumour, Nick Lowe with Dave Edmunds, Ian Dury and Dr Feelgood. On the Tuesday morning I was £150 short of the three grand. I rang up John Curd of Straight Music and asked for a loan. Although he had a reputation of being a real mean bastard, he loaned me the money. He put the cash in a taxi. He got his money back.'

On 24 September 1976, Dr Feelgood released *Stupidity*, a live LP that captured the animalism of the group in its natural environment. 'At the time our record company wasn't crazy about the idea of a live album,' says singer Lee Brilleaux. 'We'd had *Down By The Jetty*, which was kind of naïve, but had its own charm, then *Malpractice*, which was more of the same but slightly more sophisticated. What the record company would have really liked was *the* Feelgood studio album that would have helped us make the crossover into becoming a 70s rock band for the American market. The problem was, I don't think Wilko had a lot of new material up his sleeve.'

'We were booked to do our third album as soon as we got home from an American tour,' says Wilko Johnson. 'I'd got nothing, only a few ideas. Half a song here, half a song there. It was freaking me out and I was pretty bothered. We started trying to rehearse new stuff at Feelgood House but it wasn't happening. Someone suggested putting out a live album and I thought, "Of course, that's what everybody wants." It was exactly what we should have done at that point.'

'For once we were right,' says Lee Brilleaux. 'I think we had a better gut instinct about this than the record company. The title *Stupidity* could have been taken as ironic, but it was simply the title of one of the songs on the album. Many of the songs on *Stupidity* go right back to the beginning of the group. "Talking About You" and "I'm Checking Up On My Baby" were there from the start. We were also very big Coasters fans. We used to sit round Wilko's house listening to their stuff and "I'm A Hog For You Baby" and "Riot In Cell Block No. 9" lent themselves to our style and the group managed to stamp its own personality on these songs.'

A full-page advertisement for *Stupidity* in *New Musical Express* announced: 'Free collectors single with first 20,000 copies only', but the marketing stunt was hardly necessary. Dr Feelgood's fan base was now massive. Although many of these fans would switch allegiance, within the next six months, to the Sex Pistols and The Clash, they were, for the moment, completely hooked on the excitement of a Dr Feelgood show. *Stupidity* was the perfect memento for every member of this enormous teenage army who wanted a piece of the action for the home stereo. Within two weeks, *Stupidity* hit number one on the UK album chart.

'Looking at it,' says Lee Brilleaux, '*Stupidity* records our rise to fame from the pubs to the concert halls and I suppose the reason why it was a successful album was because people used to say that the Feelgoods were a great live band but there may have been something lacking on their records. *Stupidity* epitomises the whole thing and I think it goes beyond music. This was the culmination of the revolution against the stack-heel and platform-shoe brigade and everything that went with that. We said, "Bollocks to all that." This is how a live band really goes to work.'

As *Stupidity* nestled at the coveted number one spot, Dr Feelgood were in turmoil. Playing to a packed house at Hammersmith Odeon on 1 October, the group's set was dramatically interrupted by Wilko Johnson's sudden exit from the stage. 'I was in a bit of a state and four or five numbers in, everything went "Bang!",' says Johnson. 'In my mind, everything was swirling and echoing. I thought I'd try to get to the end of the number, and then I'd have to walk off. I don't know if Lee had realised there was something wrong with me. I walked off and I was upstairs in the dressing room and I thought my brain had melted. Everyone was standing round me saying, "They're shouting for you down there. Can you go back on?" I said, "You're the one with the brain. You tell me." '

Meanwhile, on stage, Brilleaux and the rhythm section were holding the fort with an improvised 'train blues'. Several minutes later, Johnson returned. 'I went back on and I think we did "Riot In Cell Block No. 9" . . . "Boom!" It went again. After the last number I keeled over. I'd been overdoing things. I felt ashamed about that. You're supposed to be professional. You're not supposed to do stuff like that. People had paid money to see us.'

'At Hammersmith, Wilko was too out of it on speed,' says the Big Figure. 'It was obvious that Wilko wasn't going to come back on at that point, so Lee called a halt to the proceedings. We went up to the dressing room and Wilko was flaked out with St John's Ambulance men all over him, saying his pulse was 170 and asking him, "What have you been doing?" At this, Wilko suddenly said, "Oh, I feel all right now . . ." and went back on. The next big headline in the music press was, "Doctor, heal thyself." '

The incident jeopardised Wilko Johnson's position in Dr Feelgood and it hardened manager Chris Fenwick's attitude. 'From a manager's point of view, I suppose it's one of your worst nightmares. An auditorium full of 3,000 people and your artist, for some reason, cannot fulfil the show. Having started it, he can't finish it. It's not really on. Obviously one is a bit nervous about doing it all again. Since that incident, I won't tolerate any troublemaker who is going to jeopardise the show. The show must have a beginning, a middle and an end. And if the aircraft is snowed in, you put your bloody skis on and get going.'

From the audience's perspective, the on-stage tension between Wilko Johnson and Lee Brilleaux added to the drama, although Johnson's days with the Feelgoods were numbered. 'It was between me and Lee really,' says Johnson. 'That was the focus. Sometimes there could be a heavy atmosphere before the gig, but when we walked on stage, a different feeling took over. Lee was so great to work with, all that anger. We had no doubts once we were on stage. I can remember once there was a row and we went on and did a really good gig. Some people said, "You two wind each other up before a show, don't you?" But it wasn't like that. We didn't.'

The Feelgoods succeeded because of their incredible live show, their radical appearance and, most importantly, the fact that they stuck to their R&B guns. While many of the Pub Rock groups offered an extremely diverse repertoire, with the Feelgoods it was black and white and you either liked R&B or you didn't. 'There were no musical differences in Dr Feelgood,' says Wilko Johnson. 'It was beat music, R&B. Whatever songs I came up with, they were always in that style. It was absolutely unambiguous and so simple you'd have to be pretty miserable to dislike it.'

Pub Rock had reached its commercial zenith. Apart from a few isolated hit singles by Ace ('How Long'), the Kursaal Flyers ('Little Does She Know') and Eddie And The Hot Rods ('Teenage Depression', 'Do Anything You Wanna Do'), the Feelgoods were the genre's sole commercial manifestation. Well accustomed to having their mugs splashed across the front of the nation's rock weeklies, Dr Feelgood had now crossed over into the commercial mainstream, while crucially priming a huge audience for the imminent punk uprising.

But Dr Feelgood may never have been given the opportunity to flex their influential muscle if it hadn't been for the groundbreaking work of the early Pub Rock pioneers. 'We'd have remained a local band,' says Wilko Johnson when asked to speculate on the Feelgoods' fate if the pub circuit hadn't existed. 'It would have lasted a year or two and then everyone would have gone off and got married!'

Dr Feelgood certainly enjoyed their moment of triumph, and would weather the Punk Rock storm better than most, but this was the fast-moving world of pop and as the orange squash and amaretto flowed at Feelgood House, a same-but-different kind of racket was biting at their heels. Dr Feelgood had become Pub Rock's most famous practitioners, but Pub Rock was about to be rendered obsolete overnight by the brat it undoubtedly spawned.

'Our energy was our legacy to the punks,' reflects Wilko Johnson. 'It was the violence of our act and the mean look that got to them. They didn't have the knowledge or the technique, but they had the attitude. They didn't have the background to come out and play R&B, but it was the same three chords.'

In October 1976, D.P. Costello received a telephone call from Stiff, who had, by now, listened to his demo tape of 'Mystery Dance'.

'I went to Stiff and met Jake Riviera for the first time,' says Costello. 'Jake was obviously very dynamic. He had a different style to everybody else in that he didn't look like he'd ever been a hippie, which wasn't actually true. I know there's photographic evidence of him with long hair, but because he had the winkle pickers on, he had a sharp operator look, with short hair and a 50s style jacket.'

After years of hustling his music, D.P. Costello had finally walked into a completely sympathetic environment. Within a short time, Costello was remodelled by Riviera to comply with the fashion dictates of the oncoming New Wave revolution. His open-neck shirt and denim jeans were supplemented by a skinny tie and a tight-fitting, narrow-lapel jacket. Into the dumper went his spectacles, to be replaced by larger, Buddy Holly-style, horn-rims. Out too went the 'D.P.' handle; Declan MacManus was now 'Elvis Costello', with the accompanying slogan: 'Four Eyes, One Vision'.

Brandishing his Fender Jazzmaster guitar, Elvis Costello did not look dissimilar to Roogalator's Danny Adler. 'It was very easy for me to adopt a new name and limit my range of expressions down to a few,' says Costello. 'Once I had people's attention, then I could diversify.'

Costello was still holding down his day job, working as a computer programmer for cosmetics giant, Elizabeth Arden, but was now taking more and more time off work to concentrate on music. Soon, he was sent to Headley Grange, once the home of Led Zeppelin and, more recently, Help Yourself, to rehearse with Clover, who had recently been brought to the UK by Robinson and Riviera.

Earlier in the decade, Clover had been a major influence on Brinsley Schwarz and now the debt was being repaid, but despite landing a new recording contract with Phonogram, Clover had come to England at the worst possible time. Their brand of countrified rhythm and blues would be an early casualty of the changing musical climate. Instead, Clover could earn their keep by clandestinely accompanying Elvis Costello, uncredited of course.

Costello and Clover soon entered Pathway Studio, with Nick Lowe producing and gradually pieced together an LP. In March 1977, Costello's debut single, 'Less Than Zero' c/w 'Radio Sweetheart', was released. Glen Colson was hired by Riviera to work on the press. 'I'd already done a bit of Damned stuff and organised the press for their gig at CBGBs. I bought them a cake and the *New York Times* said, "Mr Scabies behaved appallingly, throwing cakes into the audience." I think that was the only good review they got.'

Colson continues, 'I presented myself at the office and Jake gave me £50 a week to do the PR for everybody on the label. Jake always had good faith in me but Dave Robinson said, "No, don't employ him. He's a lazy bastard; all he likes is cricket." Jake said, "Bollocks," and played me "Less Than Zero". I said, "It must be Nick Lowe, trying to sound like someone else." I didn't believe they'd found someone who could be that good. I said to Jake, "Elvis Costello? You're winding me up. Only Nick could make music like that."'

Others quickly compared Elvis Costello to Graham Parker. 'It's obvious we both liked Van Morrison,' says Costello. 'I never thought any more of it, but we always seemed to get lumped together. He wore shades; I wore glasses. I've always thought the comparison did neither of us very much use. Graham wrote some terrific songs, but I don't think he got full credit.'

Graham Parker says, 'At the time I felt that I'd made it, but I kept being reminded that there was this other guy that was the same. He started selling more records than me and, when he did something, it made major press. I'd first seen Elvis in 1975, with Flip City, but he didn't have my aggression or energy. Now he was on stage giving it stick. Knees bent and screaming. That was probably my contribution – balls to the wall.'

Stiff was the kind of the label where the tea boy, if he had enough front, could work his way up the ladder. One such individual was Kosmo Vinyl, who went from part-time roadie to press officer and personal assistant to Ian Dury within 12 months. Vinyl recalls:

I got involved with Stiff through going to Graham Parker shows. You know how it is, you get there early and help out the roadies. I persuaded a mate of mine to come and see GP play a club in Paris. It was a fancy joint and the people weren't into it. The DJ put a record on before Graham had a chance to play an encore, so I jumped up and grabbed the record and pulled the arm off the turntable. There was a lot of shouting and shoving. Nick Lowe was there and witnessed me in action. I think it put me on the map a little bit.

Through that I graduated to knowing people and I pestered Dave Robinson for a job, although I didn't know what the jobs were. I was a fan. Tons of times I'd go all the way from Manor Park to Alexandra Street and Dave would say, 'Come back in a couple of days.' Dave would be on the phone to America. Can you imagine! 'He's on the phone to America!' But there wasn't a lot of bread about. Dave was sleeping in the office, under a desk.'

I think it was my persistence that got me the roadie job. Graham had this sound engineer named Mick and he took me under his wing. I ended up doing whatever needed doing. The first thing I had to do at Stiff was fix a door; then Dave and Jake had me fly-posting. You'd just turn up and be told what to do. It evolved. My big mouth put me in a certain direction. Jake used to get pissed off because I'd yell so much when Elvis Costello played the Nashville and it was being recorded. I used to shout, 'Get into it!'

I was around when Elvis was auditioning musicians. Terry Razor and I went and picked Steve Naïve up from his parents' house. We had to wait while Steve finished mowing the lawn. But I wasn't cut out to be a roadie really. I'm not very practical. Graham Parker was going to America and his tour manager, Rayner Jesson, told me

I wasn't going. He said, 'We're not taking that loud-mouthed lunatic kid to America just to have some fun.' I had the right hump. So I said, 'That's it. I only want to work with Ian Dury.' I liked Ian in the Kilburns and now he'd made the 'Sex and Drugs' single. I didn't know Ian at all. I remember seeing him outside the Victoria Palace at a GP gig and I said, 'Wotcha Ian' and he said, 'Fuck off!' He had the vibe.

Eventually, Kosmo Vinyl's talents were recognised by Stiff press officer, Glen Colson. 'I took Kosmo on,' recalls Colson. 'When he was told he wouldn't be going to America with Parker, I cheered him up. Within a month he was running my company. I would come in at midday with a hangover and Kosmo would be answering the phones and dishing out the records. I told him I didn't have the energy to go down to the music papers any more. I was an old man. Kosmo said, "You leave it to me!" He went into Sounds with a chain saw and cut one of the desks in half. To make them listen. He was fearless.'

'Everybody's drink was cider,' says Glen Colson. 'Jake would throw bottles through the window and I think he sent Suzanne and Cynthia and Melanie mad. They were his workers. He drove them to an early grave. He was a man possessed, just like Hitler. It was the Fourth Reich. I'm deadly serious. Everybody lived in fear. I've seen people on cocaine binges, I've seen it all, but I'd never met anybody like Jake. He was so hot, you didn't wanna touch him. He was a burning bush.

'The magic that was flowing in that first year would have made anyone famous. If you'd have walked in that office, a sleeve would have been done for you by Barney Bubbles, Nick would have produced you and Jake would have come up with ideas. You could have been anybody, as long as you were a crackpot, and had a bit of a vibe.'

Among the crackpots who walked into Stiff during the label's early months were former Hot Rod, Lew Lewis, music hall veteran Max Wall, and Eric Goulden, quickly to be rebranded 'Wreckless Eric'. Goulden, a former art student, had at least one extremely catchy song, 'Go The Whole Wide World'.

Eric Goulden says, 'When I went to Stiff, I was trying to get anything together. I basically wanted to front a pop group, but I had a massive drink problem. It happened quickly and it took me by surprise. I got a few things going that were good, but I was severely underdeveloped as an artist. Nowadays you don't go looking for a record deal unless you've got your shit together, but back then things were more lackadaisical.'

Nick Lowe recalls, 'We used to hang out at Stiff, sleeving records and drinking cider. We'd seen this guy, who looked like one of us, walking up and down outside the window. He would disappear for a while, apparently to the pub to fortify himself and then walk up and down a bit more. Finally, he opened the door and said, "Is this where any old arsehole can bring a record in and see if you wanna sign him?" He quickly handed over his tape and left immediately. He was dressed very eccentrically and righteously pissed. His tape was good. I said to Jake, "Look, I think we ought to take a listen to this bloke." '

Goulden was sent to Pathway Studio to record under the auspices of Nick Lowe and the resulting single, 'Go The Whole Wide World', sounded like a chart-bound sound, but Stiff did not yet have the distribution infrastructure in place.

'We're a record label, not a museum,' Riviera told the press, after ruthlessly deleting the first 10 Stiff singles. Collectors, who had been growing in number since Stiff revived the 45 picture bag, panicked. There was suddenly an enormous demand for all things Stiff. 'Deleting the early singles was not so much a trick as a ruthless business decision,' says Rat Scabies. 'Jake said, "It's done. We're not going to make any more money on it. Let's get some shelf space." '

'Nick got really bollocked by Jake once,' continues Scabies. 'Suzanne Spiro went out for lunch and Nick was left in the office holding the fort. A Dutch distributor phoned because he'd heard that Stiff was deleting some stock. He wanted 1,800 Nick Lowe singles. Nick, thinking he was helping out, said, "Yes, I think we've just about got that many," because he knew he'd seen a shelf full. Nick sold them to the Dutch distributor there and then. Of course, he had overlooked the fact that Jake had planned to put half of them under the bed until their rarity value grew. Nick was pleased with himself. It was quite touching. Then he got the bollocking.'

Jake and Dave were a good double act for a while [says Elvis Costello]. They could play good cop/bad cop with promoters and distributors. Even when they were caught blatantly in the wrong over something, they were so righteous, you couldn't argue with them. They had several different things on the go. Graham Parker And The Rumour and later, Rockpile, with the two main members signed to different labels so they could never record. There was a lot of cause for angst. I was often there when there was serious screaming and shouting going on, which of course soon went on in support of my career.

Jake would shout at various people on the phone. Swansong and people like that. It was a very quick education as to how the business could work as opposed to the more ordered and rather smug way that I'd previously encountered. It was very thrilling to go in there, with bottles of cider sailing through the front door at moments of exasperation. That's my favourite memory, during a heated moment of negotiation with Swansong. I don't think Jake ever felt intimidated by anybody and if he did, there was a tremendous amount of bravado going on. They were making it up as they were going along, I'm sure.

The other side of it was a communal feeling. How real it was, I don't know, but people felt very pleased to be in this club and it was a safe haven for people as wide ranging as Wreckless Eric and Larry Wallis, Richard Hell and Max Wall. There was a strange generosity to it, like, 'We know what's good and what's right.' The most brilliant thing that Stiff ever did was on the compilation *Hits Greatest Stiffs*. The inner bag showed pictures of other labels' artists' records, like Tom Petty, Abba et cetera. Other people couldn't believe they were doing it

and they rang up and said, 'What the fuck is going on?'
There was no slight. It was just, 'These are good records.
We dig 'em.' There's something so righteous about that,
what can you say?

Stiff's reputation within the record industry was growing,
although Riviera and Robinson were gambling recklessly with
Stiff's precarious finances. To promote Elvis Costello's debut
LP, *My Aim Is True*, Stiff took the unprecedented step of
booking a series of double-page ads in the music press. Dave
Robinson says:

Jake and I realised that we had to attract attention to
what was good. Barney Bubbles wanted to do big posters
and came up with some incredible silk screen designs
and the idea of the 60 × 40 poster. The size was the
thing. Nobody had done it before. At first, even I thought
they were too big. Where were the poster sites that
would take them and who would put them up?'
Barney's first 60 × 40 posters were of Nick Lowe, Larry
Wallis and Elvis Costello. As soon as we saw them, they
had to go up. Other record companies noticed them. We
then found out that the marketing departments of some
of the big labels were getting calls from their artists
saying, 'Who the hell is this Stiff Records? Why can't we
have big posters like that? Why can't we have our singles
in picture bags?' We had changed things. Today big
posters are the norm.

Stiff's promotional stunts and marketing flair forced the
major labels to take stock of their own methods and rethink
the way in which they would launch their own new acts. Stiff
was now watched by marketing executives and label managers
throughout the record industry, some of whom successfully
absorbed the Stiff influence, while others lamely imitated it.
This tickled Robinson and Riviera no end. They knew they
were the hippest cats on the block, but, despite their bravura,
a rumble in the alley was not far away.

18. PURE POP FOR NOW PEOPLE

By the summer of 1977, Stiff Records was considered by many to be the most happening record label on the planet. Actual hits were elusive, but in terms of press coverage and kudos the results were impressive. Since its inception the previous year, the development of Stiff had run parallel to the Punk phenomenon, although Stiff had superior commercial potential, offering a tuneful alternative for the more squeamish fan.

Label bosses Jake Riviera and Dave Robinson had arrived at this point after years of dues-paying on the Pub Rock scene. They were now threatening to become the record industry's worst nightmare – an independent label with the determination to bring about change. Riviera was the creative firebrand, who could summon up a snappy slogan at the drop of a cider bottle. Robinson was more of a nuts-and-bolts man, but he could close a deal in the wink of an eye. Both men were driven, but Riviera was totally manic in his pursuit of pop success. Working close to the flame were the Stiff artists. From Max Wall to The Damned, they were all fascinating characters, emerging from a virtual Ellisdon's of wacky ephemera and instant collectibles. Some were handicapped by punter-alienating quirks and general weirdness, but their music was wonderful – Nick Lowe's 'So It Goes', Elvis Costello's 'Less Than Zero', Wreckless Eric's 'Go The Whole Wide World', Ian Dury's 'Sex And Drugs And Rock 'n' Roll' – life-enhancing 45s that had been eagerly snapped up by the pop cognoscenti. Now it was time to take it to the people.

In early September the pre-tour publicity for 'Stiff's Greatest Stiffs Live' hit the front pages. 'Five Stiff acts – Elvis Costello, Nick Lowe, Ian Dury, Wreckless Eric and Larry Wallis – in 24 UK concerts, commencing 3 October . . . Each act will play a 30 minute set, with the running order changing nightly . . . A barrage of new releases, including 'Watching The Detectives', *New Boots And Panties* and *Wireless World*, the debut LP from Lowe . . . A live album of the tour will be recorded on the opening night at High Wycombe and appear in the shops four days later!'

The music formerly known as Pub Rock was about to re-emerge as New Wave.

Riviera and Robinson had envisaged a package tour reminiscent of the mid-60s Stax-Volt revue. It would be fast-moving, with short sets and shared equipment for rapid changeovers, all held together by a brace of lunatic comperes. In many ways, 1975's Naughty Rhythms Tour, also masterminded by Riviera, was the blueprint, but now the stakes were higher. In an all-Stiff show, each recording artist would be vying for his label's attention, as well as the public's. Thus, there was the likelihood of some seriously competitive stagecraft, upping the ante at every turn. And, as Riviera had discovered in 1975, there would be winners and losers.

I love my label, I love my label yeah,
And my label has high hopes in me . . .

Rehearsals took place at Manticore Studios in Fulham, where the concept of a revolving bill started to look somewhat idealistic. Wreckless Eric was undoubtedly a talented artist whose songs would one day be covered by artists ranging from Cliff Richard to Mental As Anything, but his choice of musical accompaniment was quite bizarre. His 'New Rockets' included the closerthanthis rhythm section of Ian Dury (minimal drum kit) and Denise Roudette (rudimentary bass), with Davey Payne on free-form saxophone. Eric, proudly proclaiming, 'I never play anything less than a full chord', would handle guitar duties and occupy centre stage. It was to be a lonely place for one so ill-equipped.

Larry Wallis, suffering from a shortage of songs and an inferiority complex, would fare little better. His solo repertoire was limited to the A and B sides of his lone Stiff single: 'Police Car' c/w 'On Parole'. The former 'Pink Fairy' did, however, surround himself with some musical muscle in the many shapes of Nick Lowe's Last Chicken In The Shop, the group's name for the night. Eric and Larry were no match for Elvis

Costello And The Attractions. With a mere ten weeks on the clock, The Attractions were already a lethal live force. 'We'd been once round the club circuit and we were ready to kill,' says Costello. But Dury, who had formerly been dependent on the erratic musicianship of Kilburn And The High Roads, was now older, wiser and secure in the knowledge that every night he could rely on the awesome firepower of The Blockheads.

But first, before battle could commence, there was to be one headline-grabbing incident. On Saturday, 24 September, a mere nine days before the opening show, Riviera and Robinson had a major disagreement. That afternoon, label manager Paul Conroy turned up at the Stiff HQ to find the pavement outside littered with broken glass and empty cider bottles. These had been thrown through the window by Riviera during the blazing row. The confines of Stiff were simply too cramped to accommodate the overwhelming personalities of Dave Robinson and Jake Riviera.

'Stiff's Riviera In Mystery Split' announced the *Melody Maker*, but this was no publicity stunt. A settlement was hammered out. Riviera would leave Stiff and take Lowe and Costello to a new label. Robinson, who also managed Vertigo recording artist Graham Parker, would continue with what remained of Stiff. This was an extraordinary development on the eve of what promised to be an eventful tour.

At 4 p.m. on Monday, 3 October, coach driver Trevor Wiffen parked his K reg 42-seater outside the Stiff HQ in Alexandra Street W2 to collect the motley entourage. The 18 musicians, accompanied by masters of ceremony Kosmo Vinyl and Les Prior, tour manager Dez Brown and assorted Stiff personnel, all clambered on board. The mood was upbeat as the coach crawled towards the A40, destination High Wycombe.

Two hours later a second coach departed from Alexandra Street, packed with journalists. 'It was my job to ensure that the tour got plenty of oomph on the first date,' recalls Glen Colson. 'It was massively important to get everyone grooving, because it would help to sell out the rest of the tour.' On arriving at High Wycombe Town Hall in a torrential downpour, the journalists, all wearing 'I'm Ligging With Advance-dale' stickers, marched to the front of the queue, where they were greeted by promoter Ron Watts. 'You're not bringing that lot in,' roared Watts, 'they'll all have to pay.' Riviera was furious and ordered Colson to resolve the issue promptly. 'Jake always liked a guest list,' remembers Paul Conroy, 'but for Ron, who had been doing the local Nag's Head for years, the Town Hall was the big one.'

Later that evening, a flurry of roadies were still fussing around on stage at showtime as Les Prior was sent out to keep the audience entertained. Prior, a member of the satirical group Alberto y Lost Trios Paranoias, delivered an impromptu monologue until he was given the signal to announce Nick Lowe, who appeared to be wearing a fluorescent green suit decorated with question marks.

Toting a somewhat anachronistic twin-necked guitar, Lowe launched into 'Shake And Pop', followed swiftly by the cynical 'Music For Money'. 'It was more important to have something that looked strange,' says Nick Lowe. 'I thought that if I had a weird-looking group it might get me through.' Lowe's backing group consisted of the bushy-haired Larry Wallis and the close-cropped Pete Thomas (a drummer by trade) on guitars; Terry Williams and Dave Edmunds (the well-known guitarist) banging away on drums as if they were building a shed, plus keyboard player Penny Tobin, who had been selected by Lowe to provide the tour with the much-needed 'Cherry Wainer vibe'.

Next up was Costello, looking uncomfortable in a shiny black bomber jacket. Intent on making a name for himself and prepared to take the necessary risks, Costello disappointed large sections of the audience by refusing to play material from his recently released debut, *My Aim Is True*. As Elvis rode on defiantly, matters were made worse by Ian Dury's publicist B P Fallon. 'I'd made these badges – a series of four,' says Fallon. 'One said "Sex", the next one said "Drugs &", et cetera.'

With complete disregard for Costello, who was halfway through his set, Fallon threw hundreds of the badges into the crowd like 'heavy confetti'. 'The punters started scrambling around everywhere trying to complete the set,' adds Fallon. 'Jake wasn't mad for it.'

After Wreckless Eric's brief set, Ian Dury took the stage. 'Oi Oi!' croaked Dury, cautiously. '*Oi Oi!*' The crowd responded as one. '*Oi Oi!*' This was the turning point. After years slogging away on the pub circuit, Dury's day had finally come. 'It was one of the greatest things I'd ever seen,' says Kozmo Vinyl. 'Dury just slayed 'em. Wallop! The Blockheads were a complete revelation, especially Charley Charles, and this was an amazing tour for drummers. Terry Williams, Pete Thomas . . . Ian Dury. Something for everybody! But Charley, everybody was like . . . Jesus Christ! And Ian couldn't put a foot wrong. It all happened at High Wycombe.'

Later that evening, the coach took the musicians to a motel outside Oxford, where they would spend the night before the onward journey to Wales. 'It was in the middle of nowhere,' recalls Vinyl, 'and there was no bar!' There was a certain amount of dissent about this, especially from Larry Wallis. 'Oh maan!' exclaimed Wallis, 'Where are we? This is unbelievable!' Wallis, 'a real road warrior', was so desperate for action that he walked out of the motel and crossed six lanes of dual carriageway to reach a nearby service area, where he thought he could detect signs of life. A few hours later, he was back on the coach, bereft of sleep.

'It would appear we're not paying Larry Wallis enough to afford razor blades!' yelled Riviera as the coach pulled up outside the Belle Vue Royal Hotel, Aberystwyth. Wallis checked his demeanour. It was true. If the drummers had been busy 'building a shed', Larry was sporting enough stubble to sand it down. 'I began to overhear other musicians on the coach saying things like, "Well, if I wear this shirt tonight I'll look really sharp,"' recalls Larry Wallis. 'I hadn't quite realised that I was in show business.'

But show business it was and the events of High Wycombe had given Elvis Costello something to think about. At Aberystwyth University on 4 October he reorganised his set to include more of his 'oldies' and adopted a slightly less confrontational approach.

The revolving bill concept had been a gimmick to help promote the tour and give all of the artists an equal opportunity, but after a few nights it was obviously not working. Wreckless Eric's group lacked the power to close the show successfully and Nick Lowe preferred an early slot, to allow plenty of time for a post-set drink. Conversely, Costello and Dury were both delivering riveting performances. Riviera and Robinson devised a fresh approach: Wreckless Eric and Nick Lowe would alternate in the first half of the show and Dury and Costello would alternate in the second half.

'If Nick and Dave Edmunds had chosen to put their best case out front, they certainly could have headlined,' says Elvis Costello, 'but they were playing this low-key game, constantly switching instruments and being deliberately perverse in hiding their pop potential.'

'Then there was some kind of argument,' says Dave Robinson, 'and Ian said he needed a break between drumming for Eric and performing his own set. That was agenda number two. Ian was happy to go on when he was told, but it meant a lot more plotting.' Soon, Pete Thomas was talking about putting some distance between playing in Lowe's outfit and drumming with The Attractions, so all of these factors reduced the possible programme permutations to just two: Plan A: Nick – Eric – Elvis – Ian, or Plan B: Eric – Nick – Ian – Elvis.

'It didn't take too long to decide,' confirms Lowe. 'Either Eric or I would open and Ian and Elvis would take it in turns to close.' Any other arrangement would have been the rock'n'roll equivalent of entering Charles Hawtrey and Julian Clary in a tag wrestling contest with Spider Fred Rowe and The Sulphate Strangler – two of the more colourful members on the Stiff road crew.

Throughout the next week, the tour settled into a familiar pattern. Nick Lowe would deliver a dependably rocking set, featuring Larry Wallis's modest cameo and Dave Edmunds' appearance in the front line to perform his recent Lowe-composed hit, 'I Knew The Bride'. 'Edmunds was a great drummer,' says Lowe, 'but he didn't have the stamina to play drums for the whole set.' Wreckless Eric would continue to struggle with alien equipment. 'I was told I had to use Edmunds' amplifier,' recalls Eric. 'It was about six miles away and could not be moved. Spider Fred would be standing there at the side of the stage, looking out for Ian. I'd turn round looking desperately at the amplifier, which hadn't been switched on, and Fred's looking at me, thumbs up, shouting, "Go on boy, kill 'em!"'

On 6 October, with two consecutive shows in the Avonmouth area, the entourage checked into the Bristol Holiday Inn. After a well-received show at the local Exhibition Centre, the coach delivered the musicians back to their relatively luxurious accommodation. The inevitable drinks party got off to a good start in the reception area, where Farrah Fawcett-Minor, self-styled 'Tour Nurse' and creator of a weekly tour newsletter, upended a huge glass table laden with empties and overflowing ashtrays. Immediately the highly polished floor was a sea of broken glass.

'A tour manger would have possibly seen that moment coming and averted it,' opines Wreckless Eric. 'But I can't remember any great tour manager presence.' Even though the jaunt was in its infancy, Dez Brown, a former Pink Fairies equipment handler, was becoming quite unpopular. Resembling a cross between Motorhead's Lemmy and a typical college social secretary, Brown's hirsute appearance was at odds with most of the Stiff entourage. 'I heard someone say that the reason Dez was the tour manager was to make everything more unpleasant,' continues Eric. 'But the whole vibe of the tour was becoming pretty aggressive. For example, there was a poster that said, "Dumping Music On The People . . . In Your Town". Well, Dez's manner helped to make the general vibe even more nasty.'

On 12 October the tour crossed the border into Scotland, for a show the following night at Glasgow's Apollo. The major press coverage had started to appear and both *Sounds* and *NME* published features on Ian Dury, mainly reporting the release of *New Boots And Panties*, but neither article made much mention of Dury's co-writer and musical director, Chaz Jankel. 'Chaz was somewhat taken aback that the coverage was slanted towards Ian, and not Ian and Chaz,' says Kosmo Vinyl. 'I think Chaz had seen himself and Ian as a team, but Ian was an editor's dream come true, so he was bound to get the dairy. I think this shocked Chaz, who probably thought that "talent will prevail" and "the musicians will get the credit." He'd obviously paid no attention to what had happened in the previous two years!'

But it was Jankel's musicality and fully-interlocking arrangements that had provided Dury with the crucial piece of his jigsaw. 'I preferred Ian with the Kilburns,' says Costello, 'but the Blockheads were ace players and Ian got his stories over better with this more polished music.' Jankel and the Blockheads certainly gave the material more depth and, as was about to be proven, a wider commercial appeal. In mid-October, *New Boots And Panties* entered the UK album chart, where it would remain for the next two years, giving Stiff Records some much-needed economic stability.

Meanwhile, Larry Wallis was suffering a crisis of confidence. Yet, there he was, sharing the spotlight with Elvis and Co, and basking in all the press coverage. '*Time Out* stuck us on the cover,' says Wallis. 'In the photo there's Eric being fairly serious, Ian too. Me and Nick had just drunk a pint of vodka and orange each. Right in the middle is Elvis Costello, looking straight at the camera.'

Costello, it seems, had his own private agenda. The heavily publicised tour presented the perfect opportunity for a spot of legend-building. With tough new songs like 'Night Rally' and 'You Belong To Me' peppering his set, the release of 'Watching The Detectives' imminent, and the ink drying on a lucrative US contract with Columbia, Costello oozed confidence.

While Elvis remained somewhat aloof, the young and footloose Attractions got stuck in. Last off the coach and first at the bar was Pete Thomas, whose machine-gun laughter punctuated every gathering, providing the tour with its perpetual soundtrack. Thomas was one of a small group of revellers who sought to brighten their leisure time by seeing just how far the weekly allowance of £50 would stretch, if thrown in the general direction of a bar. This determined group, which also included Bruce Thomas, Larry Wallis, Dave Edmunds, Terry Williams, Penny Tobin and Kosmo Vinyl, quickly became known as The 24 Hour Club.

Elvis Costello was rarely seen in the proximity of the 24 Hour Club. 'I was never big on communal drinking over long hours,' says Costello. 'But I did have a little blue sandwich case with my note book, a half bottle of gin and a few lemons for my throat. It was my emergency kit.' Ian Dury wasn't a club member either. 'Ian thought everyone should get on that stage sober,' says Dave Robinson. 'The Blockheads weren't allowed to drink too much before the gig. Ian had a lot of rules and regulations for his band. He was leading them very strongly. If anyone offered them a drink, Ian would say, "We don't." '

Sex and drugs and rock and roll
Is all my brain and body need . . .

On 15 October, the tour reached Leeds University. By now, Dury's 'Sex And Drugs And Rock 'n' Roll' had become the anthem of the tour and a routine had evolved whereby the entire company, or those that could be located, would join Dury on stage for a rousing finale of the song. The three principal drummers would lay down a slab of fatback funk, Blockhead Norman Watt-Roy would give it the bass from outer space and, after Chaz Jankel's signature riff, Dury would summon his fellow performers on stage one by one. 'The Sex and Drugs finale was Ian's thing,' says Robinson. 'Even if Elvis was the closing act, in Ian's mind the real headliner was himself! He had gazumped Elvis!'

As the coach rolled through the English countryside, various forms of relaxation were adopted. While some played cards or simply slept off their hangovers, Costello could often be found on the back seat dashing off a few new songs, such as 'Sunday's Best', which he would offer to Ian Dury. Another permanent fixture was Nick Lowe, holding court at a table seat. With a bottle of vodka and a Senior Service permanently on the go, Lowe would declare that everything on the tour was 'marvy' and treat those within earshot to a 'Mile Melter' – Lowe's own expression for one of his many extended anecdotes, often detailing the exploits of his former group, Brinsley Schwarz. According to witnesses, Nick's classic stories would, indeed, melt the miles.

At the University of East Anglia on 18 October, a mobile recording truck was in position to capture performances for the live LP. Elvis Costello took everyone by surprise, opening with the Bacharach and David ballad 'I Just Don't Know What To Do With Myself'. 'It's raggedy, but it sounds like we meant it,' says Costello. 'It was very much against the prevailing mood at the time.' Backstage, the prevailing mood was stormy as Jake Riviera harangued the social secretary, demanding sandwiches and drinks for the musicians. 'There was certainly a fiery atmosphere when Jake was around,' recalls Glen Colson. 'He would arrive at about 90 miles an hour, have a bit of a scream up, put everybody on edge and then leave.'

When the coach arrived at Manchester's Ardwick Apollo on 21 October, Elvis Costello's name was in lights on the marquee and local celebrities, including The Buzzcocks and John Cooper-Clark, had turned out to catch the show. After an agreeable set from Nick Lowe, Dury turned in an ecstatically received performance, followed by a blistering retort from Costello. Opening with the recently composed 'No Action', Costello's extended set included the Kilburns' 'Roadette Song', 'Go The Whole Wide World', in honour of an absent Wreckless Eric, and a raucous 'Radio Radio'.

Off-stage, tension was building between Lowe and Edmunds. 'I think Dave was disappointed that Nick was not always such an apres-gig presence as he had been in the past,' opines one 24 Hour Club member. 'Dave would say, "Look, I've come along on this for a laugh, where's Basher?"' As an occasional member of The 24 Hour Club, Basher Lowe was keeping his head down, trying to control his own excesses. 'Nick was allowed out now and again,' recalls Paul Conroy, 'then Jake would rein him in.'

'Dave Edmunds had been getting very drunk,' remembers Lowe. 'We'd all been doing it, but Dave's hangovers were now so dreadful that he couldn't really perform the next night. I sensed he was gonna blow me out or let me down. I could see it coming.' After seven years as a virtual recluse at Rockfield Studios, where he had honed his production skills, Dave Edmunds was very much enjoying being part of the Stiff circus. This, he thought, was a preferable alternative to Led Zeppelin's Swansong, the label to which he was contractually tied.

By the time the coach returned to the Manchester Post House that evening, Edmunds was so pleased to be a part of the industry of human happiness that he was banging on about it to anyone with a spare hour to kill. 'All I want is to be with Jake Riviera . . . Jake and Nick and Stiff Records,' repeated Edmunds, as if he was unaware that Jake and Stiff were history. 'I want Jake to manage me . . . this is my scene now . . . I don't want to be with Swansong . . .'

Birmingham, Cardiff and Wolverhampton flashed by in the run-up to London, with the competition between Elvis Costello and Ian Dury gaining in intensity every night. Dury, having spent years honing his performance skills, was now effortlessly wooing the crowds with tales of 'Sweet Gene Vincent', 'Billericay Dickie', 'Clever Trever' and 'Plaistow Patricia' (with its infamous lewd introduction). It was as if a whole new audience had come out of the woodwork to worship him. In response to Dury's new-found celebrity, the wired and highly unpredictable Costello was pushing himself and his group to the limit, delivering incendiary performances of 'Lipstick Vogue' and 'Watching The Detectives'. Both artists had risen to the unwritten challenge and, on stage, each of them would attempt to make it impossible for the other to follow.

Pump it up, until you can feel it
Pump it up, when you don't really need it . . .

On 4 November, the penultimate night of the tour, Elvis Costello found himself sitting out on the fire escape of Newcastle's Swallow Hotel, writing 'Pump It Up' in response to what he describes as the 'get off your face and be an asshole' side of touring. 'I can't remember anything specific,' says Costello, 'but it was anti the boring stab-you-in-the-back stuff. But it's impossible to look into the mind of someone who was out of his mind on vodka and amphetamines.'

Fully stimulated, Costello worked fast. The Attractions had no trouble in keeping up and by the following night, at Lancaster University, the freshly conceived 'Pump It Up' was in the set, after which Ian Dury closed the final show of the tour. It was Saturday, 5 November. Fireworks lit up the surrounding countryside as the exhausted musicians, themselves in a highly combustible state, filed onto the coach for almost the last time. 'Everybody finished,' recalls Kosmo Vinyl, 'in one state or another.'

Considering the volatile mix of personalities, the tour had escaped lightly. 'There were a lot of young people put together in a very confined space,' says Dury's co-manager Peter Jenner, 'and it led to a very dynamic situation in every respect, emotionally and creatively.'

For Stiff Records the tour had been a success, even though it lost money. A conservative estimate of £11,000 was bandied about – not much by today's standards – but in 1977 it was a significant sum for an independent label. 'It definitely made a loss,' says Stiff accountant Alan Parsons, 'but it was a promotional exercise. It broke Ian Dury, and that was a lifesaver for Stiff.' This is an understatement. Stiff's Greatest Stiffs Live was the launching pad for Ian Dury and a year of exceptional commercial success awaited him. Without this, Stiff Records may not have survived, especially after the disintegration of The Damned and the defection of Elvis Costello to Radar Records.

Although the Live Stiffs LP bears the message, 'Now See The Film', Nick Abson's footage has never seen the light of video and, in the opinion of Ian Dury, 'Will never be seen.' Initially, a disagreement over the editing delayed its release. In the years that have followed, the main participants have failed to reach agreement over its contents. The 50-minute director's cut is, however, a faithful snapshot of a bunch of young musicians out for a lark, with all of the self-conscious camera reactions and quaint behaviour one can imagine. It is a must-see.

Backstage scenes of impending debauchery bring into focus only too clearly those halcyon days of wine, women and petty bickering about the monitors. It's not very PC either. 'Come on Farrah. Show us your tits!' pleads a legless Attraction. Costello prepares to yawn as the poor girl's breasts are forcibly revealed. On the coach, thinly disguised insults are traded and all kinds of intoxicants are imbibed to relieve the tedium of the arduous journeys. As Trevor Wiffen drives on heroi-cally, a pale and bleary-eyed Dave Edmunds swigs the dregs of a bottle of whisky and takes a long slow hit of dream tobacco. 'You're supposed to inhale it!' wisecracks an on-looker. Edmunds leans into the camera, barely able to focus. 'Yes Mum, it's me,' he slurs.

The on-stage moments are no less entertaining: Costello's gripping reading of 'Watching The Detectives' is full of menace as he crouches down among the amps psycho style. 'She's filing her nails while they're dragging the lake,' he chillingly intones. Nick Lowe's 'Heart Of The City', a minor rock 'n' roll landmark, is knocked out with a casual swagger, climaxing with guitar solos from Edmunds and Wallis. Wreckless Eric, the runt of the litter, bravely delivers the tremendous 'Reconnez Cherie', confirming his status as one of pop's most under-valued writers and Ian Dury, his face a pallet of smudged mascara, is pure music hall. 'Fill 'er up say the Blockheads,' he screeches as his group of the same name dispense their high-octane mixture. 'How would you like to find one in your laundry basket?' he enquires.

The 'Sex And Drugs And Rock'n'Roll' finale is also captured. First up is former Kilburn, Humphrey Ocean, who dances expansively as the stage gradually fills. 'Nick!' calls Dury, then 'Elvis!' Obliged to participate for the sake of the cameras, the two deserters eventually appear. Lowe is clutch-ing a pint and grinning broadly. Costello is in Ron Mael mode, motionless and deadpan. 'I'm very grumpy by the end of it,' admits Costello. 'I was usually somewhere else when the finale was going on, but I had my arm twisted at the Lyceum. I was extremely drunk.'

Today, Nick Lowe is characteristically modest about his role in the proceedings. In the two years following the break-up of Brinsley Schwarz, Lowe had built an enviable reputation as a record producer and purveyor of 'Pure Pop For Now People', but he was a reluctant Live Stiff. 'I enjoyed wearing the Riddler suit,' he recalls, 'but I viewed my own musical contribution as an irritating interruption to the day. I didn't take it very seriously. I had to be there, but Elvis and Ian were so fantastic that I didn't really see myself as a contender.'

'Ian could have come on and read a Sainsbury's shopping receipt and everyone would have cheered,' says Humphrey Ocean. 'I think it became difficult for Elvis to come on after Ian. That's my overriding impression.' Costello stands firm on his own group's ability to ignite a show: 'There was nobody that could follow us really. I think Ian and The Blockheads had a hard time, even though Ian was so commanding. We made it difficult for them to follow us, although I think that sometimes it was better when they did. Our energy didn't really lead anywhere at that point, but Ian and his band were much more competitive than I'd expected.'

'There was a very competitive atmosphere,' confirms Jake Riviera, 'and Ian and Elvis were the most ambitious people on the tour.' When pressed to expand on the subject, Riviera agrees that the imminent departure of Lowe and Costello from Stiff had definitely created a divide between those that were going and those that were staying. Riviera also describes his relationship with his former partner Dave Robinson during the tour as 'terse'.

Although more than two decades have elapsed since 'Clever' Trevor Wiffen last had to hose down the inside of his coach, a blanket of secrecy surrounds the darker moments of Stiffs Greatest Stiffs Live. In a mass outbreak of amnesia, matched only by former associates of the Kray twins, many of the tour participants simply clam up on the subject. 'In the calmness of day,' says Peter Jenner, 'you don't want to reveal how you were thinking. It starts exposing a lot of the machinations and manoeuvrings that artists get up to. They like to pretend they're just interested in art. Once you start scratching the surface you begin to see the competitiveness.'

Reading between the lines one senses a degree of displeasure about some of the 'shenanigans' that occurred. 'I thought it was all for one and one for all,' offers Larry Wallis, 'but I didn't realise how many games were being played.' Others talk of chicanery. 'It brought out the best and worst of everything,' adds Jenner, 'and it was done on a shoestring. It wasn't an established pecking order when it went out. They had to find out who was the hierarchy, socially, professionally and musically. There was a certain amount of stitching each other up whilst pretending to be chums.'

'It was a bunch of mad people on the road,' concludes Elvis Costello. 'There was a lot of staying up late and a lot of badness. But when isn't there on a tour? What's the shock! We were young; we were free. Just like Cliff! But it was hardly *Summer Holiday*.'

Stiff's Greatest Stiffs Live had succeeded in bringing Lowe, Dury and Costello into the public eye. Over the next two years, these artists enjoyed considerable chart action in the UK and Europe, with Lowe and Costello extending their success to the USA, where they were perceived as leaders of the New Wave revolution. New Wave was a relative fad, but the values on which it was founded had their roots in Pub Rock and would soon be embraced by thousands of musicians around the world, even if nearly all of them lacked Nick Lowe's quintessential style and humour.

POSTSCRIPT

By 1981, Stiff Records had achieved an annual turnover of £3m and a strike rate of 10 hits from every 30 releases – a remarkable average. Stiff's major act throughout the early 80s was Madness, who were the most successful British singles group since The Beatles, with an unbroken run of 23 hit singles. But despite this success, Stiff's continuing chart action would not last forever. In 1986, Stiff called in the receivers and collapsed the following year with debts of £3,594,244.

Dave Robinson was named, along with EMI and the Inland Revenue, as one of the major creditors, presumably having ploughed much of his own money into the ailing company.

After departing Stiff in 1977, Jake Riviera launched Radar Records with former United Artists executives Andrew Lauder and Martin Davies. With heavy funding from Warner Brothers, Radar scored hits with Nick Lowe ('I Love The Sound Of Breaking Glass', 'Cruel To Be Kind') and Elvis Costello ('Pump It Up', 'Oliver's Army', 'Accidents Will Happen'). By 1980, the same team, minus Davies, were trading under a new name, F-Beat. Costello's success continued.

Jake Riviera's F-Beat label folded in the mid-80s, but, by then, its subsidiaries, Demon and Edsel, which specialised in roots rock and reissues respectively, were firmly established. Demon Records was sold for an undisclosed sum to Kingfisher Entertainments, part of the Woolworths group, in 1998.

Following 1977's Stiff's Greatest Stiffs Live, Nick Lowe formed Rockpile with Dave Edmunds, Billy Bremner and Terry Williams; married the singer Carlene Carter; and released a number of solo records. Rockpile disbanded early in 1981 and Lowe worked as a producer (Costello, Fabulous Thunderbirds, John Hiatt). In 1992, Lowe's 1974 song. '(What's So Funny 'bout) Peace Love And Understanding' was recorded by Curtis Stigers for the soundtrack of the Whitney Houston/Kevin Costner blockbuster movie, *The Bodyguard*.

The soundtrack recording sold over 29 million copies in its various formats, earning Lowe some richly deserved royalties.

Nick Lowe continues to record and has, in recent years, produced some outstanding, albeit low-key recordings, including *The Impossible Bird*, *Dig My Mood* and *The Convincer*.

Barney Bubbles continued to design record sleeves and promotional material, with many of his commissions coming from Jake Riviera's Radar and F-Beat labels. However, by the early 80s, Bubbles had become disillusioned with trying to meet the expectations of an increasingly more demanding record industry. He briefly took a job stacking supermarket shelves and claimed to draw inspiration from the packaging of the various breakfast cereals and soap powders he handled. He returned to graphic art (and furniture design) refreshed, via a brief period directing music videos (for Elvis Costello's 'Clubland' and The Specials' 'Ghost Town').

With the help of members of Hawkwind, Bubbles also made an LP, knowingly entitled *Ersatz*, billing himself as The Imperial Pompadours. The sleeve graphics note: 'The Imperial Pompadours are young and good looking'. But now, for the first time, some of Bubbles's visionary sleeve designs were being rejected by the major record companies.

Bubbles also had the problem of the Inland Revenue, constantly on his back for unpaid income tax. This was another major factor in his increasing bouts of depression. Following the loss of both of his parents, who died within three days of each other, just before Christmas 1980, Bubbles went into a severe three-year depression. After a number of 'cries for help' and with his personal life in turmoil, Bubbles committed suicide on 14 November 1983, his late parents' wedding anniversary.

Barney Bubbles is posthumously recognised as one of the most important graphic artists of his time. In 2001, a fine exhibition of Barney's work was staged in London by the artists Rebecca and Mike.

Dr Feelgood scored their biggest hit in 1979, with the Nick Lowe/John Mayo composition, 'Milk And Alcohol', which had been inspired by the aforementioned night in Los Angeles, when Feelgood manager Chris Fenwick was arrested shortly after the group visited a John Lee Hooker show. The Feelgoods continued to record and tour the world with various line-ups, always with Lee Brilleaux at the helm.

In February 1993, after several bouts of illness, Lee Brilleaux was called into hospital for investigations into his deteriorating health. The prognosis was not good. He was diagnosed as suffering from Non-Hodgkin's Lymphoma.

Lee Brilleaux died on 7 April 1994, aged 41. Although Lee's death was reported in the major British newspapers, with full obituaries in all of the broadsheets, it was overshadowed, in media terms, by the column inches devoted to the demise of Nirvana's Kurt Cobain, who had, two days before Lee's death, put a loaded gun to his head and pulled the trigger. It is doubtful whether Brilleaux and Cobain had heard of each other.

Ian Dury was one of the most celebrated artists to emerge from Pub Rock, although later, when fortified by hit records, such as 'Hit Me With Your Rhythm Stick' and all the attendant trappings, he became difficult. Reflecting on this, Dury said, 'Barney Bubbles told me a few straighteners towards the end of his life. Barney told me, "You were a horrible piece of work in those days, Ian." I said, "Barney, I didn't want to be."' Former manager Tommy Roberts comments, 'Ian had been waiting a long time; he was entitled to go haywire.'

After his chart success dried up, Dury branched out into acting, writing and film work, with minor roles in over a dozen movies. In 1997 he became a goodwill ambassador for UNICEF, attending mass inoculation programmes in Zambia and Sri Lanka. He was also reunited with The Blockheads, recording the warmly received *Mr Lovepants*. Dury's profile was as high as ever when he contracted cancer of the colon in 1996 and immediately underwent surgery. At first the disease abated, but unfortunately it returned in 1998. Two years of chemotherapy followed, during which time Ian continued to carry out his UNICEF duties, work with the Blockheads and spend as much time as possible with his young family. But finally he succumbed to the disease and died at home on 27 March 2000. He is frequently described in the media as 'a bona fide national treasure' and 'a diamond geezer' to boot.

Since Ian's death, the Blockheads have continued to keep the flag flying. A posthumous Dury/Blockheads CD, *Ten More Turnips From The Tip*, was released in 2002, preceded by *Brand New Boots And Panties*, a remake of Ian's most popular LP, with guest artists, including Paul McCartney and Robbie Williams, handling vocal duties. Ian's incredible work lives on and gains in stature as the years pass.

John Eichler became the landlord of the Hope & Anchor in 1977. Despite the odd foray into pop and publishing, he has stayed in the pub game pretty much ever since. Today, Eichler can be found behind the bar of the superb Three Kings in London's Clerkenwell.

Fred Grainger, the previous incumbent of the Hope & Anchor and a cornerstone of the Pub Rock phenomenon, did not fare so well. In 1977, while still tenant at the Hope, Grainger, in partnership with John Eichler, had ventured into artist management, representing the group Plummet Airlines. While away on Plummet Airlines business and unknowingly breaking the precise terms of his contract with Watneys brewery, Grainger was ousted from the Hope in a complex *coup d'état*, involving close colleagues. This sad turn of events was compounded by the arrival of a letter, from Plummet Airlines' solicitor, suing Grainger for mismanagement. 'I was fucked,' says Grainger. 'I sat on the stairs at the Hope and cried my eyes out.'

Following the collapse of Famepushers in 1970, Stephen Warwick tried in vain to complete, and find an outlet for, *Bridge-O-Rama*. He continued in the film industry, editing sound for various movies including *The Jerusalem File* (1972) and was a 'Premie' (devotee) of the Divine Light Mission for many years. Warwick disappeared from view in the 1980s, when it is said he worked in an electrical goods warehouse. It is also rumoured that he worked on a tourist boat on the Thames and, in true entrepreneurial fashion, attempted to revive the UK canal network.

Ricky Blears dragged himself, his family and his possessions back to Manchester in a rented Ford Transit. Having 'lost everything' in the Famepushers debacle, he eventually established himself as an advertising copywriter. A sadder and wiser man, he become involved in all manner of businesses and made and lost several millions in bio-technology, software, loyalty cards and media.

The whereabouts of Edward Molton are unknown.

Almost the last word on the subject of Pub Rock belongs to one of its greatest beneficiaries and probably the most famous artist to emerge from the scene, Elvis Costello.

'Pub Rock was self-defeating in the end,' says Costello, 'but I really, really hate the way in which, in more recent times, Pub Rock is still referred to in a pejorative way. If you do anything with guitar, bass and drums that isn't self-consciously new, then it is often demeaned by calling it Pub Rock. I mean, where are you supposed to play? If your band exists only on the drawing board of an advertising company, does it make it any more real? Is it actually a better group because it hasn't played in a cellar?'

Or, as Nick Lowe remarks, 'Pub Rock was a sexy and fantastic time.'

But what made Pub Rock so fantastic and so sexy? Well, at its very heart was the music – always good, often great. There are not many punters around today who can honestly claim to have seen the legendary Eggs Over Easy at the Tally Ho. The group's studio recordings are their only legacy, providing thin evidence of their musical prowess. But we have it on good authority, from reputable sources such as Barry Richardson, Nick Lowe, Dave Robinson and Ted Carroll, that there was nothing quite like hearing Eggs Over Easy knocking out great, unpredictable covers, including 'Brown Sugar', 'All Along The Watchtower' and 'Like A Rolling Stone'. We will just have to imagine it.

A far larger number of people got to hear Bees Make Honey and Brinsley Schwarz. The Bees, whatever their line-up, but always with Barry Richardson at the helm, would swing like nothing on earth. Their scorching version of Billy Lee Riley's 'My Girl Is Red Hot', left indelible goosebumps on the back of one's neck.

The Brinsleys were equally as in-the-groove, but with the added bonus of Nick Lowe's and Ian Gomm's assured songwriting. To hear 'Surrender To The Rhythm' – 'Well they danced, to every tune, the band could play . . .' – pumped out through the group's customised sound system, was a memorable musical moment. Pub Rock aficionados dream of the original Brinsleys re-forming for just one more date.

Ducks Deluxe were also special. They had the rock 'n' roll attitude sewn up, years before lesser groups adopted the stance. Sean Tyla was a whole bunch of trouble, yet he could rock for real, as on his composition, 'Fireball', a heartfelt slab of slurred vocal, complete with anthemic guitar riff.

Chilli Willi And The Red Hot Peppers were roots rock through the hippie gauze, multi-instrumentalists to the max (and the epitome of shambolic, shirkaholic ineptitude until Jake Riviera stepped in). Blessed with the swingingest rhythm section on the circuit, Phil Lithman's quirky, upbeat songs and Martin Stone's powerful bluesy guitar, Chilli Willi were a guaranteed good night out.

In my humble opinion, the Kursaal Flyers were pretty hot too. We had damn good songs like 'Speedway' and 'Pocket Money' and a brilliant front man in Paul Shuttleworth. We were a bit of a skiffle group, but once a bum note or missed cue had registered with Paul, he would give it the old sideways glance and we'd once again 'limbo under the bog door'. We even got a hit record and we occasionally reconvene for the hell of it.

Dr Feelgood reached the biggest audience of all the Pub Rock groups and there are thousands of fans around today who can testify to their on-stage dynamism. On the concert platform they were tremendous, but in the pubs they were truly dangerous. To stand just inches away from the Feelgoods, in sweat-dripping second encore mode, as they ripped up 'Route 66' at breakneck speed, was akin to seeing the words, 'I C O U L D D O T H A T T O O!' spelt out to you in giant letters. They changed the world.

Eddie And The Hot Rods, inspired by the Feelgoods, thrilled the circuit with super-fast rhythms and youthful vigour. Although discredited by the punks a few months later, the Hot Rods' arrival nevertheless represented a turning point in British rock history. In the Hot Rods' hands, rock 'n' roll was not dying, but reaching a brand-new audience, most of whom became a ready-made following for the Pistols and The Clash.

And let us not forget Ian Dury, the man who was put forward by Malcolm McLaren, to his protégé John Lydon, as a role model. Croaking out the tortured, passionate lyrics of 'Upminster Kid' with Kilburn And The High Roads – 'I could not afford the ruby snaffle tie, or the black suede Clubman shoes' – Dury reaffirmed the spirit of rock 'n' roll and the belief that the underdog could somehow make a mark, irrespective of musical ability.

That was what Pub Rock was all about and the Punk Rock revolution that followed it. They were great days indeed and, as Ian Dury once crooned, it's 'Amazing that the feeling's still around . . .'

APPENDICES

I CHRONOLOGY

1969

January	Barney Bubbles moves into 307 Portobello Road.
29 March	Stephen Warwick meets Edward Molton.
14 April	Warwick introduces Molton to Barney Bubbles and they set up Teenburger Designs.
22 April	307 Portobello Road becomes the registered office of Breydon Films Ltd.
1 May	Malcolm Addison answers Molton and Warwick's *Evening Standard* small ad for a guard at Red Sands.
8 May	Sea Tribe Ltd is registered at Companies House.
June	Molton rents room at 305 Portobello Road from Bob Wilson.
July	Dave Robinson meets Dot Burn-Forti at NEMS.
5 July	Kippington Lodge supports Village at the Marquee.
August	Dave Robinson, Dot Burn-Forti and John Eichler plan Famepushers.
September	Eichler introduces Robinson and Burn-Forti to Molton and Warwick; Famepushers moves into 305 Portobello Road.
October	Kippington Lodge becomes Brinsley Schwarz.
16 October	Famepushers (Wornet Ltd) registered at Companies House; Famepushers small ad for 'Young Songwriting Group' appears in *Melody Maker*.
October	Famepushers signs Brinsley Schwarz; Ricky Blears joins the Molton and Warwick organisation; Molton and Warwick in discussions with *Friends* magazine.
November	Molton meets Jeremy Flint and, with Warwick, conceives *Bridge-O-Rama*. Molton and Warwick meet with Omar Sharif's manager, Leon Yallouze.

5 December	Grandslam Productions Ltd registered at Companies House.
13 December	Brinsley Schwarz appear as Kippington Lodge at the Marquee, fulfilling contractual obligations.
14 December	Andrew Lauder sees Brinsley Schwarz at the Country Club.
December	Brinsley Schwarz commence recording at Olympic Studios.

1970

January	Molton moves *Friends* magazine into 305 Portobello Road.
6/10 January	Omar Sharif plays bridge at the Piccadilly Hotel. *Bridge-O-Rama* is filmed.
February	*Bridge-O-Rama* runs into financial difficulties; the 'talking up' session at Burford Villa; Ricky Blears suggests a New York launch for Brinsley Schwarz; Dave Robinson meets with Bill Graham in San Francisco; Famepushers moves to 44 Park Road.
24 March	Brinsley Schwarz filmed by Tony Palmer at the Conway Hall.
30 March	Brinsley Schwarz's Visa applications are rejected in London.
31 March	Billy Rankin and Famepushers film crew fly to New York; Robinson, Schwarz, Andrews and Lowe fly to Toronto.
3/4 April	Brinsley Schwarz make their debut at Fillmore East, New York.
17 April	Brinsley Schwarz debut LP released in UK.
June	Barney Bubbles departs Portobello Road.
July	Dave Robinson and Brinsley Schwarz part company with Molton and Warwick. The group moves to Northwood.
August	Edward Molton disappears.
September	Dave Robinson registers a new company called Dave Robinson and Dot Burn-Forti Ltd; Ian Gomm joins Brinsley Schwarz.

| November | Eggs Over Easy arrive in London to record with Chas Chandler; Ian Dury forms embryonic line-up of Kilburn And The High Roads and practises at Jubilee Studio, Covent Garden. |
| 15 November | *Sunday Times* reports on 'The Wonderful Year of Molton and Warwick'. |

1971

3 May	Eggs Over Easy debut at the Tally Ho.
2 June	The Band appear at the Royal Albert Hall.
15 June	Dave Robinson sees Eggs Over Easy at the Marquee and invites them back to Northwood.
16 June	Nick Lowe and Billy Rankin go to the Tally Ho to see Eggs Over Easy.
21 June	Brinsley Schwarz play the first 'Glastonbury Fayre'.
August	Embryonic Bees Make Honey debut at the Tally Ho; Brinsley Schwarz record *Silver Pistol*.
September	Eggs Over Easy support John Mayall on UK tour.
November	Eggs Over Easy return to the USA.
5 December	Kilburn And The High Roads debut at Croydon Art School.

1972

19 January	Brinsley Schwarz debut at the Tally Ho.
April	Brinsley Schwarz record *Nervous On The Road*.
7 May	Declan MacManus sees Brinsley Schwarz at Bickershaw Festival.
27 July	MacManus meets Nick Lowe in Liverpool pub, The Grapes.
September	Ducks Deluxe form. Manager Dai Davies spends a month in the USA as publicist for Mainman and David Bowie.
2 October	Ducks Deluxe debut at the Tally Ho.
October	Brinsley Schwarz provide backing for Frankie Miller on Ten Years After UK tour.

13 October	Death of jazz drummer Phil Seaman causes Hope & Anchor landlord Fred Grainger to rethink the pub's musical policy.
11 November	Dave Robinson and Nick Lowe see Kilburn And The High Roads at the Speakeasy.
November	*Kings Of The Robot Rhythm* by Chilli Willi And The Red Hot Peppers released by Revelation Records. Sleeve design by Barney Bubbles.
December	Chilli Willi recruit Paul Riley, Paul Bailey, Pete Thomas; Alan 'Bam' King forms Ace Flash & The Dynamos. Paul Carrack joins three months later and group becomes Ace.

1973

4 January	Dave Robinson discovers the Hope & Anchor and Fred Grainger books Brinsley Schwarz for the following week.
10 January	Kilburn And The High Roads debut at the Tally Ho.
11 January	Brinsley Schwarz debut at the Hope & Anchor.
6 February	Kilburn And the High Roads debut at Hope & Anchor.
22 February	Bees Make Honey debut at Hope & Anchor.
23 February	John Collis becomes music editor of *Time Out* and starts to publicise 'Pub Rock'.
25 March	Charlie Gillett broadcasts 'Brinsleys housing problem' on BBC Radio London's *Honky Tonk*.
April	Andrew Jakeman road manages Chilli Willi. He soon becomes the group's manager; Brinsley Schwarz move to Wilton Park Farm in Beaconsfield.
3 May	Kilburns' Van Benefit' dance at Camden Town Hall, featuring Brinsley Schwarz, Bees Make Honey and Ducks Deluxe.
May	Brinsley Schwarz support Wings on UK tour.
22 June	Dave Robinson and Brinsley Schwarz set up Down Home Ltd.
July	Brinsley Schwarz play more dates with Wings.
13 July	Dr Feelgood debut at the Tally Ho.

July	Dave Robinson and Brinsley Schwarz part company; Robinson moves into the Hope & Anchor, where he starts to build a studio and forms The Upper Street Music Company with landlord Fred Grainger; Brinsley Schwarz record *Please Don't Ever Change*; Dai Davies becomes the group's new manager.
6 November	Brinsley Schwarz record BBC2's *Old Grey Whistle Test* appearance and play Dingwalls later that evening.
December	Bees Make Honey's eponymous debut LP released by EMI.

1974
January	Kilburn And The High Roads sign to Raft Records and record their debut LP, which is shelved when Raft collapses.
March	Brinsley Schwarz and Dave Edmunds film their parts for the David Essex film *Stardust*.
April	Brinsley Schwarz record *New Favourites* with Edmunds.
June	Dave Edmunds, Brinsley Schwarz and Dr Feelgood on UK 'New Favourites' tour.
July	Dr Feelgood sign to United Artists.
6 July	Flip City debut at The Kensington.
14 July	Kursaal Flyers debut at The Kensington.
13 September	The Band rehearse at Wilton Park Farm.
September	Bees Make Honey disband; Kilburn And The High Roads sign to Dawn Records.
7 September	The 101ers debut at The Telegraph, Brixton.
November	'How Long' by Ace enters UK chart.
23 November	'Rough Kids' by Kilburn And The High Roads released on Dawn Records.
15 December	Chilli Willi's 'Big Xmas Beat Extravaganza' at the Roundhouse.

1975
11 January	The 'Naughty Rhythms Tour' opens in Bristol.

February	*Down By The Jetty*, Dr Feelgood's debut LP released by United Artists; Chilli Willi And The Red Hot Peppers disband.
18 March	Brinsley Schwarz disband after Marquee show.
March	Andrew Jakeman tour manages Dr Feelgood.
Spring	Ted Carroll starts Chiswick Records.
11 May	Charlie Gillett broadcasts Graham Parker demo of 'Between You And Me'.
17 May	Eddie And The Hot Rods London debut at The Kensington.
June	Kilburn And The High Roads disband.
1 July	Ducks Deluxe disband.
July	Charlie Gillett broadcasts Graham Parker demo.
August	Dr Feelgood play Reading and L'Orange Festivals.
7 October	Eddie And The Hot Rods and The 101ers play the Nashville.
October	Dr Feelgood's *Malpractice* LP released.
18 October	Graham Parker And The Rumour play Newlands Tavern.
6 November	Sex Pistols debut at St Martin's College of Art.
November	Chiswick releases Count Bishops' *Speedball* EP.

1976

January	Dr Feelgood play CBS conference in San Diego.
12 February	Eddie And The Hot Rods and the Sex Pistols play the Marquee.
22 February	Rough Trade record shop opens.
March	Graham Parker supports Thin Lizzy on UK tour; Nick Lowe tour manages Parker.
23 April	The 101ers and the Sex Pistols play the Nashville.
April	*Howlin' Wind*, Graham Parker's debut LP released.
10/11 May	Dr Feelgood and The Ramones play New York's Bottom Line.

31 May	'Keys To Your Heart' by The 101ers released by Chiswick; Joe Strummer soon quits The 101ers to join The Heartdrops (later The Clash).
13 August	'So It Goes' by Nick Lowe released on Stiff.
15 August	Charlie Gillett broadcasts D. P. Costello demo.
August	Eddie And The Hot Rods' *Live at the Marquee* EP released.
21 August	First European Punk Rock Festival at Mont de Marsan, Bordeaux, France.
September	The Damned sign to Stiff Records and quickly release their debut single, 'New Rose'.
10/12 September	Save The Hope & Anchor weekend, featuring Dr Feelgood, Nick Lowe, Dave Edmunds, Sean Tyla, Ian Dury, Graham Parker and Carol Grimes.
24 September	Dr Feelgood's *Stupidity* LP released.
October	Declan MacManus/D. P. Costello signs to Stiff and is renamed Elvis Costello.
November	'Little Does She Know' by Kursaal Flyers enters UK chart.
19 November	'Anarchy In The UK', the debut single by the Sex Pistols released by EMI.

1977
March	'Less Than Zero', Elvis Costello's debut single, released by Stiff.
April	*The Clash* LP released by CBS.
22 July	*My Aim Is True*, Elvis Costello's debut LP released.
26 August	'Go The Whole Wide World', Wreckless Eric's debut single released by Stiff.
10 September	'Sex And Drugs And Rock'n'Roll', Ian Dury's debut solo single released by Stiff.
September	*New Boots And Panties*, Ian Dury's solo debut LP released.
3 October	Stiff's Greatest Stiffs Live opens at High Wycombe.
14 October	'Watching The Detectives' by Elvis Costello released.

October   Jake Riviera and Dave Robinson part company;
                 Riviera takes Lowe and Costello to his new
                 label, Radar Records. Barney Bubbles is art
                 director.

II PROMINENT PUB ROCK VENUES

1. **The Tally Ho**   Fortess Road, NW5
   Tenants: Jim & Lillian Delaney
   Beer: Watneys
   Regulars: Eggs, Bees, Brinsleys, Ducks, Kilburns, Ace
   Comment: 'This is a jazz pub. Always has been; always will be.' The first on the map, where Eggs Over Easy started the ball rolling in 1971.

2. **The Kensington**   Russell Gardens, W14
   Manager: Matt Farley
   Beer: Watneys
   Regulars: Brinsleys, Bees, Ducks, Kilburns, Willies, Feelgoods
   Comment: 'Take me to Mars!' quipped Matt Farley on encountering his first enormous p.a. mixing console which was, of course, taking up valuable drinking space.

3. **The Cock Tavern**   Kilburn High Road, NW6
   Beer: Trumans
   Regulars: Brinsleys, Ducks, Kilburns
   Comment: 'Keep filling up those glasses!' was the impassioned plea of the non-rocking landlord. This soon became, 'If you lot don't buy more drinks, I'm stopping this!'

Note: Not to be confused with The Cock Tavern in Holloway Road, where Ducks Deluxe played a handful of dates, but no other groups of note appeared.

4. **The Lord Nelson**   Holloway Road, N7
   Beer: Trumans
   Regulars: Kilburns, Ducks, Feelgoods, Winkies

Comment: Opened up by Winkies manager
             Paul Kennerley, then advertising
             agent for Trumans. Kennerley
             persuaded the brewery that Pub
             Rock was the future. 'The Nelson
             had a closed-circuit TV,' recalls Ian
             Dury. 'I met my friend Denise there.
             She saw me on the telly and
             thought it was *Top of The Pops*.'

5. **Hope & Anchor**   Upper Street, N1
    Tenant: Fred Grainger (later John Eichler)
    Beer: Watneys
    Regulars: Brinsleys, Ace, Feelgoods, Kursaals,
                        Dire Straits
    Comment: 'Unfortunately it was too small,'
                        recalls Dave Robinson. 'One night
                        Fred and I got very smashed and
                        decided to enlarge the basement.
                        The next morning we propped it up
                        with steel poles and knocked all the
                        brick pillars out. We nearly
                        dropped the whole pub on
                        ourselves.'

6. **The Windsor Castle** Harrow Road, W9
    Beer: Watneys
    Comment: Little is remembered about this
                        venue, but most of the pub groups
                        played here at least once. It is still
                        going, and now regularly features
                        'exotic dancers'.

7. **The Torrington** Lodge Lane, N12
    Beer: Whitbread
    Regulars: Shakin' Stevens And The Sunsets,
                        later Brinsleys, Feelgoods
    Comment: Promoter George Blevings started
                        presenting jazz here in 1968 and
                        introduced rock two years later.

8. **Dingwalls**

	Camden Lock, NW1
Booker and DJ:	David 'Boss' Goodman, former Pink Fairies road manager
Regulars:	Kilburns, Willies, Feelgoods and, at the bar, Lemmy
Comment:	Actually a club that was, for some years, London's hottest music-biz hangout. With an admission charge and a pricey bar, Dingwalls was able to pay groups generously, compared to the pubs.

9. **Newlands Tavern**

	Stuart Road, SE15
Beer:	Bass Charrington
Regulars:	Kilburns, Feelgoods, Kursaals, Flip City
Comment:	A lone outpost south of the river run by a most charming couple, Reg and Sue Fentiman. Graham Parker And The Rumour rehearsed and made their debut here.

10. **The Nashville**

	North End Road, W14
Promoter:	Dai Davies
Beer:	Fullers
Regulars:	Hot Rods, Sex Pistols, 101ers, Elvis Costello, Rockpile
Comment:	Originally a C&W venue and larger than most, it came on stream later but is famous for early appearances by the Sex Pistols and The Stranglers.

III SELECT DISCOGRAPHY

KIPPINGTON LODGE/BRINSLEY SCHWARZ

KIPPINGTON LODGE

Kippington Lodge released five singles, all on EMI's Parlophone label, as follows:

'Shy Boy' (Hopkins/Burgess) c/w 'Lady On A Bicycle' (Schwarz), produced by Mark P. Wirtz, Parlophone R5645, released 10/67

'Rumours' (Ferdy/Wirtz) c/w 'And She Cried' (Landeman / Schwarz), produced by Mark P. Wirtz, Parlophone R5677, released 3/68

'Tell Me A Story' (Landeman) c/w 'Understand A Woman' (Leckenby/Hopkins/ Brookes), produced by Mike Collier, Parlophone R5717, released 8/68

'Tomorrow Today' (Greenaway/Cooke) c/w 'Turn Out The Light' (Landeman), produced for TIM by Gentry Records, Parlophone R5750, released 12/68

'In My Life' (Lennon/McCartney) c/w 'I Can See Her Face' (Lowe), produced by Roger Easterby and Des Champ, Parlophone R5776, released 5/69

All ten Kippington Lodge sides, along with an orderly selection of Brinsley Schwarz rarities, are collected on Hen's Teeth *Edsel EDCD546 (through Demon Records), released 1998.*

BRINSLEY SCHWARZ

SINGLES

'Shining Brightly' (Lowe) c/w 'What Do You Suggest?' (Lowe), produced by Dave Robinson and Brinsley Schwarz, United Artists UP35118, released 1970.

'Country Girl' (Lowe) c/w 'Funk Angel' (Lowe), produced by Dave Robinson and Brinsley Schwarz, United Artists UP35312, released 1971.

'Speedo' (Navarro) c/w 'I Worry ('bout You Baby)' (Lowe), produced by Brinsley Schwarz and Vic Maile, United Artists UP35588, released 1973.

'I've Cried My Last Tear' (Neville) c/w '(It's Gonna Be A) Bring Down' (Gomm), produced by Brinsley Schwarz, United Artists UP35642, released 1974.

'(What's So Funny 'bout) Peace Love And Understanding' (Lowe) c/w 'Ever Since You're Gone' (Lowe), produced and engineered by Dave Edmunds, United Artists UP35700, released 1974.

'Everybody' (Roe) c/w 'I Like You, I Don't Love You' (Gomm / Lowe), produced by Steve Verroca, United Artists UP35768, released 1975.

'There's A Cloud In My Heart' (Lowe) c/w 'I Got The Real Thing' (Gomm/Lowe), produced by Steve Verroca, United Artists UP35812, released 1975.

LPs

Brinsley Schwarz, produced by Dave Robinson and Brinsley Schwarz, United Artists UAS29111, released 1970, includes 'Shining Brightly', 'What Do You Suggest?'; CD reissue BGO Records BGOCD239 (a 2-on-1 with *Despite It All*), released 1994.

Despite It All, produced by Dave Robinson and Brinsley Schwarz, United Artists LBG83427, released 1970, includes 'Country Girl', 'Funk Angel'; CD reissue – see *Brinsley Schwarz*.

Silver Pistol, produced by Dave Robinson and Brinsley Schwarz, United Artists UAS29217, released 1972, includes 'Dry Land', 'Nightingale', 'The Last Time I Was Fooled', 'Egypt'; CD reissue Edsel Records EDCD190 (through Demon Records), released 1986.

Nervous On The Road, produced by Brinsley Schwarz, Dave Robinson and Kingsley Ward, United Artists UAS29374, released 1972, includes 'Happy Doing What We're Doing', 'Surrender To The Rhythm', 'Don't Lose Your Grip On Love'; CD reissue BGO Records BGOCD289 (a 2-on-1 with *The New Favourites Of Brinsley Schwarz*), released 1995.

Please Don't Ever Change, produced by Brinsley Schwarz and Vic Maile, United Artists UAS29489, released 1973, includes 'Hooked On Love', 'Play That Fast Thing (One More Time)'; CD reissue Edsel Records EDCD237 (through Demon Records), released 1987.

The New Favourites Of Brinsley Schwarz, produced and engineered by Dave Edmunds, United Artists UAS29641, released 1974, includes '(What's So Funny 'bout) Peace Love And Understanding', 'The Ugly Things', 'The Look That's In Your Eye Tonight'; CD reissue – see *Nervous On The Road*.

COMPILATIONS

Original Golden Greats, United Artists USP101, released 1974.

The Fifteen Thoughts Of Brinsley Schwarz, United Artists UAK29641, released 1978.

Surrender To The Rhythm, EMI CDP 7967462, released 1991.

The Fifteen Thoughts Of Brinsley Schwarz/Original Golden Greats, CD reissue, BGO Records BGOCD476, released 2000.

What IS So Funny About Peace Love & Understanding?, BBC Radio One Sessions, with guest appearance by Frankie Miller, CD on Hux Records HUX023, released 2001.

PUB ROCK REISSUED ON CD

In addition to the Brinsley Schwarz reissues noted above, the following is a selection of further Pub Rock and related titles on CD.

HELP YOURSELF

Help Yourself, produced by Dave Robinson/*Beware The Shadow*, produced by Help Yourself; originally released by United Artists 1971/72; CD reissue BGO Records BGOCD385, released 1998.

Strange Affair, produced by Help Yourself and Anton Mathews/*The Return Of Ken Whaley*, produced by Dave Charles/*Happy Days*, A Happy Daze Production; originally released by United Artists 1972/73; CD reissue BGO Records BGOCD452, released 1999.

ERNIE GRAHAM

Ernie Graham, produced by Dave Robinson, with musical accompaniment by Brinsley Schwarz, Bob Andrews, Nick Lowe, Ian Gomm, Billy Rankin and Ken Whaley, originally released on Liberty Records 1971; CD reissue Hux Records HUX032, released 2002.

DUCKS DELUXE

Ducks Deluxe, produced by Dave Bloxham/*Taxi To The Terminal Zone*, produced by Dave Edmunds; originally released by RCA 1973/1974, includes 'Coast To Coast', 'Fireball', 'Love's Melody'; CD reissue Mau Mau MAUCD610 (through Demon Records), released 1991.

KILBURN AND THE HIGH ROADS

Handsome, produced by Hugh Murphy, originally released by Dawn Records 1975, includes 'Upminster Kid', 'Crippled With Nerves', 'Rough Kids', front cover painting *'The Kilburns Near Tower Bridge'* by Elizabeth Rathmell; CD reissue with bonus tracks Dawn/Castle ESMCD775, released 1999.

CHILLI WILLI AND THE RED HOT PEPPERS

Bongos Over Balham, produced by Ron Nevison and Charlie Riley, originally released by Mooncrest Records 1975, includes 'Choo Choo Ch'boogie', 'Desert Island Woman', 'Breathe A Little', sleeve design by Barney Bubbles; CD reissue Mooncrest Records CRESTCD007, released 1991.

I'll Be Home, previously unreleased material, produced by various, including Mike Nesmith, includes 'Walking Blues', 'Midnight Bus', 'Six Days On The Road'; CD compilation by Proper Records PRPCD2, released 1996.

DR FEELGOOD

Down By The Jetty, produced by Vic Maile, originally released by United Artists 1975, includes 'She Does It Right', 'Roxette', 'Keep It Out Of Sight'; CD reissue Grand Records GRANDCD05, released 1989.

Malpractice, produced by Dr Feelgood/Vic Maile, originally released by United Artists 1975, includes 'Back In The Night', 'Going Back Home', 'Riot In Cell Block No. 9'; CD reissue Grand Records GRANDCD09, released 1990.

Stupidity, produced by Dr Feelgood and Vic Maile, originally released by United Artists 1976, includes '20 Yards Behind',

'I'm A Man', 'I'm A Hog For You Baby'; CD reissue Grand Records GRANDCD21, released 1998.

KURSAAL FLYERS

Chocs Away, produced by Hugh Murphy/*The Great Artiste*, produced by the Kursaals and JK, originally released by UK Records 1975/1976, includes 'Pocket Money', 'Speedway', 'Cruisin' For Love', *Chocs Away* sleeve design by Barney Bubbles; CD reissue On The Beach Recordings FOAMCD3 (through Grand Records), released 1991.

Golden Mile, produced by Mike Batt/*Five Live Kursaals*, produced by Vic Maile, CD reissue Columbia/Sony 5060652, released 2002.

Hit Records – The Best of the Kursaal Flyers, includes 'Little Does She Know', CD on On The Beach Recordings FOAMCD6, released 2002.

EDDIE AND THE HOT RODS

Teenage Depression, produced by Ed Hollis and Vic Maile, originally released by Island Records 1976, includes 'Teenage Depression', 'The Kids Are Alright'; CD reissue Edsel Records EDCD563 (through Demon Records), released 1998.

VARIOUS ARTISTS

Naughty Rhythms – The Best Of Pub Rock includes tracks by Eggs Over Easy, Bees Make Honey, Ace, Frankie Miller and others, compiled by Will Birch and Paul Bradshaw, EMI Premier 724383796823, released 1996.

The Chiswick Story includes tracks by The 101ers, The Count Bishops, The Gorillas and others, Chiswick Records CDWIK2 100, released 1992.

The Stiff Records Box Set includes tracks by Nick Lowe, Elvis Costello, Ian Dury, Wreckless Eric, The Damned and others, STIFFBOX1 (through Demon Records), released 1995.

A Hard Night's Day – A History Of Stiff Records, MCA/Universal Music MCD60047, released 1997.

IV BIBLIOGRAPHY

BOOKS

Baker, Glenn A. and Stuart Coupe (1980) *The New Music*, Bay Books.

Barsby, Geoff (1992) *Canvey Island*, Phillimore & Co.

Bessman, Jim (1993) *Ramones: An American Band*, St Martin's Press.

Boot, Adrian and Chris Salewicz (1996) *Punk: The Illustrated History of a Music Revolution*, Boxtree.

Clarke, Donald (ed.) (1989) *The Penguin Encyclopedia Of Popular Music*, Viking.

Clayton-Lea, Tony (1998) *Elvis Costello: A Biography*, André Deutsch.

Coon, Caroline (1982) *The New Wave Punk Rock Explosion*, Omnibus Press.

Di Lello, Richard (1972) *The Longest Cocktail Party*, Charisma Books.

Foynes, J.P. (1994) *The Battle of the East Coast 1939–1945*, published by the author.

Frame, Pete (1980) *Rock Family Trees*, Omnibus Press.

Frame, Pete (1983) *Rock Family Trees Volume 2*, Omnibus Press.

Frame, Pete (1998) *More Rock Family Trees*, Omnibus Press.

Frame, Pete (1999) *Rockin' Around Britain*, Omnibus Press.

Garfield, Simon (1986) *Expensive Habits*, Faber & Faber.

Gimarc, George (1994) *Punk Diary 1970–1979*, Vintage.

Gray, Marcus (1995) *Last Gang in Town: The Story and Myth of The Clash*, Fourth Estate.

Green, Jonathon (1988) *Days in the Life: Voices From The English Underground 1961–1971*, William Heinemann.

Green, Jonathon (1998) *All Dressed Up: The Sixties and the Counterculture*, Jonathan Cape.

Hardy, Phil and Dave Laing (1990) *The Faber Companion to 20th Century Popular Music*, Faber & Faber.

Hollis, Richard (1994) *Graphic Design: A Concise History*, Thames & Hudson.

Hoskyns, Barney (1993) *Across The Great Divide*, Viking.

Hounsome, Terry (1987) *New Rock Record*, Blandford Press.

Hunter, Ian (1974) *Diary of a Rock 'n' Roll Star*, Panther.

Kent, Nick (1994) *The Dark Stuff*, Penguin.

Larkin, Colin (ed.) (1993) *The Guinness Encyclopedia of Popular Music*, Guinness Publishing Ltd.

Lydon, John (1993) *Rotten: No Irish, No Blacks, No Dogs*, Hodder & Stoughton.

McLagan, Ian 'Mac' (1998) *All the Rage*, Sidgwick & Jackson.

Matlock, Glen, with Peter Silverton (1996) *I Was a Teenage Sex Pistol*, Virgin Books.

Moon, Tony (1997) *Down by the Jetty: The Dr Feelgood Story*, Northdown.

Morris, Gina (1984) *Happy Doin' What We're Doin': The Pub Rock Years*, Nightbird Books.

Morris, Gina (1985) *Off Beat: Pub Rock for the 80s*, Nightbird Books.

Muirhead, Bert (1983) *Stiff: The Story of a Record Label*, Blandford Press.

Muirhead, Bert (1984) *The Record Producers File*, Blandford Press.

Neville, Richard (1995) *Hippie Hippie Shake*, Bloomsbury.

Parkyn, Geoff (1984) *Elvis Costello: The Illustrated Disco/Biography*, Omnibus Press.

Ramone, Dee Dee, with Veronica Kofman (1997) *Poison Heart: Surviving the Ramones*, Firefly.

Reed, John (1996) *Paul Weller: My Ever Changing Moods*, Omnibus Press.

Reese, Krista (1981) *Elvis Costello*, Proteus Publishing.

Robbins, Ira A. (ed.) (1989) *The New Trouser Press Record Guide*, Collier Books.

Rogan, Johnny (1988) *Starmakers and Svengalis*, Queen Anne Press.

St Michael, Mick (1986) *Elvis Costello: An Illustrated Biography*, Omnibus Press.

Savage, Jon (1991) *England's Dreaming*, Faber & Faber.

Sculatti, Gene and Davin Seay (1985) *San Francisco Nights*, Sidgwick & Jackson.

Scully, Rock with David Dalton (1996) *Living with the Dead*, Little, Brown.

Shaar Murray, Charles (1991) *Shots from the Hip*, Penguin.

Sharif, Omar, with Marie-Thérése Guinchard (1977) *Omar Sharif: The Eternal Male*, W. H. Allen.

Taylor, Derek (1973) *As Time Goes By*, Davis-Poynter.

Taylor, Derek (1984) *Fifty Years Adrift*, Genesis Publications Ltd.

Turner, Frank R. (1995) *The Maunsell Sea Forts Part Two*, published by the author.

White, Susan (1994) *The History of Canvey Island*, The Bookshop, Canvey Island.

Wright, Patrick (1999) *The River: The Thames in our Time*, BBC Worldwide.

Wyman, Bill, with Ray Coleman (1990) *Stone Alone*, Viking.

Yewdall, Julian Leonard (1992) *Joe Strummer with the 101ers & The Clash 1974–1976*, Image Direct.

NEWSPAPERS AND MAGAZINES

All of the following publications were scoured for information.

Bam Balam	*Mojo*	*Select*
Daily Mail	*Music Now*	*Sounds*
Daily Sketch	*New Musical Express*	*Streetlife*
Financial Times	(*NME*)	*Sun*
Friends	*New York Rocker*	*Sunday Times*
Gandalf's Garden	*Nuggets*	*The Times*
Guardian	*Observer*	*Time Out*
Hartbeat	*Oz*	*Trouser Press*
Horseplay	*Q*	*Uncut*
International Times	*Record Collector*	*Vox*
Let It Rock	*Record Mirror*	*Who Put The Bomp*
Melody Maker	*Rolling Stone*	*Zigzag*

Specific articles that were found in these and other publications and used for research are listed below.

Anon (1970) 'The wonderful year of Molton and Warwick', *Sunday Times* 'Insight', 15.11.70.

Anon (1976) 'Pub/club rock label formed', *Melody Maker*, 7.8.76.

Aronowitz, Alfred G. (1970) 'Ricky Blears and 134 journalists', *New York Post*, 6.4.70.

Bell, Max (1976) 'Can Eddie And The Hot Rods up their wages to £25 a week and find true happiness?', *NME*, 3.8.76.

Brown, David (1977) 'Welcome to the weird, wacky, wonderful world of Wreckless Eric', *Sounds*, 10.9.77.

Brown, Geoff (1975) 'Brinsley Schwarz R.I.P.', *Melody Maker*, 29.3.75.

Brown, Geoff (1974) 'Brinsley Schwarz band breakdown', *Melody Maker*, 20.4.74.

Brown, Geoff (1975) 'Closing time', *Melody Maker*.

Brown, Geoff (1975) 'Co-op of rhythms', *Melody Maker*, 8.2.75.

Brown, Geoff (1976) 'Stiff upper lip', *Melody Maker*, 14.8.76.

Brown, Geoff and Chris Welch (1973) 'I'll drink to that – the great Pub Rock boom', *Melody Maker*, 4.8.73.

Carr, Roy (1976) 'On the down home, dusty flip side of the record biz, something stirs', *NME*, 6.11.76.

Carr, Roy (1977) 'The Ian Dury equation', *NME*, 15.10.77.

Carr, Roy (1977) 'Pub Rock', *NME*, 29.10.77.

Carr, Roy (1983) 'Barney Bubbles 1942–1983', *NME*, 26.11.83.

Clarke, Steve (1974) 'Subtle appeal of nylon shirts and string ties', *NME*, 4.5.74.

Collis, John (1973) 'The right road for Kilburn', *Time Out*, 3.8.73.

Dadomo, Giovanni (1975) 'Hard up heroes – hot poop on the new bands', *Sounds*, 15.11.75.

Darby, George (1970) 'A likely story', *Sunday Times*, 12.4.70.

Davies, Dai (1971) 'Suddenly it's Schwarz', *Music Now*.

Denselow, Robin (1973) 'Bees make money', *Guardian*, 17.3.73.

Doherty, Harry (1978) 'The last wave', *Melody Maker*, 19.8.78.

Eldridge, Royston (1970) 'Brinsley – from Kippington Lodge to the Empire State', *Melody Maker*, 18.4.70.

Eldridge, Royston and Richard Williams (1970) 'The unknown stars of Fillmore East', *Melody Maker*, 11.4.70.

Evans, Allen (1970) 'The Schwarz caper – or how to register a name', *NME*, 11.4.70.

Farren, Mick (1974) 'A thousand ugly legends', *NME*, 29.6.74.

Farren, Mick (1975) 'Money doesn't talk – the naughties of those Naughty Rhythms', *NME*, 1.3.75.

Farren, Mick (1975) 'The improbable rise of the Slaughter-house 4', *NME*, 25.5.75.

Farren, Mick (1976) 'It's only rock 'n' roll – Dr Feelgood', *NME*, 26.6.76.

Flood-Page, Mike (1975) 'Oil city slickers, honky soul and Camden cowboys', *Sounds*, 8.2.75.

Flood-Page, Mike (1975) 'The Doctor is in', *Sounds*, 5.7.75.

Frame, Pete (1974) 'Rhinos winos lunatics playboys & bums (Family Tree)', *Zigzag*, July.

Goldman, Vivien (1977) 'Stiffs strut their stuff', *Sounds*, 15.10.77.

Green, Jonathon (1970) 'Hype hype hooray', *Friends*, 15.5.70.

Hoare, Ian (1974) 'They're playing our songs', *Let It Rock*, April.

Hoare, Ian (1974) 'Urban booze', *Let It Rock*, May.

Jones, Allan (1977) 'A day in the life of a bunch of Stiffs', *Melody Maker*, 6.8.77.

Jones, Allan (1977) 'Wreckless Eric? What kind of name is that for a rock 'n' roll star?', *Melody Maker*, 3.9.77.

Jones, Allan (1977) 'Five live Stiffs', *Melody Maker*, 15.10.77.

Jones, Allan (1977) 'Nick Lowe, the last pop writer', *Melody Maker*, 22.10.77.

Jones, Allan (1977) 'From Pub Rock to New Wave', *Melody Maker*, 19.11.77.

Kendall, Paul (1976) 'Punk rock comes to town', *Zigzag*, May.

Kent, Nick (1973) 'Hardened criminals plan big break-out', *NME*.

Kent, Nick (1974) 'Ain't no warz on Schwarz', *NME*, 30.3.74.

Kent, Nick (1974) 'Rocking at the Canvey Island Oil Refinery Claimants Union Ball', *NME*, 31.8.74.

Kent, Nick (1975) 'Eat your heart out Arthur Howes – Naughty Rhythms Tour', *NME*, 18.1.75.

Kent, Nick (1976) 'Plug in to the nerve ends of the naked city', *NME*, 27.3.76.

Kent, Peter (1977) 'Spend an evening with the Stiffs', *Middlesbrough Evening Gazette*, 8.10.77.

Lake, Steve (1974) 'Nesmith shakes off a ghost', *Melody Maker*, 4.5.74.

Leonard, Deke (1991) 'Music every night', *Vox/Record Hunter*, October/November.

Marlborough, Douglas (1970) 'Life in Leeds ended my love for Whicker – Olga', *Daily Sketch*, 6.4.70.

Massey, Fraser (1974) 'Bees make honey', *Zigzag*, July.

McNeill, Phil (1976) 'Rock and roll will stand', *NME*, 18.9.76.

Nevard, Mike (1970) 'British sound stops the Bronx', *Sun*, 6.4.70.

Norman, Tony (1970) 'The Brinsley Schwarz expedition', *Music Now*, 11.4.70.

Nugent, Stephen (1973) 'Taking the low road', *Let It Rock*, April.

Palmer, Tony (1970) 'Publicity fade out', *Observer*, 5.4.70.

Parsons, Tony (1977) 'Five live Stiffs!!', *NME*, 22.10.77.

Ranson, Gerry (1996) 'Mine's a large one landlord!', *Rock 'n' Reel*, May.

Robinson, Lisa (1975) 'New York New York', *NME*, 7.6.75.

Robinson, Lisa (1976) 'Wilko Johnson hits the States. The States hit back', *NME*, 17.4.76.

Salewicz, Chris (1974) Review of Dr Feelgood at Dingwalls, *NME*, 6.4.74.

Salewicz, Chris (1974) 'The Doomwatch Report', *NME*, 27.7.74.

Shaar Murray, Charles (1974) 'God's name begins with N', *NME*, 18.5.74.

Shaar Murray, Charles (1974) 'Down in the scuzz with the heavy cult figures', *NME*, June.

Shaar Murray, Charles (1977) 'Stiffs, drugs and rock 'n' roll', *NME*, 5.11.77.

Silverton, Pete (1977) Review of Stiff tour at Lyceum, *Sounds*, 5.11.77.

Spencer, Neil (1975) 'Brilleaux agonises', *NME*, 14.6.75.

Shaw, William (1993) 'Kaleidoscopic typographic skills in 52 varieties', *Mojo*, December.

Telford, Ray (1973) 'Bees make honey – music every night', *Sounds*, 10.11.73.

Telford, Ray, Steve Peacock and Martin Hayman (1973) 'Rhythm & booze', *Sounds*, 12.5.73.

Thorncroft, Antony (1970) 'A difficult birth', *Financial Times*, 8.4.70.

Thrift, Julia (1992) 'In search of Barney Bubbles', *Eye*, June.

Tyler, Tony (1974) Review of Dr Feelgood at Lord Nelson, *NME*, 9.2.74.

Unit, Victor (1970) 'Live at the Fillmore', *Friends*, 15.5.70.

Watson, Jim (1970) 'The sound of Schwarz', *Music Now*, 25.4.70.

Whalley, Chas de (1976) 'Stiff: a label for hard up heroes', *Sounds*, August.

Williams, Richard (1973) 'We're only here for the Bees', *Melody Maker*, 5.5.73.

Worthington, Cal (Jake Riviera) (1976) 'Total unlimited credit', *Zigzag*, June/July.

CD SLEEVE NOTES

Belmont, Martin (1991) *Ducks Deluxe/Taxi To The Terminal Zone* by Ducks Deluxe (Mau Mau).

Birch, Will (1996) *Naughty Rhythms – The Best Of Pub Rock* (EMI Premier).

Birch, Will (1998) *Stupidity* by Dr Feelgood (Grand Records).

Dopson, Roger (1999) *Handsome* by Kilburn And The High Roads (Dawn/Castle).

Riley, Paul (1996) *I'll Be Home* by Chilli Willi And The Red Hot Peppers (Proper Records).

Robinson, Alan (1998) *Hen's Teeth* by Kippington Lodge/ Brinsley Schwarz (Edsel Records).

Schwarz, Brinsley (1991) *Surrender To The Rhythm* by Brinsley Schwarz (EMI Records).

Tobler, John (1994) *Brinsley Schwarz/Despite It All* by Brinsley Schwarz (BGO Records).

Tobler, John (1999) *Strange Affair/The Return Of Ken Whaley/ Happy Days* by Help Yourself (BGO Records).

MAPS AND DIRECTORIES

Barnett's Street Plan of Aylesbury, Tring and Wendover (1973)

British Telecom Directory Enquiries.

Kelly's Directories (various editions).

London A–Z Street Atlas, 12th edn (1985) Geographer's A–Z Map Co.

Port of London Authority – The River Thames from Teddington to The Tongue, 4th edn (1991) PLA.
UK Infodisc Version 4.1 Pro CD-ROM.

INTERNET WEB SITES

The World Wide Web was only a slip of a lad when I first started searching for 'Barney Bubbles'. For ages, nothing was returned, until one day I hit upon the Philm Freax site and was amazed to discover a Barney Bubbles page and much other useful information, plus some of Phil Franks's outstanding photographs. The site, produced by Malcolm Humes, is highly recommended: www.ibiblio.org/mal/MO/philn/philmfreax

Other worthwhile sites include:

Pub Rock Central	www.pubrock.co.uk
Elvis Costello Home Page	www.elviscostello.com
Nick Lowe Home Page	www.nicklowe.com
Help Yourself Home Page	www.terrascope.org/helps
Ian Dury Home Page	www.iandury.co.uk
Graham Parker Home Page	www.grahamparker.net
Dr Feelgood Home Page	www.drfeelgood.de
All Music Guide	www.allmusic.com
Delerium's Psychedelic Archive	www.delerium.co.uk
Nenne Typography	www.nenne.com/typography/bb1
Fillmore East Home Page	www.fillmore-east.com
Kursaal Flyers	www.kursaalflyers.co.uk
Hux Records	www.huxrecords.com

USEFUL ADDRESSES

BGO Records, PO Box 22, Bury St Edmunds, Suffolk IP28 6XQ
Grand Records, 107a High Street, Canvey Island, Essex SS8 7RF
On The Beach Recordings, 107a High Street, Canvey Island, Essex SS8 7RF
Hux Records, PO Box 12647, London SE18 8ZF

Proper Records, The Powerhouse, Cricket Lane, Beckenham, Kent BR3 1LW

Demon Records Ltd, West Heath Yard, 174 Mill Lane, London NW6 1TB

Chiswick Records, 46/50 Steele Road, London NW10 7AS

Diamond/Zircon Recordings, Millmead Business Centre, London N17 9QU

INDEX